THE OFFICIAL

DOWNTON ABBEY

COOKBOOK

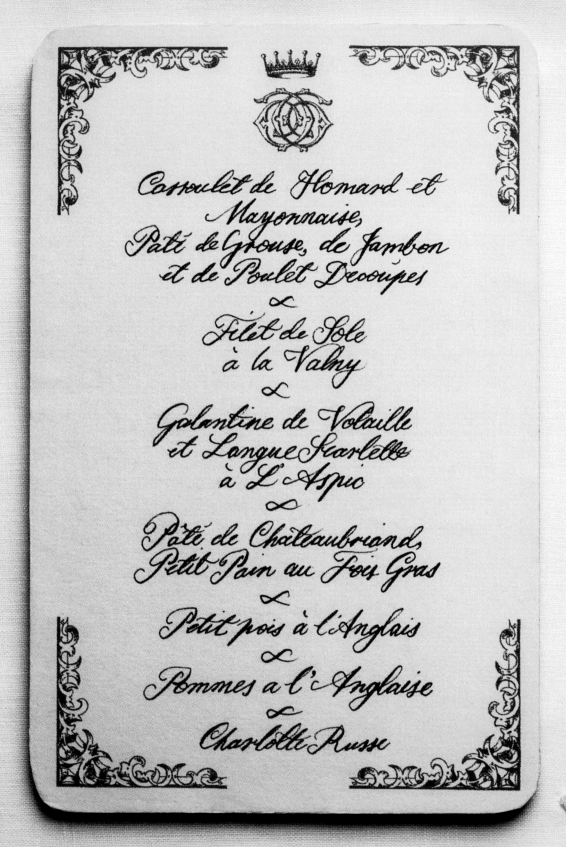

Menu card from the set of *Downton Abbey*

THE OFFICIAL

DOWNTON
ABBEY
COOKBOOK

ANNIE GRAY

weldon**owen**

CONTENTS

UPSTAIRS

DOWNSTAIRS

FOREWORD

OVER SIX SEASONS OF *DOWNTON ABBEY*, WE HAD THE PLEASURE OF WATCHING Robert and Cora Grantham and their daughters, Mary, Edith and Sybil, through romances, deaths, intrigue, marriages, the Great War, financial uncertainty, and the seeds of social change. This delicious drama played out against the backdrop of the Edwardian era, when the aristocracy defined life in England, and on into the 1920s, when the upper class faced a slow and gradual decline. They wore gorgeous clothes, had impeccable manners, and dined extravagantly upstairs on delicacies prepared downstairs. The servants, supervised by Mr. Carson and Mrs. Hughes, faced many of the same trials, tribulations, and joys—and many different ones—their lives downstairs intricately woven into the fabric of the family's life upstairs.

Food was frequently present on the show and a centerpiece around which daily events and special occasions revolved. The seasons dictated the rhythm of life at the great country houses, influencing what dishes were being served both upstairs and downstairs, and an estate like Downton Abbey would have been almost self-sufficient, providing the household with many of its daily provisions.

Esteemed food historian Annie Gray has done a remarkable job of researching and gathering recipes from historical sources for the meals seen on *Downton Abbey*—in both the grand dining room upstairs and in the bustling kitchen and servants' hall below stairs—as well as recipes for dishes that were typical of the era and have withstood the test of time. The recipes, accompanied by a wealth of historical notes about the ingredients and customs of the period, create an invaluable portrait of dining in the early twentieth century. They demonstrate that regardless of whether it was served upstairs or downstairs, food is one of life's great pleasures, and it was no different at Downton Abbey.

Gareth Neame
Executive Producer, *Downton Abbey*
London, 2019

INTRODUCTION

"SEEMS A PITY TO MISS SUCH A GOOD PUDDING"

ood is one of the universals of life: we all eat, and how and what we eat really does show who we are. It's also something we do every day, three or four times, and food marks out both the rhythm of the day and of the year, as occasions such as Christmas, birthdays, and summer parties come round, together with their seasonal specialties. Food even marks out important life events: marriages, christenings, and funerals. For a series like *Downton Abbey*, which charts the lives of a cast of characters we, as viewers, invest in and want to know better, food has to be intrinsically woven into the show.

The two main food-focused areas at Downton are the upstairs dining room, centered on a table around which all sorts of dramas unfold, and the downstairs kitchen, hub of the below stairs areas and a constant bustle of activity. Yet food and drink are also present across the wider series, be it at the village fair, where Mrs. Patmore is wooed by Jos Tufton, the new grocer, over pick-me-up cordial and cake, or at Edith's cocktail parties and intimate restaurant dinners with Mr. Gregson. The food itself is rarely the focus, with the exception of Edith's canceled wedding breakfast in season 3 and the marriage of Mr. Carson and Mrs. Hughes in season 6. On both occasions, the camera drifts lovingly over the tables piled high with food, making us long for a good pork pie

or a properly wobbly jelly. Sometimes individual dishes are central to the plot: In the very first episode, Daisy, then an inexperienced lower kitchen maid, nearly poisons the whole family when she mistakes salt of sorrel for chopped hard-boiled egg white. Later that season, while Mrs. Patmore is away having her eyes operated on, Daisy, more experienced this time, tries to sabotage the beef Mrs. Bird is cooking for the Crawleys' dinner. And in season 4, it's a sublime kedgeree that convinces Harold Levinson that English food (and English cooks) are really very good. In the main though, food forms a background, albeit an important one, to the lives being lived around it.

The period between 1912 and 1926, when *Downton Abbey* is set, was a tumultuous one. The Great War, the election of the first Labour government, the (partial) success of the women's suffrage movement, the Irish War of Independence, and the rise of the Nazi Party in Germany are just a few of the significant historical events that form the backdrop to the show. Culturally it was a time of jazz and art deco, of writers railing against what they saw as stagnant, old-fashioned Victorian values, of increasing divorce rates, and of decreasing religious belief. Meanwhile, huge technological advances were made in medicine, materials, science, and engineering. Inventions of the late nineteenth century, including electric lighting, petrol engines for cars, and airplanes, took off on a grand scale, while the pace of urbanization continued to grow.

Across all six seasons of *Downton* we see the impact of these events and advances on the Crawleys and their wider household: Downton Abbey looks solid and never changing, but this was an era in which everything changed, and did so very fast. In 1918, more country houses were bought and sold than in any year since records began, and as the 1920s rolled on and rents from land dropped dramatically, the traditional owners of stately homes struggled to make ends meet. As we see in *Downton* with Sir John Darnley's house sale in season 6, some sold up, while others, like Lord Grantham with Matthew and Mary's impetus, modernized. Some houses were stripped, demolished, or turned into schools or hotels. Others were sold to "new money": people who had made a fortune in industry, retail, or banking and who wanted a house as a weekend retreat for parties, shoots, and relaxing and who didn't particularly want or need vast estates that could no longer pay their way. And, of course, there were others, like Thomas's employers when he leaves Downton in season 6, who desperately hung on while their furniture rotted and their floors caved in. Food, too, underwent change from the late Edwardian era to the swinging twenties, and it was an especially exciting time gastronomically.

In Edwardian Britain, where the series starts, upper-class dinners were served in the late-Victorian *à la russe* style. This meant anything from seven to nine courses, sometimes broken up with a sorbet halfway through. Service at country

CORA

Mrs. Patmore, is there any aspect of the present day that you can accept without resistance?

houses was what is called "butler service" today, to distinguish it from the silver service used in restaurants and catering. Diners usually had a choice of two dishes for most courses, and they were presented on large platters, with individual servings arranged to look visually impactful: often they were piled on mounds of vegetables; other times they were elegantly placed so the dish looked as good whole as each part did on a plate. Lunches, too, were served sequentially, though these were more generally of only three or four courses. Breakfast, in contrast, had evolved over the course of the nineteenth century into a sort of hot buffet, with various elements kept warm on a sideboard from which people could help themselves.

The food of the Edwardian era, which has a modern reputation for being heavy, rich, and reliant on aspic, was phenomenal. This was the key period for the codification of French haute cuisine, and many of the dishes and techniques that we still regard as intrinsic to classical French cooking today were developed at this time. Auguste Escoffier, one of the most important figures in French cuisine, was working in London at the Carlton Hotel, having published his immensely influential *Le Guide Culinaire* in 1903. French food was regarded as the best in the world, and the very rich employed French chefs in their own homes and served French food as much as they could. The menu cards at Downton are often written in French, and even when English dishes were on the table, they were frequently given French names to be fashionable. That said,

there were some very popular British recipes, and British food was also very good. Raised pies, syllabubs, trifles, and roast meats were seen as quintessentially English, and roast beef and Yorkshire pudding was already a national dish. Families such as the Crawleys, who had been tied to the land for generations, served these alongside the fashionable French dishes and were proud to do so.

The Great War had an enormous impact on food. Rationing was brought in, in 1918, but before that, food shortages had affected everyone, including the wealthy. When the dust settled, nine-course dinners and incredibly intricate presentation seemed out of kilter with the new world. The war had also changed the workplace:

women now had more options, and the number of people employed in domestic service finally started to fall. The middle classes, in particular, struggled to afford servants, and in many cases didn't really want them: privacy and independence were increasingly more important than the constant presence of a live-in maid, and day girls, cook-generals, and charladies, who lived in their own homes and worked only during the day, became more and more common. Even among the upper classes, it was often difficult to maintain prewar standards. We see this at Downton with the employment of Ivy, and then her departure, not to be replaced. Before the war, it was rare for aristocrats of Lord Grantham's rank to employ

women as chefs, preferring men who were more prestigious (and expensive). Ickworth House, in Suffolk, however, offers a striking parallel with Downton: there the Earl of Bristol employed a Mrs. Sangster, who had been the cook to his wife, a wealthy heiress whose money had saved the estate from ruin in 1904. After the war, many more country houses employed women, and a whole army of Mrs. Patmores was born. Now, in the 1920s, they were cooking simpler food, though they could also be called upon to replicate food from the Edwardian era, particularly when entertaining. Books of the time show a marked tendency toward cook's cheats and shortcuts, such as leavening agents and food coloring, both of which had been invented in the Victorian era but were resisted by skilled cooks as they devalued their work. There was also a general move toward lighter food, with more—and more interestingly prepared—vegetables on the table and with pared-down sauces that took only a few hours, rather than a few days, to prepare. More foreign influences crept in as well: no longer just French and Indian, but now Italian, German, and, most of all, American. The predinner cocktail, long resisted as a ruiner of appetites and a bizarre American invention, was enthusiastically adopted by the young, and as Prohibition hit in America and rich Americans fled to London to drink, American bars and clubs became all the rage.

The recipes in this book reflect all the influences found on the Downton Abbey tables, upstairs and down. They are taken from original recipes published or written down between 1875 and 1930. Mrs. Patmore would have been learning her skills in the last quarter of the nineteenth century and remains very much steeped in the Edwardian style of cookery throughout the series. Daisy, in contrast, is learning in the very era portrayed in the series, and the recipes and techniques of the twentieth century are also evident at Downton. From the electric whisk to the refrigerator to the wall of packets and cans and bottles glimpsed behind the maids as they work in season 6, modernity creeps in, and with the Downton daughters (and niece) living life to the full, their influence on the food served would have been just as important as that of Violet, whose youthful fun was back in the 1860s. Any given meal could have included dishes from 1875, 1900, 1913, or 1924, reflecting the generations who lived and ate at Downton Abbey. The recipes here have all been chosen to be easily made in a modern kitchen, with only a few specialist bits of equipment (for which substitutions are available). Some are as seen on screen, some are alluded to, and others have been chosen because they are typical of the time. They would all be at home in a stately dining room, with candles and gold and tightly corseted female figures. But more important, they would be at home as part of a contemporary meal as well. These are historic recipes, and they are Downton recipes, but they are also all usable modern recipes. Bon appétit.

The table is a mass of silver and flowers. Mary shows her grandmother into the dining room.

MARY

What do you think?

VIOLET

Nothing succeeds like excess.

~ SEASON 3, EPISODE 2

KITCHEN NOTES

"THERE'S NEVER A DULL MOMENT IN THIS HOUSE"

FOLLOWING ARE A FEW NOTES ABOUT THE ingredients and pantry items that you'll see again and again in the recipes throughout this book, plus some information about the equipment and measurements that were used. In many cases, I have worked with recipes from original sources from the Downton era, testing and amending these classic dishes for modern cooks. I assume that vegetarians or those with food intolerances will be able to make their own adjustments to the recipes, such as rice flour or one of the gluten-free baking mixes on the market for wheat flour.

INGREDIENTS

Baking powder: The leavener baking powder is a compound of sodium bicarbonate (aka baking soda), an alkali, and cream of tartar, an acid, often with the addition of cornstarch to absorb moisture and thus extend shelf life. Do not confuse it with the leavener baking soda (UK bicarbonate of soda), which is used in some recipes and must be combined with an acid, such as lemon juice, to activate it.

Butter: All butter is salted unless otherwise specified in recipe.

Cream: Two types of cream are used: heavy cream (UK double cream) and half-and-half (UK single cream).

Eggs: All eggs are US large (UK medium).

Flour: All flour is all-purpose (UK plain white) unless otherwise specified. Other flours you will encounter are whole-wheat flour (UK wholemeal) and bread flour (UK strong white bread).

Gelatin: In Great Britain, we primarily use sheet gelatin, which I prefer for the clearer, more transparent final product than what I find can be achieved with powdered gelatin (which is more common in the United States). Either type of gelatin will work in these recipes. For most brands of gelatin, 4–6 sheets of sheet gelatin (depending on size and strength) is usually equal to 1 envelope (about 2½ teaspoons) of powdered gelatin and is used to gel approximately 2 cups (475 ml) of liquid. Powdered gelatin must be softened in water, then is commonly liquefied with heat (either by heating it for 5–10 seconds in a microwave or by nesting the small bowl of softened gelatin in a larger bowl of hot water) and is then added to warm liquid in a recipe; sheet gelatin is softened in water until floppy, then is added to warm liquid in a recipe. Vegetarian substitutes are available. See the pantry section that follows for my gelatin brand of choice.

Milk: All milk is whole.

Salt: All salt is fine-crystal salt unless otherwise specified in recipe.

Spices: Mixed spice is a widely sold UK blend of sweet spices (the term "mixed spice" goes back to the late Georgian period, so it has a well-established history). It generally contains allspice, cinnamon, nutmeg, mace, cloves, coriander, and ginger and is similar to the pumpkin pie spice sold in the United States, which can be used in its place. Otherwise, substitute a homemade mixture of cinnamon, allspice, nutmeg, coriander, and anything else you have in your cupboard, according to your personal taste.

Sugar: When a recipe calls simply for "sugar," granulated sugar is fine and what I tend to use, as it's cheaper than superfine sugar (UK caster). Cakes typically need superfine sugar, however. With regard to brown sugar, if light or dark brown sugar is not specified, then either is fine.

PANTRY ESSENTIALS

I assume every would-be Downton kitchen pantry—or "store cupboard"—has ready supplies of all-purpose flour, fine-crystal and kosher (large-crystal) salt, salted and unsalted butter, baking powder, cornstarch (UK cornflour), milk, cream, eggs, and lemons. Curaçao liqueur features in many of the sweet recipes and cocktails, and flat-leaf parsley and cayenne pepper are also frequently used ingredients. It's definitely worth reading a recipe through carefully a few days before you plan to make it to check you have everything on hand. Here are some of the more obscure ingredients, which you may need to order from a good butcher or may require a trip to a specialty market. Some of them will be harder to source than others, but those more-difficult-to-find items will certainly be available online with only a little searching.

Apples: It is best to avoid varieties from after 1945, for they are sweeter and less versatile. Granny Smiths and Cox's Orange Pippins are sound bets, or you could try a Braeburn, except if you wish to make a nice fluffy filling (for example, for sweet pasties). In that case, a cooking apple, such as a Bramley, the best-known cooking variety in Britain, or any other sharply acidic variety that cooks up light and fluffy, is better.

Gelatin (UK gelatine) sheets: Dr. Oetker is the most popular UK brand and is the one I used for the recipes in this book. (Four to six gelatin sheets are sufficient for about 2 cups/475 ml of liquid.) But you can also use sheets from other, more specialist producers. Just make sure you equate their weight and bloom with what I used.

Lard: The rendered fat from inside a pig, lard is generally available from butchers and from many supermarkets. Lower in saturated fat than you might think and with a very high smoke point, it was widely used in the past for frying, including deep-frying, and is the basis of hot-water-crust pastry. You can, in most recipes, substitute butter, but the effect will not be the same. If possible, purchase naturally processed lard that is not hydrogenated and contains no preservatives.

Marmalade: Always orange and preferably laced with thick-cut slices of peel.

Mushroom ketchup: The main UK brand is George (Geo) Watkins, and it is available online in the United States. If you don't have it on hand, Worcestershire sauce or the water from soaking dried mushrooms can be used in its place. The ketchup has a dark-tasting, umami-rich flavor, so you need to replicate that. Chefs tend to use Maggi or other MSG-based flavor enhancers, and these are also a good substitute. Soy sauce would not be terrible.

Suet: Fat from around the kidneys of cows or sheep, suet is widely available in the United Kingdom. The leading UK brand of beef suet is Atora, which is sold in shredded form and is available online in the United States. Alternatively, you can ask your butcher to save suet for you. A vegetarian suet, also from Atora, is available, though it's not quite as good. There are really no good alternatives, though cold shredded butter or solid vegetable shortening can usually stand in as a reliable substitute.

Treacle: For the purposes of the recipes here, what is known in the United Kingdom as golden syrup is best. It's made from cane sugar, and the main brand is Lyle's (Tate & Lyle). Some recipes (such as the gingerbread on page 245 and the beef stew on page 220) specify black treacle, which is molasses. Again, Lyle's makes a good version. The US product blackstrap molasses most closely approximates the flavor of black treacle. Lyle's brand treacle (golden syrup) and black treacle can be found in the United States online and in some well-stocked markets.

Whisky: Scottish, hence the absence of the "e," is preferred. Beyond that, the choice depends on your own preferences. American whiskey would work in most cases, but nothing too sweet.

EQUIPMENT

None of these recipes requires special equipment. The ice creams are churned in an ice cream maker, but they can also be made without one (see Recipe Note on page 203). Likewise, when I call for a 2½-cup (600-ml) or a 5-cup (1.2-l) pudding mold, or basin, a bowl of roughly equivalent size can be substituted. If it's for steaming or baking, do make sure it's heatproof. There are fixes for almost anything, and many of these are given in the Recipe Notes that accompany the recipes.

In some cases, the cooking time is given along with guidance on internal temperature, and if there's one tool I think every kitchen should have, it's a totally twenty-first-century digital probe thermometer. It consists of a thin metal rod connected to a digital display; the rod is slipped into the item being cooked, where it remains until the digital display, which sits on the counter, sounds, indicating the target temperature has been reached. I don't think I could cook without one. An instant-read thermometer is a good option in the absence of a probe thermometer.

Oven temperatures are given in both Fahrenheit and Celsius and assume the use of a conventional oven. For convection (fan-assisted) ovens, lower the temperature by 10° to 20°F (4° to 18°C). Cakes and pastries are always best baked with conventional heat.

UNITS OF MEASUREMENT

The recipes from which this collection was assembled for the most part used English imperial measurement. They have been redone to include two units of measurement: US customary and metric. The first, though related historically to the

Recipe card from the set of *Downton Abbey*

English imperial system, differs in a number of ways, and imperial measuring tools must not be used for these recipes. For example, a US pint is 16 fluid ounces, in contrast to the imperial pint, which is 20 imperial fluid ounces (or 19.6 US fluid ounces).

SERVING GUIDANCE

The recipe yields are based on an average, averagely hungry person eating a meal of two or three courses and, in the case of the savory dishes, accompanied by a side salad or other dish. You will need to use your own judgment if you are planning a five- or seven-course meal or, indeed, a one-course meal.

HAROLD

*The pâté was delicious, now the fish mousse is delicious
and all my life I've been warned off English food.*

MADELEINE

I'm glad we score in one category.

VIOLET

I'm afraid the menu is very unoriginal.

HAROLD

I like my food good. I don't want it original.

ISOBEL

So England is the right place for you.

~ SEASON 4, EPISODE 9

UPSTAIRS

 **WITHOUT THE CRAWLEY FAMILY, THERE COULD BE NO DOWNTON.** Their needs and wants drive the everyday activities of the below stairs staff, and the structure that the family choose to apply to their days dictates the timetable of those who serve them. Yet, as we see in the series, individual family members also at times feel proscribed by their social situation and the values of their class. Nowhere is this more apparent than at mealtimes. The endless need to dress for dinner, converse only on subjects deemed suitable for servants to hear when they are in the room, and entertain sometimes objectionable people on the grounds that they have been invited to dine especially affects the three Crawley daughters, all of whom at times rally against the rules.

On a normal day, the family would sit down to four meals. Breakfast was relatively informal, and a meal that was often slightly ad hoc, as different people rose at different times, but it generally took place around 9:00 or 9:30 a.m. At Downton, it's also the time when letters are delivered, which on occasion causes consternation when the letter concerned is private. Luncheon could be low key as well, but it was also a chance for people to get together in a less formal way than at dinner. Served around 1:00 p.m., it was generally only a few courses, especially after the war ended in 1918.

Tea filled the gap between luncheon and dinner and was deeply feminized. It had long been customary for the leisured classes to have a cup of tea and bite to eat in the afternoon. However, the habit was codified in the late Victorian era, as well as given a popularity boost by the much-publicized afternoon teas hosted by Queen

Victoria herself. Finally, dinner was the main meal of the day, the most important eating occasion, and the one to which the most space was devoted in both cookery and etiquette books trying to teach the middle classes how to borrow a bit of aristocratic allure.

There was a sharp contrast between food for the family and food for the servants. It was important, especially at dinner, that wealth and status were on display (even if, at times, the wealth was a little more show than real). The ingredients used were generally drawn from the estate, preferably forced and out of season if fruit and vegetables; unavailable to the masses by law, in the case of game; or sourced from shops. Local shops provided meat, fresh produce, and bulk items like flour, but it was normal to use such London-based suppliers as Harrods, Fortnum & Mason, Paxton & Whitfield, and Twinings for specialist goods. After the Great War, the reliance on shops increased, as families suffered financial problems, which meant gardening and game-keeping staffs were trimmed. Many gardens, in particular, were reduced in size, and expensive elements such as the heated greenhouses and walls that enabled the consumption of nectarines in February were scrapped, leading to a more seasonal way of eating.

At Downton, the kitchen staff is also reduced, for Ivy is not replaced when she leaves for America, and in the later seasons the family eats a somewhat more muted menu, with fewer courses at dinner and simpler presentation, in keeping with the spirit of the times.

BREAKFAST

LONG KNOWN AS THE MOST IMPORTANT MEAL of the day, it was the Victorians and Edwardians who invented the Great British Breakfast. Before then, most people simply ate toast or fruited buns, with tea or hot chocolate. By the time *Downton Abbey* opens, however, groaning tables and infinite choice were an established part of the country house routine, and the below-stairs staff would have been up for hours preparing hot food for their employers.

Published in 1898, *The Dictionary of Dainty Breakfasts* by Phyllis Browne included a quick and easy introduction (authored by "a mere man") to the basics of breakfasts. Running to five sturdy pages, it stated that you should have a "fundamental dish"; some "trifling accessories"; fruit, which could be fresh, tinned, or preserved; various drinks; and a selection of breads. Fundamental dishes were freshly prepared meats, eggs, fish, and the all-important bacon, while the "trifling accessories" were tinned, potted, or cold meats; fish; and porridge. Your aim, as a discerning breakfaster, was apparently to base your meal around a fundamental dish, filling up the cracks with your trifles, having cleansed your palate with fruit. The author closes by recommending tea, coffee, cocoa, white wine, and/or beer, and stacks of hot buttered toast.

While a full breakfast table would have been laid out for the family and their guests in the breakfast room on a daily basis, some people preferred individual trays. In *Downton Abbey*, Lady Mary and Cora regularly breakfast in bed, a habit that was well established and that enabled ladies to eat before they faced the rigors of dressing for the day. At Downton, only the married ladies, with their own maids, take breakfast alone and in bed. Mrs. Patmore can sometimes be seen laying out the breakfast trays at the end of her evening's work, a common way to save a little time the next morning.

By the 1920s, the breakfasts rich in meats and carbohydrates of the later Victorian era were changing. Lighter and more exciting options were being embraced, especially by ladies who faced pressure to be slim. One author even suggested trying American dishes, such as marmalade with bacon, or molasses added to fried ham and eggs. Meanwhile, the Hollywood diet recommended eating only half a grapefruit and a cup of black coffee.

At Downton, the usual options, laid out on a sideboard at the back of the room, are scrambled eggs, hot buttered toast, a selection of jams, and several types of stewed fruit. It was the only meal that was not served by footmen (though they were on hand to replenish empty dishes), and the family and their guests all helped themselves. For a heartier option, there is kedgeree, a favorite, along with sausages, bacon, and the occasional tomato. If you are cooking up your own version, don't forget to have oodles of proper leaf tea, coffee, and a glass or two of freshly squeezed orange juice on hand for those who want it.

KEDGEREE

No breakfast at Downton would be complete without a dish of kedgeree, kept warm on a burner on the sideboard. The name and the concept come from an Indian recipe called *khichri*, a mixture of dal and rice that was quickly adopted and altered to suit the British palate. Modern versions often use smoked fish, and the dish is especially associated with finnan haddie, a lightly smoked fish from Scotland that was popularized in Britain once the Victorian railway boom made it possible to transport it to London without spoiling.

SERVES 4

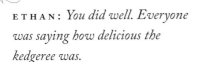

ETHAN: *You did well. Everyone was saying how delicious the kedgeree was.*

MRS. PATMORE: *Well that were Daisy's work.*

ETHAN: *Mr. Levinson had three helpings. And he always thought he wouldn't care for English food.*

MRS. PATMORE: *Ey, you've converted him, Daisy, and that's something to be proud of.*

~ SEASON 4, EPISODE 9

INGREDIENTS

1 lb (450 g) skin-on firm white fish fillets, such as turbot, haddock, or cod

1 cup (240 ml) milk

4 tablespoons (60 g) butter

5 cups (775 g) cooked white or brown rice, cold

¼ cup (60 ml) fish or chicken stock or water, or as needed

1 teaspoon cayenne pepper

Salt and black pepper

2 eggs

⅔ cup (160 ml) heavy cream

FOR GARNISH

1 small bunch fresh flat-leaf parsley, chopped

2 hard-boiled eggs, peeled and sliced

Put the fish into a saucepan with the milk and bring to a gentle simmer. Cook the fish until it flakes when prodded with a fork and is opaque at the center. The timing will depend on the thickness of the fillets. Remove the fish from the pan and discard the milk. Let the fish cool until it can be handled, then remove and discard the skin and break up the flesh into large flakes, removing any errant bones. Set aside.

Melt the butter in a high-sided frying pan over medium heat. Add the rice and stir to coat with the butter. Add the stock and continue to stir, adding more stock if necessary to prevent the rice from sticking, until piping hot. Add the cayenne and the salt and black pepper to taste and stir well. Add the fish, turning it gently with the rice to mix it in. Break the eggs into a bowl, add the cream, and mix roughly with a fork. Keeping the heat very low, add the egg mixture to the pan and cook very gently, turning occasionally, until the egg is just cooked through but remains slightly runny, 5–6 minutes.

Remove from the heat and serve on warmed plates, garnished with the parsley and hard-boiled eggs.

TRUFFLED EGGS

Scrambled eggs are another staple at the Downton family breakfast. They are usually served as part of the classic full English, which also includes bacon, sausages, black pudding (blood sausage), tomatoes, and leftover cooked potatoes, all fried and accompanied with condiments and sauces. The full English remains one of Britain's most recognizable plates of food, and there's a strong argument that it's one of the most universal national dishes. Done badly or with poor ingredients, however, it's terrible. Eggs, in particular, are deceptively simple yet easy to overcook. It's not surprising that in season 4 when Mary makes perfect scrambled eggs for Charles Blake after their night saving the badly dehydrated new pigs, she once again belies his first impressions.

SERVES 2

INGREDIENTS

I small black truffle

2 tablespoons butter

4 very fresh free-range eggs

Kosher salt and black pepper

I tablespoon Madeira

This recipe is ideally made in a double boiler. If you don't have one, you can improvise with a heatproof glass or ceramic bowl set over (but not touching) simmering water in a saucepan.

Chop half of the truffle, cut the remainder into thin slices, and set aside both halves. Melt I tablespoon of the butter in the bottom of the heatproof bowl. Break the eggs into a separate bowl or a pitcher and roughly break them up with a spoon, then season with salt and pepper. Add the eggs to the bowl with the melted butter and leave them for about I minute so they start to cook on the bottom. With a spatula or wooden spoon, scoop the cooked curds from the bottom and mix into the rest. Repeat, letting the eggs begin to cook, then scooping up the curds and mixing them into the rest. After about 4 minutes, add the Madeira. Aim to cook the eggs very gently, not stirring too often but firmly mixing in the curds whenever a layer is cooked. It should take 8–10 minutes for the eggs to be just cooked through but still soft and creamy.

Remove from the heat and quickly add the remaining I tablespoon butter and the chopped truffle, mixing firmly and well to stop the eggs from continuing to cook.

Serve on warmed plates, covered with the truffle slices.

MARY: *I can scramble eggs but that's about it.*

~ SEASON 4, EPISODE 7

BREAD AT DOWNTON

Until the 1860s, flour in Britain was stone-ground and then sifted to remove the bran. Depending on the fineness of the mesh, the flour was labeled according to six grades, with "firsts" being the best and "sixths" being mainly bran. The first roller mills began operating in the second half of the nineteenth century and revolutionized the industry. Roller milling made white flour cheaper and more consistent and also removed the germ, which caused flour to go rancid after a few months. At the same time, advances in yeast technology meant that longer-life "German yeast" became available in blocks for the trade, reducing the reliance on brewer's yeast—or even on sourdough, which was generally disliked both for its flavor and its association with the poor.

Throughout most of history, including the Downton era, white bread was very much preferred to brown. It was easier to digest and therefore seen as healthier, and because, until the invention of roller milling, it took time and lots of effort to produce white flour, it cost more and was associated with gentility. Brown bread tended to be coarse and was thought to cause flatulence—never a comfortable condition in good company. White bread started to gain a bad reputation in the Victorian period, however, as it was often adulterated with alum, which both whitened the lower grades of flour and enabled the baker to add lots more water (which was free). Reports of the time showed that plaster of Paris or other fillers, many of them equally inedible, were also mixed in. When the price of white bread fell because of cheaper flour, due to both roller mills and new, better-quality flours being imported from Eastern Europe, North America, and Canada, the rich started to reconsider brown bread.

By the 1920s, brown bread was newly fashionable, albeit not as popular as white. National manufacturers such as Hovis and Allinson returned to stone grinding and marketed their brown breads with health slogans. Big houses like Downton had long since stopped making their own bread, buying it instead from a local bakery, and trade manuals of the time strongly suggested even small bakeries add a brown, malted, or whole-wheat "health bread" to their offerings.

ENGLISH MUFFINS

English breakfasts in the *Downton Abbey* era invariably included a wide choice of baked goods, some of which can be seen both filling the kitchen table as Mrs. Patmore and her staff work, and on the sideboard in the breakfast room itself. Muffins were a classless food, and even made their appearance in a classic English nursery rhyme, "The Muffin Man," first recorded in 1820. Muffin sellers were familiar figures on urban streets, and bakers worked through the night to prepare hot muffins for people to buy as they walked to work. They were usually served simply split in half and spread with lots of salted butter, but they also made their way into later recipes for eggs Benedict and eggs Florentine. This recipe comes from a ca. 1911 edition of *Domestic Cookery and Household Management*, which mentions neither the author nor the first edition from 1806. The original recipe included the suggestion that if the muffins aren't all eaten immediately and go stale, they "may be made to taste new, by dipping in cold water, and toasting, or heating in an oven." Modern cooks can wrap the muffins airtight and freeze.

MAKES 14 MUFFINS

INGREDIENTS

3¾ cups (450 g) flour, plus more for the work surface

1 cup (240 ml) milk

2 tablespoons butter, plus more for the bowl

1 egg, lightly whisked

2 teaspoons active dry yeast

2 teaspoons salt

Put the flour into a large bowl. Heat the milk in a small saucepan to blood-warm (about 100°F/38°C) and melt the butter in it. Pour the warm milk into the flour, add the egg and yeast, and mix with a wooden spoon until a shaggy dough forms. Mix in the salt, then turn out the dough onto a floured surface and knead until smooth and elastic, 15–20 minutes. Alternatively, in a stand mixer fitted with the dough hook, knead the dough on low speed until smooth and elastic, about 10 minutes.

Lightly butter a large bowl and transfer the dough to it. Cover the bowl with a damp kitchen towel, set it in a warm spot, and let the dough rise until almost doubled in volume, about 2 hours.

Divide the dough into about 14 pieces, each weighing about 2 oz (60 g). Roll and shape each portion into a smooth 2-inch (5-cm) ball. As the balls are formed, put them on a well-floured work surface. With your hand, flatten each ball into a 2½-inch (6-cm) round about ½ inch (12 mm) thick. Cover and let rest for 30 minutes. The rounds will rise only slightly.

Heat a well-seasoned cast-iron griddle or lightly greased large frying pan over medium heat and gently place the muffins on it without crowding. (You may need to cook them in batches.) When the bottoms are dry, after a few minutes, gently turn the muffins over with a spatula. Reduce the heat to low and continue to cook, turning regularly, until the muffins are nicely puffed, lightly browned on both sides, and cooked through, about 20 minutes. When done, the center of a muffin should register about 200°F (95°C) on a thermometer.

Turn them onto a rack to cool only briefly, for they are best served hot. Use your fingers or a fork to split each muffin in half.

DEVILED BISCUITS

The British have long loved a good devil, as deviled mixtures were sometimes known. The term refers to a spicy mixture, usually made with paprika or cayenne pepper, and boosted with a condiment, such as Worcestershire sauce, vinegar, or mustard. Devils were popular in the late eighteenth century, and they've continued to be consumed with joy up to the present day. This recipe first appeared in *The Cult of the Chafing Dish* (1905), whose title refers to a handy device aimed at the bachelor-about-town that incorporated a spirit burner, a deep-sided dish, and various attachments, including one to make toast and an egg poacher. It was ideal for gentlemen in the style of *Downton*'s Henry Talbot: men who came from wealth but couldn't live on family money alone; men who had a servant but at times needed to be able to fend for themselves.

MAKES 50–60 SMALL BISCUITS

RECIPE NOTE

The biscuits are particularly good with soft cheese or used as a crispy topping for Kedgeree (page 34) or scrambled eggs. You can vary the deviling mixture as you desire. Some recipes call for curry powder, and others boost the heat by using different types of chile.

INGREDIENTS

FOR THE BISCUITS

1¾ cups plus 2 tablespoons (225 g) flour, plus more for the workspace

1 teaspoon baking powder

1 teaspoon salt

⅔ cup (160 ml) milk

2 tablespoons unsalted butter, plus more for frying

FOR THE DEVILING MIXTURE

1 tablespoon mustard

1 tablespoon Worcestershire sauce

2 anchovy fillets in olive oil, finely minced

2 tablespoons olive oil

1 teaspoon paprika

Stir together the flour, baking powder, and salt in a bowl. Heat the milk in a small saucepan to blood-warm (about 100°F/38°C) and melt the butter in it. Pour the warm milk into the flour mixture and mix until a dough forms. Shape the dough into a ball.

Preheat the oven to 400°F (200°C). Line a large sheet pan with parchment paper.

Transfer the dough to a well-floured work surface and knead briefly until evenly mixed. Divide the dough in half. Cover half loosely with plastic wrap and set aside. Flatten the other half into a disk, then roll it into a round ⅛ inch (3 mm) thick. Using a 2-inch (5-cm) round biscuit cutter, cut out as many biscuits as possible and transfer them to the prepared pan. Gather up the scraps and press onto the remaining dough. Lightly prick the surface of the biscuits all over with a fork.

Bake the biscuits until almost golden, about 6 minutes. Meanwhile, roll out the remaining dough and cut out more biscuits. Transfer the first batch of biscuits to wire racks to cool while baking the second batch. Transfer the second batch to the wire racks and let cool completely.

To make the deviling mixture, mix together all the ingredients in a small bowl. Transfer to a large plastic bag, add the biscuits, and shake the bag to coat them thoroughly. Leave them in the bag for at least 10 minutes or up to 1 day to soak up the mixture.

Melt about 1 tablespoon butter in a large frying pan over medium heat. In batches and adding more butter as needed, fry the biscuits, turning them once or twice, until lightly browned, about 4 minutes total. Serve right away.

PIKELETS

Pikelets, the Welsh cousins of crumpets, are classic British breakfast fare. The glory of them is in the pattern of small holes on their surface, which means they can take a satisfyingly large amount of butter before they become saturated and the butter drips down your arm. They are not only good for breakfast but are also excellent toasted as a late-night snack, and any leftovers would have been happily consumed by servants in a house such as Downton—by the early 1920s possibly even using an electric toaster of the rather beautiful type seen on screen in Mrs. Hughes's room in season 3. They are good with butter, great with jam, and sublime with a sharp cheese.

MAKES 10–12 PIKELETS

INGREDIENTS

1¾ cups (210 g) flour

2 teaspoons active dry yeast

½ teaspoon superfine sugar

½ teaspoon salt

1¼ cups (300 ml) milk, warmed

Butter, for frying and serving

Stir together the flour, yeast, sugar, salt, and milk in a bowl until well mixed. Cover the bowl with plastic wrap or a damp kitchen towel, set it in a warm spot, and allow the batter to rise for 2 hours. The mixture should be very airy and full of bubbles.

Heat a cast-iron griddle or large, heavy frying pan over medium heat and brush with a small amount of butter. To make each cake, scoop a scant ¼ cup (60 ml) of the mixture onto the heated surface, allowing it to spread out to form a flattish round and being careful not to crowd the pan. When the sides start to dry out but the top is still tacky, flip each cake over with a spatula to cook the top. The bottom normally takes 3–4 minutes and the top takes 2–3 minutes. The cakes should be lightly browned on both sides when ready. Transfer to a warmed plate and repeat with the remaining batter.

Serve them hot with lots and lots of butter.

CARSON: *What in God's name is it?*

MRS. HUGHES: *An electric toaster. I've given it to myself as a treat. If it's any good, I'm going to suggest getting one for the upstairs breakfasts.*

CARSON: *Is it not enough that we're sheltering a dangerous revolutionary, Mrs Hughes? Could you not have spared me that?*

~ SEASON 3, EPISODE 4

DAIRY AT DOWNTON

Country houses like Downton nearly all had dairies. Sometimes they were situated near the house, or in the service wing itself, but by the twentieth century, they were more often at the home farm (the farm most closely associated with the estate and from which fresh eggs and produce came directly, as opposed to the other farms on the estate that were tenant occupied and did not supply the house except through local butchers). Upper-class food relied on cream and butter, which was generally used salted, unless a recipe specified "sweet" butter, that is, unsalted. The cream would be left in settling pans overnight, and in the morning, the fat would be skimmed from the top and churned for butter. The remaining milk, now called skimmed milk, would be consumed by the servants or sold cheaply to local villagers. Meanwhile, it was unthinkable upstairs to drink tea without whole milk.

Cream itself went into everything from sauces to blancmange, ice cream to kedgeree. Butter, as well as being used for frying, baking, and pastry, was also an essential component of the cook's emergency arsenal. Flavored with herbs, fish, spice, or even sugar and perfumed waters, compound butters were a handy pantry fallback, ideal for sudden emergencies or spontaneous picnics. Meals were planned very precisely, with the cook sitting down with the mistress of the house on a daily or sometimes weekly basis to go through the menus and receive instructions as to the specific needs of any guests. However, there had to be some leeway, and at Downton we regularly see people eating unplanned meals, including the impromptu supper where Mary and Matthew first start to come together. Having easy edibles on hand for hungry family members was an obligatory part of the cook's duties.

Some houses made their own cheese, though this was very rare by the twentieth century, when it was more often bought. Cheese was vital, and a wide range was always on hand, to be used for everything from rich, cheap Cheshire cheese sauces for the servants to delicate Parmesan toppings for an upstairs gratin. French cheese and expensive English cheeses such as Stilton were sometimes eaten as part of a family dinner, and cheap rounds of Cheddar were always present at the servants' supper.

LUNCH & SUPPER

LUNCH, OR LUNCHEON, IS A RELATIVE NEW-comer to Britain. It's first recorded at the end of the eighteenth century: a tumultuous time with Britain and other European countries allied against the newly established French First Republic and the country militarized and heavily taxed. In a more domestic context, mealtimes were in a state of flux, with dinner gradually moving from midafternoon to around 8:00 p.m. for the upper classes. Given that breakfast was generally around 9:00 a.m., it was a long time to go without eating, and while what would later become afternoon tea could fill some gaps, it was hardly a substantial repast.

Lunch, therefore, was inevitable. It was originally known by many names, including nooning and the rather poetic noonshine. It was never as formal or as lengthy as dinner, which remained the main focus of the eating day and the meal to which guests were generally invited. It was a proper sit-down meal, but there was no need to dress specially for it, and frequently not everyone living in a house would be at the table, as there were always those who were off visiting friends, shooting, or conducting business and would therefore have lunch elsewhere. Naturally, it was slightly geared more toward women than men, for women were most likely to be in to eat it. The implications of this are made clear in season 3 when Isobel has Ethel cook lunch for Cora, Violet, and the Downton daughters, and they stand firm against Robert's intrusion into their ladies' lunch and their feminine concerns.

The meal itself was a hot one, though the dishes tended to be simple and were often based on leftovers or used pantry items. In keeping with its feminine overtones, as well as its place as a less important meal than dinner, the food was light and, especially after the Great War, was the most likely place to find dishes based on eggs and salad, both very easy to prepare. Unlike dinner, with its many courses and complicated cutlery etiquette, lunch was sometimes served buffet-style, with dishes laid on the table for people to help themselves. That meant fewer servants were required—useful if you are planning to host a Downton-style lunch yourself. At Downton Abbey itself, footmen are generally on hand to serve, but even there, when the financial situation is at its most dire and the number of staff reduced, Robert dining alone is served by Jane, who, as a woman, was of much lower status than one of the liveried manservants.

> **ISOBEL**
>
> *I was wondering if I . . . might try to take her out of herself. Perhaps give a little lunch party, nothing formal. Just Lady Grantham and the girls.*
>
> ~ SEASON 3, EPISODE 6

SARDINE SALAD

The 1920s saw a new vogue for fresh, zingy flavors and lighter dishes than those of the Edwardian era. The first calorie-controlled diet was introduced in 1918, and women's fashions of the time emphasized a slender, boyish figure. At lunches, in particular, which were very much feminized meals, light dishes and salads were popular. Houses such as Downton all had extensive kitchen gardens, which meant that the elements of leaf salads, known to lose their crunch rapidly, could be picked at their best and served within a few hours. This recipe, which comes from *A Book of Scents and Dishes*, published in 1927, makes use of one of the staples of the twentieth-century pantry: tinned sardines. The original also calls for garnishing the salad with lemon slices and nasturtiums.

**SERVES 4 AS A SIDE SALAD
OR 2 AS A MAIN**

INGREDIENTS

2 heads Belgian endive, stem end trimmed and sliced crosswise

3 oz (90 g) watercress, roughly chopped

1½ tablespoons fresh flat-leaf parsley leaves, finely chopped

1 tablespoon capers

1 can sardines (about 3 oz/90 g drained weight)

FOR THE DRESSING

1 hard-boiled egg yolk

1 teaspoon Dijon mustard

¼ teaspoon cayenne pepper

Pinch of salt

Black pepper

1½ tablespoons olive oil

1 tablespoon fresh lemon juice

Combine the endive, watercress, parsley, and capers in a salad bowl. Drain the sardines and break them up with the back of a fork. Add them to the salad greens.

To make the dressing, put the egg yolk, mustard, cayenne, salt, and a little black pepper into a small jar and mash together with a fork. Add the oil and lemon juice, put the lid on, and shake the jar to combine the ingredients well.

Drizzle the dressing over the salad, toss well, and serve.

FOOD FOR THOUGHT

Sardines were one of the first foods to be successfully canned, in the 1830s in France. By the time *Downton Abbey* opens in 1912, cookery book authors were advising discerning sardine eaters to look for pilchards instead, for sardines were so popular that unscrupulous merchants were canning any old fish and labeling them as the finest sardines. Pilchards are the same fish, but slightly bigger.

ISOBEL: *There's no need to cook. Just fetch some ham from Mr. Bakewell and make a light salad. You can't go wrong with that and Lady Grantham won't want more.*

~ SEASON 3, EPISODE 6

LOBSTER CUTLETS

After Edith's wedding to Sir Anthony Strallan ends in tears, the carefully prepared dishes that were to form her wedding breakfast are whisked away and end up as the servants' dinner. Many gloriously extravagant foods are on offer, but the lobster dish is particularly striking, garnished as it is with whole lobster shells in a gravity-defying pyramid. The edible elements are, indeed, almost lost beneath it. However, as the servants tuck in, they find they are eating lobster rissoles, a dish that was a Victorian favorite, and, despite appearances, is both quick and easy to prepare—ideal for a celebratory wedding breakfast.

SERVES 2–4

RECIPE NOTE

The cutlet shape was very popular with the Victorians, complete with leg-to-look-like-bone. (In Britain, the terms *cutlet* and *chop* are used interchangeably. In the US kitchen, cutlet is used for a thin, boneless piece of meat that is often breaded and fried.) If you form the mixture into balls, you have rissoles, and if you bake it in small pastry shells, you have patties. Spread it on toast and it's a *croûte*, which works as an hors d'oeuvre. The mixture can also be made with fresh or canned crabmeat. If the mixture is too sloppy to shape, add bread crumbs until it is more manageable.

INGREDIENTS

1 lobster, cooked	Salt and black pepper
⅔ cup (160 ml) milk	Grated zest and juice of ½ lemon, plus 1 lemon, cut into wedges, for garnish
2 tablespoons heavy cream	
2 tablespoons butter, plus more for frying	1 egg
¼ cup (30 g) flour	½ cup (20 g) fresh bread crumbs
⅛ teaspoon cayenne pepper	Small fresh flat-leaf parsley sprigs, for garnish

Holding the lobster flat on a cutting board, insert the tip of a large, sharp knife where the head and body sections meet and cut through the shell to halve the head lengthwise. Rotate the lobster 180 degrees and cut the body and tail in half lengthwise. Twist off the claws and legs from the lobster. Lift out the meat from the tail and reserve. Crack the claws and the large sections of the legs and remove all the meat. Save the ends of the legs for serving, if desired. Chop all the lobster meat finely and transfer to a bowl.

Combine the milk and cream in a small saucepan, heat over medium heat until hot, and pour into a heatproof measuring pitcher with a spout. To make a roux, melt the 2 tablespoons butter in a saucepan over medium heat, then whisk in the flour until smooth. Reduce the heat to low and stir for 2–3 minutes to cook off the raw flour flavor. Add the hot milk mixture, little by little, to the roux, stirring constantly. You should finish with a very thick, smooth sauce. Add the cayenne, a little salt, some black pepper, and the lemon zest and juice and stir to mix well, then remove from the heat and let cool completely.

Add half of the sauce to the finely chopped lobster meat, and stir well. Then add the rest of the sauce, spoon by spoon, until you have a very thick paste that holds its shape when formed into a lump (you may not need all the sauce). Cover and chill for at least 1 hour or up to overnight.

Whisk the egg in a shallow bowl and spread the bread crumbs in a second shallow bowl. Form the lobster mixture into 8 small balls, then mold each ball into the rough shape of a meat cutlet (a flat pear shape). Brush the cutlets on all sides with the egg and then turn them in the bread crumbs to coat evenly.

Recipe continues

Line a large plate with paper towels. Heat 2 tablespoons butter in a large frying pan over medium heat and lay the cutlets in the pan. If the fat is too hot, the bread crumbs will burn before the cutlets are heated through, so keep the heat moderate and turn the cutlets once they are browned on the underside. When the cutlets are cooked, which should take 5–6 minutes, drain them briefly on the towel-lined plate, then transfer to a warmed serving platter.

Garnish the cutlets with the parsley. The ends of the lobster legs can be inserted gently into the pointy end of each cutlet to resemble the bone that would stick out of the end of a lamb or pork cutlet. Accompany with the lemon wedges.

FOOD FOR THOUGHT

Sometimes whole meals did indeed have to be scrapped. In 1902, Edward VII was rushed to the operating table and his coronation feast was put on hold. Some dishes were saved—the Champagne jellies were melted down and put into bottles—but those that would spoil, including anything made with lobster, were discreetly handed to charity and went to feed the poor in London's East End.

HAM WITH RED WINE AND ALMONDS

Boiled gammon is a standard dish at Downton at both lunch and dinner. Inevitably, large joints of meat didn't always get eaten when first served, and that means recipes for using up ready-cooked meat would have been part of every cook's repertoire. Refrigeration was slow to catch on in large houses, which often didn't have electricity—Downton is very modern in this respect, as it has just been installed when the series opens—and so recipes such as this one were vital. Waste was frowned on, though peelings and other kitchen refuse that really couldn't be eaten would have been fed to the pigs as swill. The idea that leftovers were something inferior, to be used up and annoying to store, is very modern: at Downton uneaten meat would have been looked at as an ingredient for another dish. This recipe is very simple and very effective and is representative of the lighter take on lunches characteristic of the 1920s. Serve with rice or a salad of bitter leaves, such as chicory or Belgian endive.

SERVES 4

INGREDIENTS

4 thick slices cooked ham, 4–5 oz (115–140 g) each

1¼ cups (300 ml) fruity, medium-bodied red wine (I tend to use a Côtes du Rhône, but a middle-of-the-road drinking plonk is fine)

Grated zest and juice of 1 orange

1 oz (30 g) ratafia biscuits or small almond macaroons (see Recipe Notes)

Put the ham slices into a saucepan. Combine the wine and orange juice in a large measuring cup. Pound the ratafia biscuits to a powder, add them to the wine mixture, then add the wine mixture to the pan. Bring slowly to a gentle simmer and warm very gently until the ham is heated through, about 5 minutes. Stir in the orange zest at the end. Do not allow the liquid to come to a full boil or the ham will be tough. Serve warm.

RECIPE NOTES

A type of British ham, gammon is salt- or brined-cured leg of pork that must be cooked before eating. Any fully cooked ham will work here. Earlier versions of this recipe, often listed in books as a "hash," simply involved reheating the cold cooked meat in gravy or thickened stock. Other good ways to use up leftover ham include replacing the usual sausages in toad-in-the-hole (baked in a Yorkshire pudding–like batter; see page 216), adding it to stuffings, or using it in sandwiches.

Small, crisp, golden-brown ratafia biscuits are almond-flavored cookies that are often served with after-dinner coffee or used in making cakes and pies. Small almond macaroons, such as Italian amaretti, can be substituted.

ROBERT: *Is this the refrigerator?*

CORA: *It is. Mrs. Patmore hates it.*

ROBERT: *Of course she does.*

~ SEASON 6, EPISODE 1

RECIPE NOTE

You can use almost any filling in these, but you do need a balance between meat and vegetables. Other Downton-era possibilities include squab (pigeon) and rutabaga (swede), chicken and mushroom, and, of course, beef and potato. The crust is good for sweet pasties, too: mincemeat works well (see Lemon Mincemeat, page 105), as does apple, especially with a little dried fruit and some spice added.

CORNISH PASTIES

Cornish pasties are a food about which many myths circulate. The modern version generally contains beef, potato, and onions, with a rich, fat-based pastry, and has been given protected status. However, pasties have medieval origins and were widespread in the United Kingdom until the nineteenth century. Early pasties could contain any number of things, and most had very little meat, as it was so expensive. The Cornish pasty as we now know it emerged in London in the late nineteenth century and was more middle class than its vegetable-based country cousin. It spread rapidly throughout Britain and abroad, to the extent that earlier versions were almost forgotten. However, during the First World War, some authors revived pasties, as they were practical to make, could be filled with all sorts of ingredients, and were suitable for both elegant luncheons and marching off to the front, depending on their size, filling, and the chunkiness of their pastry. These are of the former type.

SERVES 4–6

INGREDIENTS

FOR THE PASTRY

4½ cups (540 g) flour, plus more for the work surface

1¼ teaspoons salt

7½ oz (210 g) suet, solid vegetable shortening, or butter, shredded or cut into bits

1 cup plus 2 tablespoons (270 ml) cold water

FOR THE FILLING

2 small apples, such as Granny Smith or Cox's Orange Pippin, peeled, halved, cored, and cut into ½-inch (12-mm) cubes

7 oz (200 g) boneless pork shoulder, trimmed of excess fat and cut into ½-inch (12-mm) cubes

¼ lb (115 g) bacon, minced

1 tablespoon mushroom ketchup or Worcestershire sauce

1 teaspoon dried sage, or 1 tablespoon minced fresh sage

Salt and black pepper

To make the pastry, combine the flour, salt, and suet in a large bowl and quickly mix with your fingertips until the mixture resembles coarse crumbs. Using a pastry blender or fork, mix in the water a bit at a time until the dough can be formed into a ball. Divide the dough in half and pat each half into a disk. Wrap each disk in plastic wrap and refrigerate while you make the filling.

To make the filling, combine the apples, pork, bacon, ketchup, and sage in a bowl, season with salt and pepper, and mix well.

Preheat the oven to 375°F (190°C). Line 2 sheet pans with parchment paper. Flour a work surface generously. Roll out 1 disk about ⅛ inch (3 mm) thick. Using a saucer as a guide, cut out 6 circles, each about 6 inches (15 cm) in diameter. (If needed, gather the scraps and re-roll until you have 6 circles.) Divide half of the filling evenly among the circles, spooning it onto half of each circle and leaving ½ inch (12 mm) uncovered around the edge. Dampen the edge of each circle with water, fold the circles in half, and press down on the edge to seal. Crimp the edges with a fork or with your fingers. Prick the tops several times with a fork to vent and arrange on a prepared sheet pan. Repeat with the remaining pastry and filling.

Bake until barely golden on top and a thermometer inserted into the center of a pasty registers 165°F (74°C), about 20 minutes. Serve the pasties warm or at room temperature.

EGGS À LA ST. JAMES

Delicate molded individual creams and egg-based items appear on the table at Downton at many meals. Sometimes sweet but more often savory, they are far removed from modern dish presentation. Instead, they are ideal for service *à la russe*, for they look good presented on a large dish en masse but are easily portioned out. Any self-respecting country house kitchen would have had a wide range of molds in copper, tin, and ceramic, and a bewilderingly large number of foods were cooked in them. Visitors to historic kitchens today may be forgiven for thinking that the Victorians and Edwardians ate vast amounts of aspic, but while that's nearly the only food we habitually mold today, in the past if it could be molded, then it was. These eggs are best done in dariole molds, which are tall and narrow, but if you don't happen to have a full complement of gleaming copper molds, they can also be made in a muffin pan.

SERVES 6

INGREDIENTS

Butter, for the molds

3 tablespoons finely chopped fresh flat-leaf parsley

2 teaspoons smoked paprika

6 anchovy fillets in olive oil

1 cup (240 ml) heavy cream

6 eggs

¼ teaspoon cayenne pepper, or 1 teaspoon hot-pepper sauce

Boiling water, for the bain-marie

6 thin slices white sandwich bread

Small watercress sprigs for garnish (optional)

Preheat the oven to 325°F (165°C). Butter 6 standard muffin cups (about 3 inches/7.5 cm in diameter and ¾ inch/2 cm deep) or metal dariole molds. Sprinkle the bottoms with the parsley and smoked paprika, dividing them equally, and curl an anchovy around the base (if you are using muffin cups, you may need to cut the anchovy fillet in half lengthwise to make it go fully around). Add 1½ teaspoons of the cream to each mold, then crack an egg into each mold.

Combine the remaining cream and the cayenne in a bowl and, using a whisk or a handheld mixer on medium speed, whip until stiff peaks form. Set aside in a cool spot or in the fridge.

Set the muffin pan or molds in a roasting pan and pour boiling water into the pan to reach two-thirds of the way up the sides of the muffin pan or molds. Bake until the whites of the eggs are fully set and the yolks have thickened but are still runny, 10–12 minutes, or until done to your liking.

Meanwhile, cut out a circle from the center of each bread slice, making the circle about 1 inch (2.5 cm) larger in diameter than your eggs. Toast the circles.

Arrange the toasted bread circles on a large plate. Turn out an egg onto each bread slice. Garnish with watercress, if using. Just before serving, spoon or pipe some of the whipped cream onto each egg. The cream will start to melt immediately, so serve quickly.

RECIPE NOTE

You can vary this recipe, which is essentially coddled eggs, by substituting mushrooms for the anchovy fillets or changing the spice. If you bake the eggs until they are just hard boiled, they will last fairly well and are transportable for a picnic, in which case serve them with mayonnaise.

FOOD FOR THOUGHT

Curries like this form part of a
distinct Anglo-Indian repertoire
of cookery. Totally unlike anything
served in either country at the
time, they were utterly scorned
by writers in the second half of
the twentieth century for being
inauthentic and a weird mishmash
of ingredients. That's very unfair,
for they were never billed as
being representative of the food
eaten by Indians, but rather
were a vaguely raj-flavored set
of dishes for the British palate.
As such, they are often delicious
and were extremely popular.

VEGETABLE CURRY

The kitchen at Downton is always full of people bustling about. Often the food itself is merely a background to the conversations happening around the table, and one of the challenges of filming is to provide the actors with enough to do that they look busy, and that the tasks they are doing are replicable take after take. Chopping vegetables is a favorite activity, particularly good for the various extras who don't have named parts but are there to give an impression of the number of staff that would have been present in a house like Downton. Although the series focuses on Mrs. Patmore and Daisy, plus Ivy in seasons 3 and 4, country house kitchens of the status of Downton would usually have four or five kitchen staff, including a scullery maid who did the plucking, gutting, and washing up, and would also hire extra staff for large events. All those vegetables have to go somewhere, and this dish is an excellent way to use a large variety of carefully diced props.

SERVES 4-6

2 firm apples, such as Granny Smith or Cox's Orange Pippin, cored and diced

2 small yellow onions, minced

1 cucumber, peeled and diced

¼ cup (30 g) flour

4 tablespoons (60 g) butter

1 tablespoon curry powder

1 teaspoon ground ginger

1 teaspoon salt

1 teaspoon tomato paste

2 tablespoons unsweetened shredded dried coconut, plus more for garnish

1 cup (240 ml) milk

½ cup (120 ml) heavy cream

About 4 cups (600 g) diced mixed vegetables, in pieces about ⅓ inch (9 mm) square, such as carrot, parsnip, turnip, rutabaga, green beans, cauliflower, and broccoli, and/or whole shelled fava beans and peas, in any combination

Put the apples, onions, and cucumber into small separate bowls and dust them with the flour. Melt the butter in a saucepan over medium-high heat until it foams and throw in the apples and onions. Turn the heat down to medium-low and cook, stirring often, until the onions are just starting to brown, which should take about 10 minutes. Add the cucumber and continue to cook, stirring often, for 5 minutes longer.

Add the curry powder, ginger, salt, tomato paste, coconut, milk, and cream and stir well. Raise the heat to medium-high and bring to a boil. Turn down the heat to a gentle simmer and add any root vegetables, such as carrot, parsnip, rutabaga, or turnip, and cook, stirring occasionally, for 5 minutes. Add all the remaining vegetables and cook, continuing to stir regularly, for about 10 minutes longer. Check that the vegetables are tender (exactly how crunchy you like your vegetables is a personal thing).

Transfer the curry to a warmed serving dish, garnish with a little more coconut, and serve immediately.

RECIPE NOTE

If your curry powder is mild, this makes a good side dish. But it can also be served as a main course if accompanied with rice. You can use cooked vegetables as well, and it's an excellent way to use up niggly amounts of leftover vegetables.

MACARONI WITH A SOUFFLÉ TOP

Macaroni cheese was a much-loved British dish in the eighteenth century. It was also one that early settlers took with them to America, where it was enthusiastically adapted and became more American than British (and very different from the original). This version, with a soufflé top, comes from *English Country House Cooking*, recipes collected between the wars from cooks at country houses. It originated with Viscount Dalrymple, a Scottish peer who was a prisoner of war during the Great War, which forms the background to much of season 2 at Downton. He was later repatriated through Switzerland and, like many returning soldiers, brought back a recipe he'd acquired on his way home. Soufflés are phenomenally popular at Downton and appear regularly throughout all six seasons.

SERVES 4–6

MRS. PATMORE: *It can't be going out!*

DAISY: *Well, it is. There must be a block in the flue.*

MRS. PATMORE: *But the dinner's not cooked. We haven't even put in the soufflés.*

DAISY: *There'll be no soufflés tonight.*

~ SEASON 3, EPISODE 2

INGREDIENTS

2 cups (475 ml) chicken stock or water

Salt

½ lb (225 g) macaroni

2 tablespoons olive oil

Black pepper

3 tablespoons unsalted butter, plus more for the dish

½ cup (2 oz/60 g) grated Parmesan cheese, plus more for the dish

2 tablespoons flour

1¼ cups (300 ml) milk, warmed

½ teaspoon English mustard powder

2 eggs, separated

¾ cup (3 oz/90 g) grated Gruyère cheese

Combine the stock and 2 teaspoons salt in a saucepan and bring to a boil over high heat. Throw in the macaroni and cook, stirring occasionally, for just under the time recommended on the package. (The macaroni will cook further in the oven.) Scoop out and set aside 2 tablespoons of the stock, then drain the macaroni and return it to the pan. Add the 2 tablespoons stock and the oil, season with salt and pepper, toss to mix, and set aside.

Meanwhile, preheat the oven to 350°F (180°C). Butter a 2-quart (2-l) baking dish, then coat the inside of the dish with Parmesan, turning and tipping the dish to cover it evenly.

Melt the butter in a saucepan over medium-low heat. Add the flour and cook, stirring, for 2 minutes. Whisk in the milk and cook, stirring often, until thickened, about 3 minutes. Stir in the mustard powder. Remove from the heat and stir in the egg yolks, one at a time, beating well after each addition. Add the Parmesan and Gruyère cheeses and stir until melted. Season with salt and pepper and let cool.

Whisk the egg whites with a pinch of salt by hand or with a handheld mixer on medium-high speed until stiff peaks form. Gently fold the beaten whites into the now-cool cheese mixture. Gently add about half of the soufflé mixture to the macaroni and fold together until evenly mixed. Spoon the macaroni mixture into the prepared baking dish. Spoon the remaining soufflé mixture on top, making sure it is no higher than 1 inch (2.5 cm) or so below the rim.

Bake until puffed and browned, about 25 minutes. Serve immediately.

AN ITALIAN WAY OF COOKING SPINACH

During the Great War, large numbers of ordinary people traveled abroad for the first time, eating and drinking French and Italian food along the way. This, plus the determination of governments afterward to emphasize shared values and preserve peace, led to a definite postwar expansion of culinary influences into mainstream British cooking. Books on Italian cookery had been published before, but now books such as *The Gentle Art of Cookery*, by Hilda Leyel and Olga Hartley, contained lots of recipes for slightly exotic-sounding ways to transform boring British vegetables. British vegetable cookery was centered largely around boiling, mashing, and gratins, with sauces usually based on butter and cream. Although vegetables served in this way can be sublime, the cooking times given in books suggest they were habitually overcooked. At Downton, many of the upstairs dishes are served with watercress or spinach, which gives the plates color but, more importantly, gives the cast something practical to eat in front of the cameras when they are repeating scenes many times over. The triangular shape of the croutons is traditional, but you can vary it as you wish.

SERVES 4

INGREDIENTS

4 slices white bread, as thin as possible

I tablespoon unsalted butter or vegetable oil, for frying, plus ½ teaspoon, at room temperature

2 lb (I kg) spinach, hefty stems removed

2 anchovy fillets in olive oil, minced

½ cup (90 g) mixed golden and dark raisins

First, make the croutons. Cut the bread slices into neat triangles about I inch (2.5 cm) on each side. Melt the I tablespoon butter in a frying pan over medium heat. Working in batches, fry the triangles, turning as needed, until golden brown on both sides. Set aside. (If you prefer not to fry the croutons, shake the bread cutouts with a little oil in a shallow baking pan and bake them in a preheated 400°F (200°C) oven until golden brown, 5–10 minutes.)

Rinse the spinach well and transfer to a large saucepan. Cook over medium heat in just the rinsing water clinging to the leaves until tender, a few minutes. Drain well and then press the leaves gently between paper towels or a clean kitchen towel to remove most of the moisture. Chop the leaves roughly and return them to the pan.

Using a fork, mix together the ½ teaspoon butter and the anchovies until thoroughly blended. Add the anchovy butter and raisins to the spinach, set the pan over medium heat, and heat, stirring often, until the mixture is piping hot.

Transfer to a serving dish, garnish with the croutons, and serve immediately.

FOOD FOR THOUGHT

The instruction, so common to spinach cookery, to cook the leaves after washing with no extra water goes back to at least 1806, when Maria Rundell, author of a hugely popular cookery book, said you should use "no water but what hangs to the leaves from washing." It remains a highly evocative—and accurate—piece of cookery prose.

AFTERNOON TEA & GARDEN PARTIES

DAINTY AFTERNOON TEAS ARE A FIXTURE IN the world of *Downton Abbey*. From the robust, cake-heavy library teas of Lord Grantham to the refined setting of a genteel tearoom, the variety of experiences seen on screen reflects the enormous range of tea-taking occasions in British life.

Having a cup of tea and something light to eat in the afternoon was well established as part of the daily pattern of meals by the early twentieth century. Tea itself had been introduced to the country in the mid-seventeenth century, when it was very expensive. The price gradually came down over the course of the next one hundred years, however, and by the Victorian era, it was enjoyed by all.

Right from the beginning tea was often drunk with a slice of bread, a biscuit, or a piece of cake, and in the Regency era, as written about by Jane Austen, the habit of taking tea was a key part of the social whirl for wealthy ladies who visited one another in the afternoon. It wasn't until the 1870s that this habit gained not only a name—afternoon tea—but also more devotees, as the lower classes enthusiastically adopted what they perceived to be an elegant occasion with a whiff of the aristocratic about it. A myth even started to circulate that the custom had somehow been "invented" in the 1840s by a duchess.

By the Edwardian era, tea wasn't just something you had at home. Tearooms boomed, including chains such as ABC and Lyons. They were seen as intrinsically feminine and therefore unthreatening, and were ideal places for women of all classes to gather and chat away from male intrusion. Some became key locations for the women's suffrage movement, and violent campaigns were often hatched and launched over the seemingly innocuous swirl of steam off a hot cup of tea. They were also useful for courting couples, who could, especially in the more relaxed atmosphere of the 1920s, meet unchaperoned in the protected surroundings of a genteel tearoom. *Downton*'s Rose, ever the modern woman, meets Jack Ross in a tearoom in Thirsk.

By this time, teas came in more forms than just afternoon tea. There were meat teas, family teas, high teas, tennis teas, and the very specific "at homes," when ladies, generally titled or at least moneyed, were officially at home to callers and dropped in on one another. Afternoon tea could easily morph into a large-scale garden party as well, and parties of this type were well liked, for they were fairly informal, easy to cater, and could accommodate a large number of people. A garden party usually involved a great deal more than just sandwiches, cake, and tea. An invitee could expect to see punches and endless Champagne, plus ice creams and water ices. The food was light, easy to digest, and deliberately fairly bland, as befitted a proper, ladylike meal at which the central beverage was not strongly flavored.

DUNDEE CAKE

Miss M. M. Mitchell, author of *The Treasure Cookery Book*, published in 1913, was the superintendent of the Polytechnic School of Cookery on London's Oxford Street. Her recipes are clear and easy to follow, and she continued to write during the Great War, advising girls who had little knowledge of cooking on how to get started. When Sybil bakes a cake for the first time in season 2, she's echoing the experience of many women who threw themselves into learning new things. For Sybil, as with so many women of the era, the war changed everything: cakes were merely the tip of the iceberg. Dundee cake was promoted heavily by Keiller's, a Scottish marmalade company, who mass-produced it. Its almond-studded top appears regularly at teas and fairs in *Downton Abbey*.

SERVES 8–10

MRS. PATMORE: *Now steady. Even the most experienced cook can burn themself if they're not careful.*

SYBIL: *Do you think it's ready?*

MRS. PATMORE: *I know it's ready.*

DAISY: *Go on. You don't want to spoil it.*

~ SEASON 2, EPISODE 1

INGREDIENTS

1 lb (450 g) mixed golden and dark raisins

6 tablespoons (90 ml) Scotch whisky

1 cup (225 g) butter, at room temperature, plus more for the pan

1 cup (225 g) firmly packed Demerara sugar

Pinch of salt

4 eggs

2¼ cups (285 g) flour

¼ teaspoon ground cinnamon

¼ teaspoon ground nutmeg

1 cup plus 2 tablespoons (115 g) ground almonds

½ cup (160 g) orange marmalade

Finely grated zest of 2 oranges

⅔ cup (90 g) whole blanched almonds, for decorating

Put the raisins and the whisky into a pan and heat over low heat, stirring once or twice, until hot, 10–15 minutes. Remove from the heat and leave to steep for 2 hours.

Preheat the oven to 325°F (165°C). Grease a 9-inch (23-cm) round cake pan. Line the bottom with parchment paper and butter the parchment.

In a large bowl, using a handheld mixer on medium speed or a wooden spoon, cream together the butter, sugar, and salt until smooth and creamy. Add the eggs, one at a time, together with a spoonful of the flour with the first egg to stop the mix from curdling, mixing well after each addition. Then beat in the remaining flour and the cinnamon and nutmeg until incorporated. Finally, stir in the raisins and whisky, the ground almonds, marmalade, and orange zest until evenly distributed.

Spoon the batter into the prepared pan and smooth the top with the back of the spoon. Arrange the whole blanched almonds on top in concentric circles, with the pointed end of each nut directed toward the center. Bake until a skewer inserted into the center of the cake comes out clean, 1½ – 1¾ hours.

Let cool completely in the pan on a wire rack, then carefully turn out the cake, peel off the parchment, turn the cake upright, and serve. This is a fairly dense cake that can be made a few days in advance and stored tightly covered at room temperature.

GAMES CAKE

The annual cricket match that takes place at the end of season 3 is a very serious business. Sports were an opportunity not just to get fit but also to entertain, in this case the wider community of Downton Abbey. Enterprising bakers quickly realized there was an opportunity to market cakes specifically for such occasions, and, with the Downton kitchens stretched as usual, this may have been an occasion for which an outside caterer was used—perhaps Bettys of Harrogate, where Rose first meets Atticus while shopping for cakes (the company still exists). This recipe is for the basic cake, and the decorated icing used should be appropriate for the occasion, whether it's tennis, cricket, or even a game of chess. Be warned: it makes two good-size cakes, so if you aren't baking it to feed the entire local populace, it is worth halving the recipe.

SERVES 20–30

INGREDIENTS

FOR THE CAKES

2½ cups (570 g) butter, at room temperature, plus more for the pans

4½ cups (570 g) flour, plus more for the pans

2¾ cups (570 g) superfine sugar, plus more for the pans

1 cup plus 2 tablespoons (115 g) ground almonds

2 teaspoons baking powder

8 eggs

1 lb (450 g) golden raisins

1 lb (450 g) dried currants

½ lb (225 g) mixed candied citrus peel, roughly chopped

½ lb (225 g) glacéed cherries, roughly chopped

FOR THE DECORATION

1½ lb (680 g) marzipan, plus more for leveling the cake if needed

½ cup (140 g) red currant or raspberry jam

1½ lb (680 g) ready-to-roll white fondant icing

1 package (1 lb/450 g) royal icing mix, or sugar icing (see Recipe Note, page 115, using four times the amount of each ingredient)

Food coloring, in assorted colors

Preheat the oven to 325°F (165°C). Butter two 9-inch (23-cm) square cake pans or two 11 x 7-inch (28 x 18-cm) pans, then dust with a mixture of equal parts flour and sugar, tapping out the excess.

In a bowl, stir together the flour, almonds, and baking powder. Using a stand mixer fitted with the paddle attachment, or in a large bowl with a handheld mixer, cream together the butter and sugar on medium speed until smooth and creamy. On low speed, gradually add the flour mixture, beating until fully incorporated. Increase the speed to medium and gradually add the eggs, beating until incorporated. Using a rubber spatula or a spoon, fold in the raisins, currants, citrus peel, and cherries. Divide the batter evenly between the prepared pans and smooth the tops.

Bake until a skewer inserted into the center of each cake comes out clean, about 1¾ hours. If the tops start to darken too much, lay a piece of brown paper or aluminum foil on them.

Remove the cakes from the oven, let cool in the pans on wire racks for 15 minutes, then turn them out onto the racks, turn them upright, and let cool completely.

Transfer the cooled cakes to a large board, pushing them together to form an oblong cake. If the assembled cake has any large holes or if the corners or sides slope downward too much, pad the flaws with a little marzipan so the top is as even as possible. Now roll out the marzipan and trim it so it will cover the entire top of the cake. In a small saucepan over low heat on the stove top or in a small heatproof bowl in the microwave, heat the jam until it melts, then strain through a fine-mesh sieve to remove any fruit chunks or seeds. Brush the melted jam on top of the cake, covering it evenly. Lay the marzipan on top and trim the edges if needed to fit exactly. You need only cover the top of the cake and not the sides. Roll out the fondant icing and trim it so it will cover the entire top of the cake. Lay the fondant on top of the marzipan, trimming once again as needed to make a nice, neat, smooth layer.

Now you can go to town with the icing. Mix up the royal icing according to the package instructions (generally ¼ cup/60 ml water to 1 lb/450 g mix). Divide up the icing into as many portions as you like, color each portion a different color, and pipe designs of your choice on top of the cake. Or you can mix a little more water into some of the icing, divide it into portions, color them, and flood parts of the cake. When you've created a masterpiece, run a suitably sized ribbon around the edge and pin it in place.

RECIPE NOTE

This recipe, which appeared in the 1903 *The Art of Confectionery* by George Cox, was originally called Tennis Cake and was intended as a light fruitcake for summer tennis teas. But Cox suggested to his audience of professional bakers that "games cakes to suit the requirements of any season or district can be made from the recipe given for the Tennis Cake . . . substituting the word 'golf' and piping golf clubs on the top, or 'football,' 'hockey' or 'boating,' when a small boat or yacht could be placed upon the top as well." Ingenious icing is the way to make this recipe look its most Downtonesque. It's iced only on top so it can be cut into equal-size squares and everyone will have the same proportions of cake and topping.

MRS. WIGAN: *It comes down to priorities, Lord Grantham. Which is more important, a game of cricket or the loss of a son in the course of his duty?*

~ SEASON 5, EPISODE 2

PINEAPPLE AND WALNUT CAKE

Every time Downton breaks out into a party, there are lots of cakes. Generally plainly decorated, they fill the kitchen and then the cake stands at the village fair, the church fund-raiser, and the memorable garden party at the close of season 1, which ends with the announcement that Britain is at war. This recipe's use of glacéed pineapple reflects the growing availability of previously exotic products in the twentieth century: pineapple still carried a certain cachet from the time when it was unaffordable for all but the rich. Pineapple recipes proliferated in cookery books in the early to mid-twentieth century after Jim Dole founded the Hawaiian Pineapple Company in 1901. In the nineteenth century, Downton would likely have grown its own fresh pineapples in pits or heated greenhouses, but in the more financially straitened times in which the series is set, such expensive practices would all have been history.

SERVES 6–8

INGREDIENTS

I cup (225 g) butter, at room temperature, plus more for the pan

I heaping cup (115 g) walnut halves and pieces, plus ½ cup (60 g) walnut halves for decorating

½ lb (225 g) glacéed pineapple

2¾ cups (340 g) flour

I teaspoon baking powder

½ teaspoon ground nutmeg

Pinch of salt

I cup plus 2 tablespoons (225 g) superfine sugar

5 eggs

⅛ teaspoon pure pineapple or pure vanilla extract

2 tablespoons milk

Preheat the oven to 325°F (165°C). Butter an 8-inch (20-cm) round cake pan with 2-inch (5-cm) sides. Line the bottom with parchment paper and butter the parchment.

Spread the heaping cup of walnut halves and pieces on a small sheet pan and toast until brown and fragrant, 8–10 minutes. Pour onto a cutting board and let cool. Reduce the oven temperature to 300°F (150°C).

Chop the cooled nuts finely. Cut the pineapple into pieces about twice the size of the walnut pieces.

In a medium bowl, combine the flour, baking powder, nutmeg, and salt. Whisk gently to blend.

In a large bowl, using a handheld mixer on medium speed or a wooden spoon, cream together the butter and sugar until smooth and creamy. Add the eggs, one at a time, together with a spoonful of the flour mixture with the first egg to stop the mix from curdling, mixing well after each addition. Mix in the pineapple extract. Beat in half of the remaining flour mixture, all of the milk, and then the remaining flour mixture. Quickly fold in the reserved chopped nuts and pineapple.

Scrape the batter into the prepared pan and smooth the top. Decoratively arrange the walnut halves on top. Bake until the cake begins to pull away from the sides of the pan and a skewer inserted into the center comes out clean, about 1¼ hours.

Let cool completely in the pan on a wire rack, then carefully turn the cake out onto the rack, loosening the edges with a blunt knife if needed. Peel off the parchment, turn the cake upright, and serve.

MADEIRA CAKE

Named for its usual accompaniment rather than an ingredient, Madeira cake was a favorite throughout the nineteenth and twentieth centuries, and a slice of cake with a glass of Madeira was both a slightly more fortifying alternative to afternoon tea and a suitable way of staving off hunger pangs in the early evening if you'd missed tea. There are many, very slightly different recipes, but it was nearly always made in a loaf pan and is instantly recognizable whenever it appears on *Downton*—usually on the side table during the family's tea. Cakes of this type were often made in pans greased with butter and lined with sugar rather than flour. It gives them a slightly crunchy exterior and keeps the eater from having the occasional alarming mouthful of flour.

SERVES 8–10

INGREDIENTS

½ cup (115 g) unsalted butter, melted and cooled, plus room-temperature butter for the pan

¾ cup plus 2 tablespoons (170 g) superfine sugar, plus more for the pan

1 cup (128 g) flour

Grated zest of 1 large or 2 small lemons

½ teaspoon baking powder

3 eggs

½ teaspoon pure vanilla extract

Preheat the oven to 350°F (180°C). Butter an 8½ x 4½-inch (21.5 x 11.5-cm) loaf pan, then lightly coat with sugar, tapping out the excess.

Whisk together the flour, lemon zest, and baking powder in a bowl. In a separate, larger bowl, whisk the eggs until thick and creamy. Continuing to whisk, gradually add the sugar until fully incorporated. While whisking constantly, very slowly add the melted butter just until incorporated. (Alternatively, use a handheld mixer on medium-high speed to beat the eggs, then beat in the sugar, and finally the butter.) Carefully fold in the flour mixture just until thoroughly combined. Pour the batter into the prepared pan.

Get the pan into the oven quickly, before the eggs have a chance to collapse. Bake until a skewer inserted into the center comes out clean, about 30 minutes.

Let cool in the pan on a wire rack for 10 minutes, then carefully turn the cake out onto the rack, turn the cake upright, and let cool completely before serving.

RECIPE NOTE

You can use orange or lime zest instead of lemon. You can also add a few chopped glacéed cherries to the batter and garnish the top with whole glacéed cherries to make a cherry Madeira cake (in which case you could serve it with cherry liqueur instead of Madeira). A light glaze of confectioners' sugar, lemon juice, and a little bit of hot water will boost the lemon flavor and add a bit of interest to the top, but it's not essential.

SUPER-CHOCOLATE CAKE

Chocolate cakes were comparatively new in Britain in the Edwardian period but caught on quickly. The writer of this recipe, Agnes Jekyll, was the daughter of a politician, the sister of one of Britain's most influential gardeners, and a strong supporter of the arts. She was one of many strong-minded, talented women who forged careers for themselves in the years after the Great War, and her book, *Kitchen Essays*, was aimed at well-born ladies, like Edith, who found life in the 1920s both liberating and confusing. The carnage of 1914 to 1918 wiped out a large proportion of the male population, leaving many women to face life without marriage. But they were determined that life as a spinster would not be a life with no meaning. Like Edith, Agnes was a journalist, who wrote for *The Times*.

SERVES 8

MRS. PATMORE (TO DAISY): *Fold it in, don't slap it! You're making a cake, not beating a carpet!*

~ SEASON 2, EPISODE 2

INGREDIENTS

FOR THE CAKE

I cup (225 g) butter, at room temperature, plus more for the pan

¾ cup (90 g) flour, plus more for the pan

I cup plus 2 tablespoons (225 g) superfine sugar, plus more for the pan

I cup plus 2 tablespoons (115 g) ground almonds

I teaspoon baking powder

Pinch of salt

½ lb (225 g) bittersweet chocolate (70 percent cacao), chopped

6 eggs

I teaspoon pure vanilla extract

FOR THE ICING (optional)

I cup (115 g) confectioners' sugar

2–3 tablespoons maraschino, orange, or other liqueur

Preheat the oven to 250°F (120°C). Line the bottom of a 9-inch (23-cm) springform or round cake pan with parchment paper. Butter the paper, then dust with a mixture of equal parts flour and superfine sugar, tapping out the excess.

In a bowl, combine the flour, almonds, baking powder, and salt. Whisk gently to blend.

Melt the chocolate either in a microwave oven (the twenty-first-century way) or in a heatproof bowl over a pan of simmering water (the Downton way). Set aside to cool.

Separate the eggs, releasing the whites into a large bowl and the yolks into a medium bowl. Beat the yolks briefly to blend, then stir in the vanilla. Whisk the egg whites by hand or with a handheld mixer on medium-high speed until stiff peaks form.

In a bowl, using a handheld mixer on medium speed or a wooden spoon, cream together the butter and superfine sugar until smooth and creamy. Beat in the melted chocolate until well mixed. Beat in a spoonful of the flour mixture to prevent curdling, then gradually beat in the egg yolk mixture. Gradually fold in the remaining flour mixture. Add about one-fourth of the beaten egg whites, folding in just until no white streaks remain. Fold in the remaining egg whites the same way. Spoon the batter into the prepared pan and smooth the top.

Bake until the cake begins to pull away from the sides of the pan and a skewer inserted into the center comes out clean, about 1¼ hours. Let cool completely in the pan on a wire rack, then turn out onto the rack, peel off the parchment, turn the cake upright, and place on a serving plate. If you have used a springform pan, let cool as directed, then unclasp the pan sides and carefully slide the cake onto a serving plate, peeling away the paper as you do.

If making the icing, put the confectioners' sugar into a bowl, whisk in enough of the liqueur to make a soft, pourable icing, and slowly pour the icing over the cake. Alternatively, use only enough liqueur to make a stiffer icing and spread it on with a palette knife or offset spatula.

RECIPE NOTE

This cake is excellent plain or iced. If you want a fancier cake to serve at dinner, top it with a layer of cherries soaked in brandy or maraschino liqueur. It is particularly nice with a dollop of softly whipped cream or crème fraîche.

FAIRY CAKE BASKETS

Fairy cakes are a British teatime classic. Smaller than modern cupcakes, they nevertheless have similar origins and are essentially a flavored sponge cake. This delightful version takes a simple recipe and elevates it to a suitably high-class context. The cakes are particularly good fun to make with children, and both Sybbie and George can be seen in the *Downton* kitchen in season 6 making much of licking the bowl.

MAKES 12 BASKETS

INGREDIENTS

¾ cup (170 g) butter, at room temperature, plus more for the muffin cups

¾ cup plus 2 tablespoons (170 g) superfine sugar, plus ½ teaspoon for the espresso mixture and more for the muffin cups

1¼ cups (155 g) flour, plus more for the muffin cups

3 eggs

1 generous teaspoon baking powder

3–5 drops red food coloring

3–5 drops yellow food coloring

¼ teaspoon pure rose extract

¼ teaspoon pure orange extract

2 teaspoons espresso powder

1 teaspoon hot water

14–16 thin strips candied angelica, each 4–5 inches (10–13 cm) long

Boiling water, to cover

2 tablespoons plus 4 teaspoons strawberry jam

4 teaspoons cold water

¼ cup (1 oz) sweetened shredded dried coconut, finely chopped, or ground almonds

2 tablespoons plus 4 teaspoons orange marmalade

4 teaspoons chocolate spread

⅔ cup (160 ml) heavy cream

Preheat the oven to 350°F (180°C). Butter 12 standard muffin cups (about 3 inches/7.5 cm in diameter and ¾ inch/2 cm deep), then dust with a mixture of equal parts superfine sugar and flour, tapping out the excess.

In a large bowl, using a handheld mixer on medium speed or a wooden spoon, cream together the butter and sugar until smooth and creamy. Add the eggs, one at a time, together with a spoonful of the flour with the first egg to stop the mix from curdling, mixing well after each addition. Then fold in the remaining flour and the baking powder, mixing thoroughly.

Divide the mixture into three equal portions, putting each portion into a separate small bowl. Color one portion with the red food coloring and one with the yellow food coloring. Stir the rose extract into the red portion and the orange extract into the yellow portion. For the third portion, stir together the espresso powder, hot water, and ½ teaspoon sugar in a small cup until the espresso powder and sugar are dissolved, then fold into the remaining plain batter until evenly blended. Divide the mixtures evenly among the muffin cups, filling 4 cups with each color.

Bake until a skewer inserted into the center of a cake comes out clean, 16–18 minutes. Let cool in the pan on a wire rack for 10 minutes, then turn out onto the rack, turn upright, and let cool completely.

Meanwhile, put the angelica strips into a small heatproof bowl, add boiling water to cover, and let stand until softened, about 20 minutes. (You'll have a few spares in case of breakage.)

Using a paring knife held at a 45-degree angle, a small spoon, or a melon baller, hollow out the center of each cake, being careful not to pierce the bottom. In a small bowl, mix the 2 tablespoons strawberry jam with 2 teaspoons of the cold water. Brush the outside and sides of each red cake with the jam and then roll the cake in the coconut to coat evenly. Repeat with the 2 tablespoons marmalade, mixing the marmalade with the remaining 2 teaspoons water, then brushing and coating the yellow cakes. Leave the brown cakes plain. Now fill each red cake with 1 teaspoon strawberry jam, each yellow cake with 1 teaspoon marmalade, and each brown cake with 1 teaspoon chocolate spread.

Whisk the cream by hand or with a handheld mixer on medium-high speed until stiff peaks form. Transfer to a piping bag fitted with a star or plain tip and pipe a little cream into the center of each basket. Finally, bend each angelica strip into a half-circle to form a "handle" and gently push the ends into the sides of each cake.

RECIPE NOTE

Specific amounts are included for the flavorings and colorings, but all flavorings and colorings are different, so make sure you use the amount you need according to the type you have, adding them gradually and judging the intensity of the flavor or the color as you go. These little cakes can be as varied as you like, so let your imagination run wild with your jams, flavors, and colors. The secret is to ensure your basic cake is light, delicate, and small, so that whatever you add doesn't make the cake too rich.

ORANGE LAYER CAKE

While the Victoria Sandwich (page 77) is the most famous layered cake of the era, it's by no means the only such cake to make an appearance at Downton. Layered cakes appear in the background of lots of scenes, especially those set during afternoon tea, which at Downton is often taken informally in the library. Tea-taking also happens on the lawn, with the house itself in the background; in tearooms; and in other people's houses. Both Isobel and Violet are regular afternoon tea-takers. Orange cakes were one of the staples of the period and appear in many books. This version, from Margaret Black's *Superior Cookery* (1887), uses oranges and lemons and packs a very citrusy punch indeed.

SERVES 8–10

FOOD FOR THOUGHT

Baking powder wasn't invented until the middle of the Victorian era. Before then, sponge cakes were raised by beating as much air as possible into the eggs. Many cooks looked down upon raising agents and resisted using them, fearing, like Mrs. Patmore, that such modern cheats were a slippery slope to the devaluing of cooks, eventually replacing them entirely.

INGREDIENTS

1 large or 2 small oranges

2 lemons

½ cup (115 g) butter, at room temperature, plus more for the pans

1 cup (200 g) superfine sugar, plus more for the pans

1¾ cups plus 2 tablespoons (225 g) flour, plus more for the pans

1¾ teaspoons baking soda

Pinch of salt

5 egg yolks

FOR THE CANDIED PEEL

1 cup (240 ml) water

1 cup (200 g) granulated sugar

FOR THE ICING

2 cups (250 g) confectioners' sugar, sifted

Pinch of salt

FOR THE FILLING

2 tablespoons orange marmalade, puréed in a blender or by hand

Using a paring knife, remove the peel from the orange and lemons, leaving as much of the white pith behind as possible. You need the peel in strips, ideally about 3 inches (7.5 cm) long and ¼ inch (6 mm) wide, though chunks will do. Just don't grate the zest. Put the orange peel and lemon peel into separate small bowls. Now juice the orange and add the juice to the bowl of lemon peel and juice the lemons and add the juice to the orange peel. Leave the peels to steep for 1 hour, then strain the juices into separate small bowls and reserve along with both peels for later.

Preheat the oven to 350°F (180°C). Butter the bottom and sides of two 9-inch (23-cm) round cake pans. Line the bottoms of the pans with parchment paper and butter the parchment. Dust the sides with a mixture of equal parts superfine sugar and flour, tapping out the excess.

In a bowl, combine the flour, baking soda, and salt. Whisk gently to blend.

In a stand mixer fitted with the paddle attachment, or in a large bowl with a handheld mixer, cream together the butter and superfine sugar on medium speed until smooth and creamy. Add the egg yolks, one at a time, mixing well after each addition, then beat for 10 minutes. The mixture should be pale and fluffy. On low speed, beat in 2 tablespoons of the flour mixture to

Recipe continues

prevent curdling, then add the remaining flour mixture in three batches, alternating with the reserved orange juice in two batches, beginning and ending with the flour and mixing well after each addition. Divide the batter evenly between the prepared pans, spreading to the edges of the pan.

Bake until a skewer inserted into the center of each cake layer comes out clean, 20–25 minutes. Let cool completely in the pans on wire racks. Using a blunt knife, loosen the edges of the cakes from the pan sides, then invert the pans onto the racks, lift off the pans, and gently peel off the parchment. Work carefully, as the layers are very light and delicate.

While the cake layers are cooling, candy the citrus peel for decorating the top of the cake. Put the orange and lemon peels into a small saucepan, add cold water to cover, and bring to a boil over high heat. Boil for a couple of minutes, then drain, discarding the water, and return the peels to the pan. Repeat twice, discarding the water each time. Meanwhile, line a large sheet pan with parchment paper.

When you have boiled the peels three times, return them to the pan, add the I cup (240 ml) water and the granulated sugar, and bring to a boil, stirring to dissolve the sugar. Adjust the heat to maintain a simmer and simmer until the peels are tender and any pith has become translucent, 25–30 minutes. Drain well and use a fork to spread the peels in a single layer on the prepared sheet pan to cool. Finally, dry the peels in a gentle oven—250°F (120°C) is perfect—until they are crisp but not browned, about 30 minutes. Set aside.

To make the icing, put the confectioners' sugar, reserved lemon juice, and the salt into a bowl and beat together until smooth.

Place a cake layer on a serving plate and spread the top with the marmalade. Top with the second layer, then, using a palette knife or offset spatula, frost the top and sides of the cake with the icing. Sprinkle the top with the candied peel. Let the cake stand for 15 minutes to set the icing before serving.

VICTORIA SANDWICH

Split sandwich cakes often make an appearance in the kitchen and drawing room at Downton Abbey. This is probably the best-known cake of that type in Britain, but the original version was not the large round cake visible at Downton and usually served under the name today, but a delicate pile of finger sandwiches made with sponge cake and spread with what the recipe in Isabella Beeton's *The Book of Household Management* calls "nice preserves." The Beeton book is, like the Victoria sandwich, iconic, and was the first to call the cake the Victoria sandwich, named, of course, after Queen Victoria. It's very middle class, aimed at families such as one in which Matthew grew up, and a Victoria sandwich can be seen on the table when Isobel is having tea with Lord Merton during the budding romance of season 5. Although Beeton's book isn't one that would have been used much in the aristocratic context of Downton, the recipe, with its simple measurements and ingredients, is a classic. The modern Victoria sandwich includes whipped cream along with the jam.

SERVES 6–8

INGREDIENTS

Unsalted butter, at room temperature

Flour

Superfine sugar

4 eggs, at room temperature

Pinch of salt

½ teaspoon baking powder (optional)

¼ cup (70 g) jam of choice

Preheat the oven to 350°F (180°C). Generously butter an 8-inch (20-cm) square cake pan. Line the bottom with parchment paper, butter the paper, then dust with a mixture of equal parts flour and sugar, tapping out the excess.

Weigh the eggs in their shells. Then weigh their equivalent in butter, flour, and sugar. In a medium bowl, gently whisk together the flour, salt, and baking powder (if using, for a lighter cake; for a denser, more authentic cake, leave it out). In a large bowl, using a handheld mixer on medium speed or a wooden spoon, beat the butter until creamy, then beat in the sugar until well blended, 2–3 minutes. Beat in 1 tablespoon of the flour mixture to prevent the mix from curdling, then add the eggs, one at a time, beating well after each addition. Continue to beat until light and fluffy, about 2 minutes. Gradually add the remaining flour mixture, on low speed if using a mixer, and beat only until incorporated. The batter will be thick and creamy. Scrape into the prepared pan and smooth the top.

Bake until golden brown, the sides begin to pull away from the pan, and a skewer inserted into the center comes out clean, 30–40 minutes. Let cool in the pan on a wire rack for 20 minutes, then turn out onto the rack, peel off the parchment, turn upright, and let cool completely.

Trim off the browned edges from the cake, if desired. Using a serrated knife, cut the cake in half horizontally to make 2 layers. Spread the bottom half with jam, then return the top half and press together gently. Slice the cake into 6 equal strips about 1¼ inches (3 cm) wide and then crosswise into thirds to create 18 "nice finger pieces"—ideal for eating in a couple of delicate bites. For an Edwardian presentation, on a serving plate, stack the sandwiches in rows of three, with each row at a 90-degree angle to the previous one.

AFTERNOON TEA

Afternoon tea was a low-key occasion on which everyone could come together. It lacked the formality of dinner and was an ideal way to introduce new friends or potential suitors to a family group, without the nerve-racking test of a full meal. It was usually consumed sitting down on sofas or chairs, with handy side tables for placing cups and saucers, and it lent itself easily to semiprivate conversation, as large groups typically broke down into smaller gatherings. At Downton, the Dowager Countess frequently uses the calm, intimate atmosphere of afternoon tea to give out advice, especially to the women of the family.

Meeting for tea in the afternoon was seen as being very feminine, with men the decided interlopers. In the late nineteenth century, a fashion for wearing tea gowns developed that emphasized both the informal and feminine aspects of afternoon tea: they were usually worn without corsets and had a whiff of the dressing gown (known as a wrapper) about them. Pretty yet comfortable, they were not intended as garments in which a lady would leave the house. They lasted until the early 1930s, by which time fashion itself had veered away from the heavily shaped and boned figures that were common in the years before the Great War.

Like every social occasion, even informal afternoon tea was surrounded by an apparent plethora of rules in the etiquette guides of the time. However, such guides didn't apply at houses like Downton: if you needed the book, you weren't born to it, and you were definitely not the right person to be doing it.

ROBERT: *Where have you been?*

ROSE: *I went out for tea with Atticus.*
We met half way, in Ripon.

ROBERT: *It's getting quite serious, then?*

ROSE: *Fingers crossed.*

~ SEASON 5, EPISODE 7

MADELEINES

A classic of French cookery, madeleines are delicate sponge cakes traditionally made in a special pan with shell-shaped molds. Families such as the Crawleys, seasoned travelers to France as they are, would have known them well. They're served in season 1, when Matthew is still coming to terms with having a valet to serve him and helps himself to them, much to Molesley's chagrin. Quick and easy to make, they were perfect for delicate, feminine afternoon teas but were also suitable for late-night snacking, and often filled the biscuit jars kept by Mary, Edith, and Sybil's beds.

MAKES 12 MADELEINES

ANNA: *Have you had any breakfast?*

DAISY: *Not a crumb.*

ANNA: *Here.*

She takes the biscuit jar beside the bed and hands it to Daisy.

GWEN: *You can't take her biscuits.*

ANNA: *She never eats them. None of them do. They're just thrown away and changed every evening.*

DAISY: *Thanks. She won't mind anyway. She's nice, Lady Sybil.*

~ SEASON 1, EPISODE 5

6 tablespoons (90 g) unsalted butter, melted and cooled, plus room-temperature butter for the molds

6 tablespoons (80 g) superfine sugar, plus more for the molds

⅔ cup (80 g) flour

¼ teaspoon orange flower water

Grated zest and juice of ½ small lemon

2 eggs, separated

Pinch of salt

Confectioners' sugar, for serving

Preheat the oven to 350°F (180°C). Butter 12 madeleine molds. Dust them with superfine sugar, tapping out the excess.

Put the melted butter, superfine sugar, and flour into a bowl and stir to mix well. Add the orange flower water and lemon zest and juice and again mix well. Stir in the egg yolks until blended.

In a separate bowl, combine the egg whites and salt. Whisk by hand or with a handheld mixer on medium speed until stiff peaks form. Gently fold the egg whites into the batter just until no white streaks remain. Divide the batter evenly among the prepared molds.

Bake until very lightly browned at the edges, 10–12 minutes. Let cool in the molds on a wire rack for 5 minutes, then turn out of the molds onto the rack and let cool completely. Sift the confectioners' sugar over the madeleines just before serving.

BEST GRANTHAM

Grantham is a small town in Lincolnshire, about one hundred miles (160 kilometers) from the area in Yorkshire where Downton, home of the earls of Grantham, stands. It was not unusual for titled families to live hundreds of miles from the town or county from which their title derived, however, for families frequently owned land—and houses—in many different counties. Land holdings were often consolidated in the twentieth century and estates sold off, leaving a number of anomalies like this. Grantham was also a type of gingerbread, which was named, like the family, for the town that was the center of its production from the Victorian period onward. Unlike many gingerbreads, this one is what was known as a white gingerbread, as it was made with white sugar rather than brown sugar or molasses. It has medieval roots, though it started life more as a spiced marzipan than a cake or cookie. Like many regional specialties, it died out in the late twentieth century and is now almost forgotten. It is an excellent addition to an afternoon tea party, however, especially if lots of people are expected, for it is easy and quick to make and stores very well.

MAKES 18 SQUARES

INGREDIENTS

1¾ cups (210 g) flour, plus more for the work surface

¾ cup (150 g) superfine sugar

2½ teaspoons ground ginger

½ teaspoon ground nutmeg

7 tablespoons (150 g) cold butter, cut into cubes, plus more for the pan

½ teaspoon baking soda

1 tablespoon milk

1 egg, lightly whisked

Candied citrus peel, for decorating

Put the flour, sugar, ginger, and nutmeg into a large bowl and stir together. Scatter the butter cubes over the top and, using a pastry blender or your fingers, work the butter into the flour mixture until the mixture is the consistency of bread crumbs. Dissolve the baking soda in the milk, add the milk and the egg to the flour mixture, and mix until thoroughly combined. Shape into a ball, cover with a bowl or wrap in plastic wrap, and leave to rest at room temperature for 2–4 hours.

Preheat the oven to 350°F (180°C). Butter a large sheet pan.

On a floured work surface, roll out the dough into a 12-inch (30-cm) square. Trim the edges as needed to make them even, then cut the square into nine 4-inch (10-cm) squares. Transfer them to the prepared pan, spacing them well apart, as they will expand. Put a piece of candied peel on the top of each square.

Bake until the tops and bottoms are golden brown but the gingerbread is still flexible and yielding when you press it with your fingertip, about 15 minutes. The pieces may expand into one another a bit, but you should be able to break them apart easily. Transfer to a wire rack and let cool completely before serving.

RECIPE NOTE

The candied peel is suggested in the original recipe, but the gingerbread also lends itself to a bit of basic icing. These gingerbread squares are intended to be cheap and cheerful, sold, according to the author of this particular version of the recipe, "at two, three, or four a penny, according to thickness and size."

SCONES

A staple of the twentieth-century tea table, scones have become a British classic, and, as befits such a simple recipe, they are the subject of fierce debate. They are generally eaten with cream and jam, a habit popularized by the rise of Cornish and Devonshire cream teas, heavily marketed to the modern leisure motorist in the 1920s and 1930s. In this case, the argument centers on whether the eater puts jam on first or cream on first (there is also debate over what type of cream, but it should always be clotted cream, and the more lumps the better). It's not a question *Downton* illuminates, however, since even though scones appear frequently both in the kitchen and upstairs, we never quite see the moment of consumption. There's also a question over how the word *scone* is pronounced—either as "skon" or "scohwn"— and this is settled in *Downton*: when Mrs. Patmore serves them up to Lord and Lady Grantham at her B and B in season 6, both she and Robert pronounce it "skon."

MAKES 16 SCONES

INGREDIENTS

3¾ cups (450 g) flour, plus more for the work surface

2 tablespoons plus 2 teaspoons superfine sugar

2 tablespoons baking powder

2 tablespoons cold solid vegetable shortening or lard, cut into cubes

2 tablespoons cold butter, cut into cubes

I egg

I cup (240 ml) milk, plus more for brushing

½ cup (90 g) dried currants (optional)

Preheat the oven to 425°F (220°C). Have ready an ungreased large sheet pan.

Put the flour, sugar, and baking powder into a large bowl and stir together. Scatter the shortening and butter cubes over the top and, using a pastry blender or your fingers, work in the butter and shortening until the mixture is the consistency of bread crumbs. Whisk the egg in a small bowl until blended, then whisk in the milk. Add the milk mixture to the flour mixture and mix until a slightly crumbly but cohesive dough forms. Add the currants, if using, and gently knead into the dough.

Divide the dough into 16 equal portions weighing about 2 oz/60 g each and shape each portion into a ball. Arrange the balls on the sheet pan, spacing them well apart, and press down lightly on each ball to flatten the top. Make two cuts almost all the way through at right angles to each other, so that you form four wedges, which can easily be torn apart when served. (Alternatively, on a floured work surface, roll out the dough to about 1½ inches (4 cm) thick and use a 2-inch (5-cm) round biscuit cutter to cut into rounds.) Brush the tops with milk.

Bake until golden brown, about 15 minutes. After 10 minutes, it is worth turning them over to brown the bottoms, if you like. Transfer to a wire rack and let cool before serving.

RECIPE NOTE

Scones are fairly bland, and it's the topping that makes them: lots of jam, even more clotted cream, and that's it. If that's not possible, butter spread so thick you leave teeth marks in it and jam or honey also work.

MACAROONS

More like Bakewell tarts than macaroons in the conventional sense, these are delicate little tartlets that lend an air of sophistication to the tea tray. Be Ro was a brand of flour, predominantly selling self-rising flour that struggled to find a market in the late nineteenth century. To help market its products, Be-Ro, beginning in 1923, produced a recipe pamphlet that rapidly became a fixture in many homes. It was much cheaper than a full cookery book, and it made Be-Ro a household name in the north of England, where its efforts were concentrated. Unlike hardcover books, few of the millions of pamphlets that were produced survive today. The impact of small-scale manufacturer-led recipe pamphlets is often underestimated, but for many people, they were the key way they learned to cook. Branded products are often in view on the kitchen shelves at Downton, and increasingly so as the series moves forward in time. Although cooks like Mrs. Patmore would have had high-end French cookery books, the Be-Ro pamphlets would have been familiar to the younger staff at country houses, who were brought up in a more brand-focused time.

MAKES 12 MACAROONS

INGREDIENTS

FOR THE PASTRY

1 cup (115 g) flour, plus more for the work surface

¼ teaspoon salt

4 tablespoons (60 g) cold unsalted butter, cut into cubes

2–3 tablespoons ice-cold water

FOR THE TOPPING

7 tablespoons (90 g) superfine sugar

¾ cup (90 g) ground almonds or almond flour

½ teaspoon orange flower water

1 egg

¼ cup (70 g) good-quality jam of choice

To make the pastry, put the flour and salt into a bowl and mix well. Scatter the butter cubes over the flour mixture and, using a pastry blender or your fingers, work the butter into the flour mixture until the mixture is the consistency of bread crumbs. Add 2 tablespoons water and stir and toss just until the dough comes together in a rough mass, adding more water if needed. Shape into a ball, wrap in plastic wrap, and refrigerate for 30 minutes.

While the pastry chills, make the topping. Combine the sugar, almonds, orange flower water, and egg in a bowl and mix well.

Butter 12 tartlet pans each about 2½ inches (6 cm) in diameter. On a lightly floured work surface, roll out the pastry as thinly as possible. Using a small, sharp knife or a cookie cutter, cut out 12 rounds ¾–1 inch (2–2.5 cm) larger in diameter than your pans. Transfer the pastry rounds to the prepared pans, pressing them onto the bottom and up the sides and trimming away any excess. Refrigerate the pastry-lined pans for 30 minutes. Gather together any pastry scraps and wrap and chill at the same time.

Preheat the oven to 425°F (220°C). Put 1 teaspoon of the jam in the bottom of each pastry-lined pan, spreading it evenly. Divide the almond topping evenly among the pans. Roll out the pastry scraps and cut into decorative shapes, such as crosses or stars, and decorate the top of each tartlet.

Place the tartlets on a large sheet pan and bake until the pastry is golden and the topping is puffed and dry to the touch, about 12 minutes. Let cool completely in the pans on a wire rack, then carefully remove from the pans to serve.

PICNICS, SHOOTS
& RACE MEETS

DOWNTON ABBEY IS VERY GOOD AT SHOWING the everyday lives of the Crawley family and how the rituals of the day, and the year, were signposted by meals. Much of the upstairs action takes place in the sumptuous interiors of the house itself, though the village is also well represented. On occasion we see the family elsewhere, however, either engaged in the seasonal pastimes of shooting or hunting, which invariably involve a lavish lunch as the autumn shadows stretch in the early afternoon, or taking part in picnics. Mary rides point-to-point in a steeplechase in season 5 while her family (and suitors) look on from a refreshment tent, and when she falls in love with Henry Talbot she's drawn into the world of car racing, which also involves a catered spread.

These occasions all had one thing in common: they required good food presented in the usual exacting standards of the upper-class table, but with the added condition that it needed to be transported and served in a temporary setting that was often at some considerable distance from the kitchen. On shoots, the personnel were divided into guns, the well-born men who shot the game; their loaders, usually their valets; and the beaters, who were estate workers and hired hands tasked with flushing the quarry from the bushes. The party would sometimes be out from an early breakfast to the end of the light around four in the afternoon, and their tea then had

to be substantial enough to make up for missing lunch (but not so heavy as to ruin dinner, to which visiting guns would invariably be invited). By the 1920s, however, it was more usual to have a sit-down lunch instead. These meals were often served in a large tent (marquee) at a properly set table with chairs and with a semiformal style of service attended by footmen.

Picnics could be just as formal, such as the one held at Eryholme in season 3 when the Earl is thinking of downsizing. Alternatively, they could be chances to relax and sprawl (in a limited fashion), as Harold Levinson and Madeleine Allsopp do in the park in season 4. It was rare for the upper classes to sprawl quite as much as Anna and Bates do when they have their much more muted picnic by the river in season 3.

Race meets, with their catered refreshment tents, combined elements of both the picnic and the shooting lunch and generally involved a buffet. The food for all these occasions was carefully planned to fill, though not too much; to please the eye without being impossible to set up (especially without cooks on hand); and to last for several hours packed in straw-lined hampers en route to its destination. It also had to be practical to eat, which, given that the preferred dress for a summer picnic tended toward white muslin and cream linen suits, was not easy to manage.

POTTED CHEESE

When the fridge arrives at Downton in season 6 it's yet another sign of encroaching modernity. Although ice caves and chests had been around since the mid-nineteenth century, it took the arrival of electricity and the development of (relatively) efficient artificial chilling processes to allow what we call fridges to develop. In the United Kingdom take-up of the new technology was slow: most houses did not have electricity, and the system of wet, dry, and cool larders that had developed over hundreds of years, together with the ability to have regular butcher shop and milk deliveries, meant there was little need for them. Additionally, meat consumption was much lower, with many people eating meat only once or twice a week. Even in the 1960s, less than half of the national population had a fridge. This meant that age-old preserving methods, including salting, smoking, jamming, and potting, remained important, especially in rural areas such as Yorkshire, where *Downton* is set. This recipe, which originates in the early nineteenth century, is ideal for making use of nub ends of hard cheese and is a practical way to add pizzazz to a picnic.

SERVES 4–6

INGREDIENTS

¼ lb (115 g) Cheshire or similar hard, crumbly cheese

4 tablespoons (60 g) unsalted butter, at room temperature

I teaspoon sugar

½ teaspoon ground mace

½ teaspoon white pepper

6 tablespoons (90 ml) dry white wine

2 tablespoons clarified butter

Bread or hot toast, for serving

Pound the cheese in a mortar with a pestle until smooth or purée it in a food processor. Add the room-temperature butter, sugar, mace, pepper, and wine and mix well. Firmly pack into a small crock, then melt the clarified butter and pour it on top. Cover and chill in the fridge to set.

Serve with plain or freshly toasted bread.

RECIPE NOTE

A similar technique can be used to pot ham, shrimp, or cooked beef, though in these cases leave out the wine and increase the unsalted butter to 6 tablespoons (90 g). Anything potted is particularly good on hot toast, as the butter in the spread melts into the bread, leaving the slightly spiced top behind.

CORA: *I've come down to persuade you.*

MRS. PATMORE: *I just don't see why it's better than an icebox.*

CORA: *Well, a refrigerator is more efficient. It keeps food fresh longer, [and] we won't need ice to be delivered.*

~ SEASON 4, EPISODE 5

SAUSAGE ROLLS

Along with fox hunting, shooting features as a sport at Downton on a number of occasions. We see not only the excitement of bringing down a bird but also the tedium of waiting for the other guns and the beaters to get into position before the beaters flush out the pheasants and partridges from the undergrowth. Edwardian shooting parties generally involved a substantial breakfast and an expansive late lunch, though sometimes lunch was replaced by an even later tea, as shooters sought to make the most of the short hours of daylight in the winter. These sausage rolls, which use bread dough instead of pastry, were ideal for slipping into a pocket and nibbling on during the waits.

MAKES A BAKER'S DOZEN (13 ROLLS)

FOOD FOR THOUGHT

Sausage meat, or forcemeat as it was often called, was a staple of the nineteenth- and early-twentieth-century kitchen. Every cook had his or her own recipes and could turn out cheap forcemeats for servants or more expensive ones for the family. Veal was the most usual meat, but there were forcemeats made from fish, game, or vegetables, all flavored with herbs and spices. If you decide to make your own, a good proportion of fat, along with meat or vegetable and a bit of filler (usually bread crumbs), is vital, and an egg is useful to bind everything together.

INGREDIENTS

3¾ cups (450 g) flour, plus more for the work surface

2½ cups (600 ml) water

I teaspoon active dry yeast

I teaspoon salt

Vegetable oil, for the pan

13 oz (370 g) high-quality bulk sausage meat

Chutney and/or relishes, for serving (optional)

Put the flour into the bowl of a stand mixer or into a large bowl and make a well in the center. Add ½ cup (120 ml) of the water and the yeast to the well, then sprinkle some of the flour from the sides of the well onto the water-and-yeast mixture, covering it lightly. Leave until the yeast starts to bubble through this floury layer, 15–20 minutes.

Add the salt along the edges of the bowl and then add the remaining 2 cups (480 ml) water to the well. If making the dough by hand, mix with a wooden spoon or your hands until it forms a rough mass, then turn it out onto a floured work surface and knead until smooth and elastic, 10–15 minutes. If using a mixer, fit the mixer with the dough hook and knead on low speed until smooth and elastic, 5–8 minutes. Put the dough into a clean large bowl and cover with plastic wrap or a damp kitchen towel. Leave to rise in a warm spot until doubled in size, 2–3 hours. You can do this stage the day before baking and leave the dough to rise in the fridge overnight, removing it about 30 minutes before it is needed.

Oil a large sheet pan. Divide the dough into 13 equal portions, each weighing about 2 oz (60 g). Flatten each portion slightly, set a 1-oz (30-g) ball of sausage on the center, and enclose the meat completely in the dough, sealing it well and forming a log. Arrange the finished rolls, well spaced, on the prepared pan and cover loosely with a damp kitchen towel or plastic wrap. Leave in a warm spot until slightly risen, 15–20 minutes. Meanwhile, preheat the oven to 425°F (220°C).

Bake the rolls until golden brown, about 20 minutes. They will split slightly, but the meat should stay intact. Serve them accompanied with chutney and/or relishes if desired.

VEAL AND HAM PIE

Some recipes were part of the country house repertoire for centuries, including a range of incredibly versatile pies. In the medieval period, the pies were made with tough, almost inedible crusts, which meant the upper classes ate only the filling, leaving the pastry to be eaten by servants or distributed to the poor as edible alms. As we see in *Downton Abbey*, many ladies and their staff still regarded feeding the destitute as part of the duty of a grand house, and the practice continued well into the twentieth century, when a government-led benefit system was introduced. This pie, however, which is adapted from a recipe in the 1900 book *Savoury Pastry* by Frederick Vine, has a delicate crust intended to be eaten with the filling. In season 3, when the oven malfunctions before Mary and Violet's party for Martha and the great and good devour everything edible in the house, it's a veal pie that saves the day for the starving servants below stairs. Such pies were also popular picnic fare and can be served hot or cold.

SERVES 10–12

INGREDIENTS

FOR THE PASTRY
7½ cups (900 g) flour, plus more for the work surface

1½ tablespoons salt

1 cup (225 g) cold unsalted butter, cut into cubes, plus more for the mold

2 eggs, lightly whisked

1¼ cups (300 ml) ice-cold water

FOR THE FILLING
10 oz (280 g) ground veal

9 oz (250 g) ground pork

9 oz (250 g) fatty smoked bacon or ham, minced

1 egg, lightly whisked

½ cup (120 ml) brandy

2 teaspoons black pepper

½ teaspoon cayenne pepper

½ teaspoon ground nutmeg

3 or 4 hard-boiled eggs, peeled (optional)

FOR THE GLAZE (optional)
1 egg

1½ teaspoons water

IF SERVING COLD
2 cups (480 ml) veal or chicken stock

1 package (about 2½ teaspoons) powdered gelatin, or 5 gelatin sheets

To make the pastry, mix the flour and salt in a large bowl. Scatter the butter cubes over the top and, using a pastry blender or your fingers, work the butter into the flour until the mixture is the consistency of bread crumbs. Whisk together the eggs and water in a bowl, then stir into the flour mixture, stirring constantly until the dough comes together in a shaggy ball. (You can instead put the flour and butter into a stand mixer fitted with the paddle attachment and beat on low speed until the mixture is the consistency of bread crumbs, then add the remaining ingredients and beat until the dough comes together in a shaggy ball.)

Turn the dough out onto a floured work surface. Using the base of both palms, push the far edge of the pastry mound hard away from you, smearing it against the work surface, then bring it back into the main ball, repeating the action until the pastry is firm and has a clay-like consistency. (Do not knead it as you would bread dough.) The pushing technique used here works the pastry hard to ensure it won't collapse once the pie is out of its mold. Shape the dough into a ball, wrap in plastic wrap, and let rest in the fridge for at least 30 minutes and for up to a few days.

To make the filling, combine the veal, pork, bacon, beaten egg, brandy, black pepper, cayenne pepper, and nutmeg in a bowl and mix well. Set aside.

Generously butter a 14 x 3-inch (35 x 7.5-cm) meat pie mold or 9 x 5 x 3-inch (23 x 13 x 7.5-cm) loaf pan. If you are using a loaf pan, lay two 2-inch (5-cm) wide strips of parchment paper in the pan, forming a cross and overhanging each side by 4–5 inches (10–13 cm). These strips will allow you to lift the pie out of the pan when it is done. If you are using a traditional meat pie mold that has clips and whose sides are easily removable, there is no need to use the strips (and they will spoil the pattern on the mold). Cut off one-third of the dough and put it into a plastic bag or under a bowl so it doesn't dry out.

On a well-floured surface, roll out the remaining dough into a rough rectangle or oval about 2 inches larger than the mold or pan you are using. Fit the dough into the bottom of the mold, pressing it into the corners and up the sides of the pan. You should aim for a nicely lined mold with the pastry about ¼ inch (6 mm) thick at the sides and slightly thicker at the bottom, and an overhang at the rim of at least ½ inch (12 mm). Trim any excess pastry and gather up, cover, and reserve the scraps.

Recipe continues

RECIPE NOTE

This basic recipe can be used for any filling— mutton and apple, chicken and ham, or even pork. There was a working-class pie tradition, too: at the Carsons' wedding, the tables groan under the weight of stacked pork pies. These would have been made with a hot-water crust (boiled water, lard, flour, and salt) and filled with chopped and minced pork and with a thick pig trotter jelly. They were usually bought from butchers who specialized in such pies, and they remain popular today.

If using the hard-boiled eggs, put half of the meat mixture into the pastry-lined mold, packing it firmly and smoothing the top. Lay the eggs in a line down the center of the meat mixture, add more meat mixture around them, and then put the rest of the meat mixture on top, packing it firmly and smoothing the top. If you are not using the eggs, add all the meat mixture at once and smooth the surface.

Preheat the oven to 325°F (165°C). To make a lid, on a well-floured work surface, roll out the reserved dough into a rectangle or oval ⅛ inch (3 mm) thick and about 1 inch (2.5 cm) larger on all sides than the top of the mold. Trim off any excess pastry and gather up, cover, and reserve the scraps. Dampen the edges of the lid with water, then carefully transfer it, dampened side down, to the top of the mold and seal the edges well. If the filling is below the rim of the mold, fold the edges of the pastry in under the lid. But if, as intended, the filling sits level with the rim of the mold, the edges of the lid will sit nicely on the overhang of the bottom crust. To create the pie edge, trim the top and side pastry edges so they are even, then press the dough edge between your forefinger and thumb, with your other thumb on the other side of the dough, crimping well as you go. Trim off any raggedy edges with a sharp knife and then go back around the edge to make sure there are absolutely no gaps.

To make chimneys for venting the pie, cut 3 holes, each a scant 1 inch (2.5 cm) in diameter, spacing them at even intervals along the center of the lid. Using pastry scraps, make a wall of pastry about 1 inch (2.5 cm) high around the edge of each hole, sealing each wall securely at its base to the lid with a little water. The wall needs to be tall enough to stop the juices from bubbling over it as the pie bakes. If in doubt, insert a tube of buttered aluminum foil into each chimney to add extra height.

Bake the pie for 2–2½ hours. The easiest way to check if it is done is to insert a thermometer through a chimney into the center of the filling. It will register 165°F (74°C) when the pie is ready. You can also check for doneness by pushing a metal skewer down the chimney, leaving it for 1 minute, pulling it back out, and testing the temperature on the back of your hand. It should be piping hot. If in doubt, give the pie another 15 minutes in the oven.

RECIPE NOTE

To make your own chicken or veal stock, put a chicken carcass or 6–8 chicken wings or some veal bones and trimmings and a slice of ham into a large pot. Add a couple of celery ribs, a carrot, and water to cover, and bring to a boil, skimming off any foam that forms on the top. Reduce the heat to a simmer and simmer for 1 hour. Strain the stock, taste it, and add salt if needed. There is no need to clarify the stock for this pie.

Remove the pie from the oven and, if serving it hot, resist the urge to remove it from the mold straightaway. Let it stand for 15 minutes, then carefully remove the sides of the mold or lift the pie out of the loaf pan with the ends of the parchment strips. If you want to glaze the pie, whisk together the egg and water, brush the top and sides with a thin layer of the beaten egg, and put the pie into a 400°F (200°C) oven until the glaze sets, 3–5 minutes. To serve, cut into portions with a large, sharp knife.

If serving the pie cold, remove it from the oven, cover it loosely with a kitchen towel, and let it cool overnight in the mold at room temperature. The next day, carefully remove the sides of the mold or lift the pie out of the loaf pan with the ends of the parchment strips. If you want to glaze the pie, refrigerate the pie until well chilled, then, as directed for the hot pie, make the glaze, brush it on the pie, and put the pie into a 400°F (200°C) oven for 3–5 minutes. Let cool while you prepare the jelly.

A jelly is typically added to a cold pie because the filling settles. Bring the stock to a boil in a small saucepan over high heat and remove from the heat. If using powdered gelatin, in a small cup, sprinkle the gelatin over 2 tablespoons water and let stand until softened, about 2 minutes. (If using gelatin sheets, put the sheets into a bowl, add cold water to cover, and let soak until floppy, 5–10 minutes.) Add the softened gelatin to the warm stock and stir until dissolved. Let the stock cool to room temperature. The jelly should be thick and gloopy but still pourable. If it hasn't thickened enough, put it in the fridge for 15 minutes. The jelly is intended to be softer than usual, as it's posher that way.

When your jelly is gloopy, add it to the pie through the chimneys. A small funnel is helpful, but it's manageable with a teaspoon and a great deal of dexterity. Add the jelly very slowly, allowing each addition to settle into the gaps in the pie before adding more. When all the jelly has been added, put the pie into the fridge and chill for at least 2 hours to set the jelly before serving. To serve, cut into portions with a large, sharp knife.

MRS. HUGHES: *Is there anything for our supper?*

MRS. PATMORE: *I've hidden a veal and egg pie.*

~ SEASON 3, EPISODE 2

CHICKEN STUFFED WITH PISTACHIOS

Showpiece meat dishes were a mainstay of the aristocratic table, but unless they were roasted and destined for expert carving at the sideboard, they also needed to be easy to cut up and serve. One solution was to bone them and stuff the gap with a rich forcemeat, which meant the meat could then be easily sliced and served with the obligatory sauce. This recipe has a particularly fun stuffing inspired by the *Arabian Nights* and with flavors reminiscent of the Middle East, and is typical of the fresher flavors becoming fashionable in the 1920s. It can be served hot or cold, though the original suggests cold with "cold well-seasoned rice."

SERVES 8

RECIPE NOTE

If the mere thought of galantining (boning) the chicken makes you quake, ask your butcher to do it for you. Alternatively, halve the stuffing recipe and use it to stuff a bone-in whole chicken for roasting (pictured left): Sauté the stuffing mixture in a frying pan over medium heat until the sausage is no longer pink, 3–4 minutes. Let cool, then loosely stuff the chicken cavity. Put the chicken, breast side up, on a rack in a roasting pan, add ½ cup (120 ml) stock to the pan, and roast in a 325°F (165°C) oven, basting occasionally with the pan juices, until a thermometer registers 165°F (74°C) for the chicken and the stuffing, about 2½ hours.

INGREDIENTS

1 whole chicken, about 6 lb (2.7 kg)

2 ribs celery, roughly chopped

2 carrots, roughly chopped

2 cloves garlic (unpeeled is fine)

FOR THE STUFFING

¼ lb (115 g) ground veal

1 cup (225 g) butter, chopped

1 cup (115 g) pistachios, chopped

¼ cup (30 g) ground almonds

½ apple, such as Granny Smith, finely chopped

Grated zest of 1 lemon

1 teaspoon ground coriander

½ teaspoon ground allspice

1 teaspoon kosher salt

1 teaspoon cracked black pepper

2 eggs, lightly whisked

FOR THE SAUCE

2 tablespoons butter

2 tablespoons flour

White pepper

Handful of pistachios, for garnish

Start by boning the chicken (see Recipe Note). Turn the bird breast side down on a cutting board and, using a small, sharp knife, cut along the backbone from the neck to the tail. Using your fingers and the knife as needed, carefully remove the meat from both sides of the ribcage. Pull out the legs and the wings and detach them from the carcass, leaving them with the body. The breastbone is the only really tricky bit, as you need to be careful you do not tear the skin. If necessary, cut off the cartilage with the meat and then carefully remove the cartilage with a small pair of kitchen scissors or a knife afterward. Remove the carcass (save it for making stock) and scrape the thigh bones clean. Wrap the corner of a kitchen towel around the top joint to get a good grip on the leg bone so you can remove the flesh from the lower part of the leg. Cut the leg off at the joint, leaving the very lowest bone (the one with the thick yellow skin) intact. Cut the wings off neatly (save them for making stock). You should now have a fully boned chicken except for 2 inches (5 cm) or so of leg bone.

To make the stuffing, combine the veal, butter, pistachios, almonds, apple, lemon zest, coriander, allspice, salt, black pepper, and eggs in a bowl and mix well.

Recipe continues

Spread the chicken, skin side down, on a work surface. Form two-thirds of the stuffing into a thick sausage shape in the middle of the chicken. Use the remaining one-third to stuff the legs, working it well into the space where the bones once were. Now fold the chicken around the stuffing, enclosing it completely to make sure it will not ooze out of the ends. Truss it securely with kitchen string, forming a neat meat package. The easiest method is to make loops at intervals around the bird and then wrap the string snugly round the remaining leg bones, using them to anchor the string.

Now wrap the chicken package, parcel-style, in parchment paper, being careful to cover it fully. Wrap this parchment parcel in turn in cheesecloth or a clean kitchen towel and tie the whole thing up tightly with more string.

Put the chicken into a large saucepan and add water just to cover (8–10 cups/1.9–2.1 l). Add the celery, carrots, and garlic and bring to a boil over high heat. Reduce the heat to a gentle simmer, cover, and cook until a thermometer inserted in the stuffing registers 165°F (74°C), about 1½ hours.

Remove from the heat and transfer the chicken to a large plate. Leave it to rest for about 15 minutes. It must be cool enough so you don't burn your fingers when you take off the cloth and paper. Unwrap the chicken but leave the trussing intact, then let cool completely, cover, and chill in the fridge. Strain the cooking liquid and reserve 2 cups (480 ml) for making the sauce.

To make the sauce, which is served hot, first make a roux. Melt the butter in a saucepan over medium heat, then whisk in the flour until smooth. Reduce the heat to low and stir for 2–3 minutes to cook off the raw flour flavor. Add the reserved cooking liquid, little by little, stirring constantly to avoid any lumps. You'll need to add about 1 cup (240 ml) of the reserved liquid (you'll have extra just in case). You should finish with a smooth sauce. Season with the white pepper (you can use black, but you'll have specks in your sauce) and keep warm for serving.

Snip and remove the trussing string from the chicken and transfer to a serving plate or platter. Garnish with the pistachios and serve with the hot sauce.

RECIPE NOTE

At shooting lunches, generally served in a marquee, or tent, some distance from the house, it was hard to keep poultry or roasts warm, so serving them cold with a hot sauce was a good solution for hungry shooters who wanted a hot meal. Vacuum flasks, which were invented in 1898 and were widespread by the time *Downton* opens in 1912, were much in use for this kind of thing. If you want an alternative 1920s way of serving your chicken, soak 3 gelatin sheets in cold water until softened and stir them into your hot sauce after removing it from the heat. Allow the sauce to cool to room temperature and thicken, then spread it over the chicken, masking the bird completely. Sprinkle with chopped pistachios (or perhaps decorate it with your family crest cut out of truffles, if you feel particularly inspired) and put it in the fridge to set. This is rather more suited to a cold supper or lunch, as it is difficult to transport.

MANY WAYS WITH SANDWICH FILLINGS

The concept of putting a filling between two slices of bread is hardly new, as pictures of medieval field hands eating this way attest. However, it wasn't until the mid-eighteenth century that the term *sandwich* started to be used for it, initially in the context of a delicate and lightweight snack for men busy late at night with work or, more usually, gambling. It's named for John Montagu, the fourth Earl of Sandwich, who was one such man. By the late eighteenth century, sandwiches had moved onto dinner tables, still in a very light and tasteful form, but inevitably the term expanded used to describe everything from ladylike finger food to the doorstep sandwiches of the modern pub. They were very practical for picnics and for shooting teas, as they could be served in a way that appeared genteel yet were easy to transport and to eat.

Many of the recipes in this book make excellent sandwich fillings with a bit of mashing up and sometimes mixing with other things. Salmon Mousse (page 143), Potted Cheese (page 88), Fish Cream (page 142), and Flavored Butters (page 256) work as spreads; Eggs à la St. James (page 56) makes a base for a superb egg mayonnaise; and the various poached and roasted meats work cold, especially with a little of their respective sauces. Cold ham, lamb, beef, puréed game, and chicken were all fairly standard options, often with sliced pickles and watercress, or with sauces such as horseradish (for beef), mustard (for ham), or chutney (for game). Cheese of various types was also common. Most fillings were pounded or puréed and mixed with a little sauce or butter to make them easier to apply and safer to eat (no one needs accidental beef down their décolletage, especially in a corset).

If you want some more Downtonesque fillings, however, here are some contemporary suggestions. For all of these, and for the ultimate aristocratic flourish, the bread should be very thinly sliced, and don't merely cut off the crusts. Instead, stamp out your bread slices with pastry cutters and serve your sandwiches as fluted circles, perfect squares, stars, ovals, leaves, or anything else that comes to hand.

CHEESE & BUTTER

2 oz (60 g) Gruyère or Cheddar cheese, grated, mixed with an equal amount of butter, 1 teaspoon each white wine vinegar and Dijon mustard, and a little black pepper and cayenne

EGG & CAPER

2 hard-boiled eggs, finely minced, mixed with 1 teaspoon each minced capers and fresh flat-leaf parsley and layered with cucumber strips

PROPER CUCUMBER

Peeled and thinly sliced cucumber, marinated in white wine vinegar well seasoned with salt and black pepper, then drained well and used in a sandwich spread with butter mixed with a tiny bit of grated lemon zest

WINDSOR

2 oz (60 g) cooked beef tongue, 2 oz (60 g) Parmesan cheese, 2 tablespoons butter, and a pinch of cayenne or red chile flakes pounded together to a paste, spread between the bread slices; brush the outside top and bottom with melted butter, press some grated Parmesan onto the buttered surfaces, and fry until light brown on both sides

BONE MARROW

Roasted bone marrow well seasoned with salt and pepper and layered with nasturtium flowers

DELHI

6 anchovy fillets in olive oil, 3 canned sardines, 1 teaspoon chutney, 1 egg yolk, 2 tablespoons butter, and 1 teaspoon curry powder combined in a saucepan and simmered until thick; best used with bread that has been toasted on one side only, with the spread on the untoasted side

ADDITIONAL COMBINATIONS

Shredded chicken, chopped almonds, cream, salt, and paprika

Mashed cooked navy or butter beans, horseradish sauce, a very small amount of minced yellow onion, mustard, and a little minced celery and fresh flat-leaf parsley

Olives and cream cheese, spread on buttered brown bread

Chopped bell peppers, mayonnaise, shredded lettuce, and cream cheese (called an American salad sandwich; possibly a rather harsh indictment of American salads)

Mango chutney, watercress, and hard-boiled egg, all finely chopped and well mixed

Finely chopped cooked oysters and beer

Sliced sweetbreads layered with pickles

Cooked small sausages, cut lengthwise and casing removed, with mustard and a squeeze of lemon

Layers of thinly sliced beef tongue and black truffles

Cooked veal and asparagus tips, minced and mixed together

Cooked cod and mussels, chopped very finely and spread on buttered bread

Lobster curry with sorrel leaf and a dash of fresh lemon juice

FESTIVE FOOD

DOWNTON ABBEY **IS FULL OF CELEBRATION AND** over the course of nearly two decades, we witness many significant life events—marriages, christenings, and balls—and also the yearly festivities for birthdays and, of course, Christmas and New Year's. The modern Christmas was born in the late nineteenth century, when such obligatory elements as the Christmas tree, crackers (attractively decorated cardboard tubes filled with bonbons or other small prizes), Father Christmas, and the sending of cards were all either invented or popularized. Queen Victoria and Prince Albert did a lot to promote the idea of a family-focused celebration centered on a large dinner.

At country houses, the usual seven or eight courses were served, and meals almost always included such seasonal favorites as roast turkey, mince pie, and a Christmas pudding flambéed in brandy. Seasonal vegetables were served as well, though the super rich also liked to set out such delicacies as asparagus, which was not in season but would have been forced in the kitchen garden. Indeed, it would be served precisely to make the point that if you were rich enough, you need not be hampered by mere seasons. Below stairs, the servants also celebrated—and with broadly similar food. They often had their own party, to which many of the estate workers would be invited. The British Christmas still includes these elements, along with a rich, dark fruitcake and always a great deal of dried fruit.

The Christmas cake appears at Downton in another guise as well, for the same recipe was the basis of the wedding cake of the time. Wedding food, of course, could consist of almost anything, as long as it was showy and delicious. We see many of the preparations for Edith's first wedding, and then see a different perspective when Mrs. Hughes and Mr. Carson marry. In both cases, though, the showpiece is the cake, made in the Downton kitchens with a great deal of pride.

Cake also featured at Easter, which, while never as significant a celebration as Christmas, was nevertheless associated with specific foods. Hot cross buns were (and are) the food most closely linked with Easter. They derived from late seventeenth-century breakfast breads and were, inevitably, reliant on dried fruit and spice, both of which had been very expensive in previous centuries. There were various regional Easter cakes and breads as well, often made with saffron and linked to the idea of rebirth through their use of eggs and their rich golden color. The most universal of them, however, was simnel cake, which survives today. Easter was when the first of the new-season lamb started to be available, too, and lamb was often eaten as the centerpiece roast.

BRUSSELS SPROUTS WITH CHESTNUTS

Brussels sprouts are one of those vegetables that everyone claimed to dislike yet everyone served at Christmas anyway. The first British recipe for them appeared in the 1840s, served in "the Belgian mode," and they have a long association with Flanders. Essentially tiny cabbages, Brussels sprouts once had the reputation of being impossible to cook: they were generally boiled whole, and the middle tended to remain raw while the outside turned to mush. To avoid that outcome, they were traditionally overcooked, and the British used to start muttering darkly about needing to get the sprouts on for Christmas dinner from early November onward. This recipe is rather less of a trial, although the original, true to form, left the sprouts whole.

SERVES 4–6

INGREDIENTS

6 oz (170 g) lardons (optional)

Lard or vegetable oil, for frying, if using lardons

1 lb (450 g) Brussels sprouts

2 tablespoons butter

2 tablespoons water

6 oz (170 g) canned or jarred roasted and peeled whole chestnuts (about 1 cup)

Salt and black pepper

Adding lardons (bacon cut into strips about 1 inch/2.5 cm long and ¼ inch/6 mm wide and thick) to this recipe is optional but recommended. If you decide to use them, start by frying them in a very hot frying pan with a little lard until they are very crisp, then drain them on paper towels while you cook the sprouts.

Discard the outer leaves of each sprout, trim off the very bottom, and then cut each sprout lengthwise into thin slices. Melt the butter with the water in a large saucepan over medium-high heat. Add the sprouts and mix well to cover them with a thin layer of butter. Break up each chestnut into 6–8 pieces and add them to the sprouts. Cover the pan and simmer until the sprouts are just hot through but still crunchy, 4–5 minutes. Season with salt and pepper.

Transfer to a serving dish, sprinkle with the crisp lardons, if using, and serve immediately.

RECIPE NOTE

This method works with any cabbage. For extra richness, stir in 1 tablespoon heavy cream just before serving.

STUFFING FOR TURKEY OR GOOSE

Although turkey, first introduced in the sixteenth century, was a relative newcomer to British shores, it was firmly established as a Christmas dish by the *Downton* era. For aristocratic families such as the Crawleys, roast game and a huge roast beef with Yorkshire puddings were as obligatory as the turkey, and for the lower classes, goose or chicken was a more common choice (turkey being rather large as well as expensive). However, with Cora's American influence at work, it's all about the turkey in the *Downton* Christmas specials, and Mrs. Patmore's kitchen table is loaded with huge golden turkeys being basted and stuffed for the festive table. This stuffing uses another seasonal favorite, chestnuts, and it is good not only baked in the cavity of the bird but also made into sausages and balls that are fried for garnishing it.

MAKES ENOUGH STUFFING FOR ONE 15-LB (6.8-KG) TURKEY

VIOLET: *A peer in favour of reform is like a turkey in favour of Christmas.*

~ SEASON 6, EPISODE 3

INGREDIENTS

2 cloves garlic, unpeeled

Olive oil, for drizzling

1 jar or can (1½ lb/680 g) roasted and peeled whole chestnuts

2 teaspoons butter, at room temperature

1 lb (450 g) bulk pork sausage meat

2 cups (90 g) fresh bread crumbs

Leaves from 1 small bunch fresh flat-leaf parsley, finely minced

6 fresh sage leaves, finely minced

1 egg, lightly whisked

Preheat the oven to 400°F (200°C). Line a ramekin or other small baking dish with parchment paper, add the garlic cloves, drizzle with a little oil, and roast until the cloves are squidgy, soft, and fragrant, 15–25 minutes. Let cool, then squeeze the cloves out of their skins and set aside. Leave the oven on.

Purée two-thirds of the chestnuts in a food processor until smooth. Roughly chop the remaining chestnuts. In a small baking dish, mix the chopped chestnuts with the butter to coat. Bake until lightly browned, 5–10 minutes. Let cool.

Combine the sausage meat, puréed chestnuts, baked chestnuts, roasted garlic, bread crumbs, parsley, sage, and egg and mix until a sticky paste forms.

Use this mixture to stuff your turkey and roast it as you normally would. Any leftovers can be shaped into small balls or sausage shapes, fried gently in butter until cooked through, and then used to garnish the bird.

RECIPE NOTE

A slightly old-fashioned but popular way to garnish roast turkey was to use ornamental hâtelet skewers. Balls of stuffing (and whole truffles, cooked cockscombs, and quail eggs) were threaded onto the skewers, which were then plunged into the bird. Alternatively, fried balls of cooked stuffing were arranged around the edge of the turkey. The stuffing mixture can also be baked in an ovenproof dish and served as a side dish.

LEMON MINCEMEAT

Mincemeat started life in the Middle Ages as a filling for rich, beautiful pies. In those days, it was based on meat, as the name suggests, and cooks could use anything from beef to mutton to fish to, occasionally, eggs. Over the course of several centuries, the meat content dwindled until, by the Edwardian era, most recipes didn't include any meat at all. Mincemeat is an absolutely obligatory part of the British Christmas and is generally used for making tarts. This lemon-based version was a popular variant on the usual mixture, which contained large quantities of dried fruit, some chopped apple, candied citrus peel, cherries, and lots of alcohol to preserve it. It is highly versatile and keeps well, making it perfect for a busy country house kitchen where as much as possible needed to be prepared in advance. Mincemeat tarts are present in every Christmas episode of *Downton Abbey*.

MAKES ABOUT TWO 1-PINT (480-ML) JARS

INGREDIENTS

1 lemon

1 cup plus 2 tablespoons (225 g) sugar

½ lb (225 g) shredded suet (about 2 cups)

1⅓ cups (225 g) dried currants

⅔ cup (115 g) raisins

2 tablespoons brandy

2 tablespoons port

1 tablespoon plus ¾ teaspoon mixed spice

Put the lemon into a small saucepan with water to cover, bring to a boil over high heat, and boil until tender and easily pierced with a fork, about 30 minutes. Drain the lemon and either pound it in a mortar with a pestle until smooth or purée it in a blender. Transfer to a bowl large enough to accommodate all the ingredients, stir in the sugar, cover, and let stand at room temperature for 12 hours.

Add the suet, currants, raisins, brandy, port, and mixed spice to the lemon and sugar and stir well. Use the mincemeat right away, or pack it into jars, cap tightly, and refrigerate. It will keep for up to 1 year.

RECIPE NOTE

Mincemeat is used for mincemeat tarts, which can be made with shortcrust, puff, or sweet pastry. They are typically made in tartlet pans, which are lined with pastry, filled with 1 heaped teaspoon mincemeat, and then baked. Some people top them with pastry, too, but they are equally good without—or with meringue on top. You can also make a suet pastry following the recipe on page 222, roll it out into a rectangle, spread it with mincemeat, roll it up like a jelly (Swiss) roll, tie it securely in a dampened and floured cloth, and boil it for 1½ hours to make a mincemeat roly-poly pudding. It's good used in toasted sandwiches or cooked up with oatmeal for a Christmas breakfast, too.

CHRISTMAS PUDDING

No British Christmas table would be complete without a flaming Christmas pudding. Originally called simply plum pudding (in the past, *plum* referred to any type of dried fruit), it was eaten throughout the winter and was so utterly associated with roast beef that the two were used as visual shorthand for Britishness in satires of the eighteenth century. They were served simultaneously and work very well eaten together. Roast beef and plum pudding were celebration dishes, which meant Christmas, among other occasions, and even in the Edwardian era, many people still served beef for dinner and plum pudding for afters on Christmas. The pudding had now changed its name to Christmas pudding, however, and it was rarely eaten apart from the holiday. We see stupendous puddings at every *Downton* Christmas, adorned, as was obligatory, with a generous sprig of holly. Puddings destined for the family table would generally have been cooked in an elaborate mold. Those for the servants would have been plainer, made in just a simple basin.

SERVES 8

INGREDIENTS

1 cup (225 g) cold butter, plus more for the mold and parchment

¾ cup (90 g) flour, plus more for the cheesecloth

¾ cup (150 g) sugar

2 cups (90 g) fresh bread crumbs

Scant 1 cup (160 g) raisins

¾ cup (130 g) dried currants

1 cup (115 g) peeled and chopped apple (about 1 apple)

⅓ cup (60 g) chopped candied citrus peel

½ teaspoon mixed spice

Pinch of salt

½ cup (120 ml) brandy, plus ¼ cup (60 ml) for serving

3 eggs, lightly whisked

1 holly sprig without berries, for decorating (optional)

Butter a 5-cup (1.2-l) steam pudding mold. If you are using a patterned mold, make sure to butter all the corners so the pudding does not stick. Cut a piece of parchment paper just to cover the top of the mold and butter one side of the paper.

Combine the flour, sugar, bread crumbs, raisins, currants, apple, candied peel, mixed spice, salt, ½ cup brandy, and eggs and mix together very well. Using a cheese shredder, shred in the cold butter while a helper stirs it into the batter, stirring until evenly mixed. Pack the mixture into the prepared mold. Place the parchment, buttered side down, on top of the mold. Cover the mold lid and clip into place, or cover with aluminum foil and secure with kitchen string.

Fill a saucepan large enough to accommodate the mold with water to reach about 1 inch (2.5 cm) below the rim of the mold once the mold is added. Bring the water to a boil and carefully lower the mold into the pan. Allow the water to come back to a full boil, cover the pan, and then turn down the heat so the water is still at a rolling boil but not bubbling so vigorously that it splashes over the rim.

Recipe continues

Boil the pudding for 4 hours, keeping an eye on the water level and adding more boiling water as needed to maintain the original level. If the water level drops too much, the pudding won't cook properly.

After 4 hours, turn off the heat and carefully remove the mold from the water. Remove the covering, turn the pudding out onto a serving plate, and stick the holly sprig in the top, if using. (You can make the pudding several days in advance and store it in the fridge; when ready to serve it, cover it again with a fresh layer of buttered parchment and floured cheesecloth or foil and boil it for 1 hour to heat it through.) Just before serving, heat the ¼ cup brandy in a small pan on the stove top, pour it over the pudding, and carefully ignite it with a long match. Enter the dining room bearing the warm flaming pudding to wild applause.

RECIPE NOTE

If you are lacking a steam pudding mold, the pudding can be baked in a regular Bundt pan using the same ingredients plus more flour (with the addition of baking powder) and eggs: Mix together all the ingredients except the sugar, butter, flour, and eggs, then set aside. Using a handheld mixer, beat together the sugar and butter (softened to room temperature) on medium-high speed until light and creamy, about 5 minutes. Beat in 6 eggs, one at a time, beating well after each addition. Sift 1 cup (115 g) flour with 1 teaspoon baking powder into the butter mixture. Using a spatula, fold in the flour mixture until incorporated, then fold in the reserved ingredients. Spoon into a buttered and floured 10-inch (25-cm) Bundt pan and bake in a 350°F (180°C) oven until a skewer inserted into the center comes out clean, about 40 minutes.

Carson carries in the flaming pudding.

EDITH: *Sybil's favorite.*

Carson brings it to Violet's left. She holds a spoon up.

VIOLET: *A happy Christmas to us all.*

~ SEASON 2, EPISODE 9

YULE LOG

The yule, or yuletide, log seems to have originated in France and reached Britain in the last years of the nineteenth century. It was never as popular as a proper weighty fruitcake, but it was a lightweight alternative for those who wanted something a bit different. This recipe comes from Frederick Vine's *Saleable Shop Goods for Counter-Tray and Window*, published in 1907 and aimed at professional bakers. It suggests making the cake as an enormous slab, which can then be cut up and rolled into many identical cakes. The author says they are by no means reserved for Christmas and will sell well simply as "logs" throughout the year.

SERVES 6

INGREDIENTS

Butter, for preparing the pan

4 eggs

½ cup plus 1 tablespoon (115 g) superfine sugar

½ teaspoon fresh lemon juice

¾ cup (90 g) flour

Pinch of salt

Confectioners' sugar, for dusting

½ cup (140 g) cherry preserves

2 tablespoons water

FOR THE BUTTERCREAM

2 oz (60 g) dark chocolate, chopped

½ cup (115 g) butter, at room temperature

1½ cups (170 g) confectioners' sugar, sifted

Pinch of salt

3 tablespoons dark rum

1 tablespoon superfine sugar, for finishing

Preheat the oven to 350°F (180°C). Line the bottom of a 10½ x 15½ x 1-inch (27 x 39 x 2.5-cm) jelly roll (Swiss) pan with parchment paper and butter the parchment and pan sides generously.

In a bowl, using a stand or handheld mixer on medium-high speed or a whisk, beat together the eggs, superfine sugar, and lemon juice until thick, creamy, and tripled in volume, about 10 minutes. Sift the flour and salt over the egg mixture, then fold in just until combined. Pour the batter into the prepared pan (it should be about ½ inch/12 mm deep) and smooth the top.

Bake until the surface is golden and the cake springs back when pressed with a fingertip, 15–20 minutes. Remove from the oven and let cool in the pan on a wire rack just until cool to the touch, 10–15 minutes. Use a blunt knife to loosen the edges of the cake from the sides of the pan.

Lay a kitchen towel on a work surface and dust the towel with confectioners' sugar (to prevent the cake from sticking). Invert the warm cake onto the prepared towel and carefully peel off the parchment. Starting from a long side, roll up the cake in the towel, then leave seam side down to cool completely.

While the cake is cooling, make the filling. Combine the preserves and water in a blender and process until smooth (or beat by hand).

Recipe continues

Unroll the cooled cake and spread the filling evenly on the cake, making sure it extends to the edges. Now, starting from the same long side, roll up the cake as before and place it seam side down on a serving plate.

To make the buttercream, melt the chocolate in a small heatproof bowl over a pan of simmering water or in a microwave. Set aside. In a bowl, using a handheld mixer on medium speed or a wooden spoon, beat the butter until smooth and fluffy. Gradually beat in the confectioners' sugar and salt until incorporated. Add the melted chocolate (which should have cooled slightly by now) and the rum and beat until well mixed and a good piping consistency.

Frost the log with a thin layer of the icing. Transfer the remaining icing to a piping bag fitted with a star tip and pipe several lines onto the length of the log to look like bark. Just before serving, sprinkle the superfine sugar onto the icing so it glistens and looks like frost.

RECIPE NOTE

If you aren't keen on rum in the icing, you can replace it with another spirit or liqueur, such as Scotch whisky, kirsch, or Calvados. Alternatively, trade it out for milk and a bit of pure vanilla extract for flavor. The cherry preserves can, of course, be swapped out for any type of preserves you like.

HOT CROSS BUNS

Cross buns first became associated with Easter in the seventeenth century, which was boom time for rich yeast-risen doughs like this one. Popular for breakfast, they were sold hot in the streets by enterprising bakers and eventually became known as hot cross buns. They remain indelibly associated with the festival in the United Kingdom, though modern versions often have a pastry cross on top. Buns like these can be seen cooling on the *Downton* kitchen table in several episodes, and they would have been consumed by family and servants alike. They were also a popular street food.

MAKES 12 BUNS

INGREDIENTS

3½–4 cups (430–480 g) flour, plus more for the work surface

¼ cup (50 g) superfine sugar

½ teaspoon ground nutmeg

½ teaspoon ground cinnamon

¼ teaspoon ground ginger

Generous pinch of salt

4 tablespoons (60 g) butter, plus more for the pan and for serving

1¼ cups (300 ml) milk

1 teaspoon active dry yeast

1 egg, lightly whisked

½ teaspoon grated lemon zest

½ teaspoon grated orange zest

½ cup (90 g) dried currants

½ cup (90 g) mixed candied citrus peel or golden raisins

Mix together 3½ cups (430 g) of the flour, the sugar, nutmeg, cinnamon, ginger, and salt in a large bowl and make a well in the center. Combine the butter and milk in a small saucepan and heat over medium heat just until the butter melts. Remove from the heat and let cool to blood-warm (about 100°F/38°C), then add the yeast. Let stand until the yeast is softened, about 5 minutes, then add the egg and citrus zests and stir until blended. Pour the yeast mixture into the well in the flour mixture and stir together with a wooden spoon until a shaggy dough forms.

Turn out the dough onto a floured work surface and knead until smooth, soft, and elastic, about 20 minutes, adding only as much of the remaining ½ cup (60 g) flour, a little at a time, as needed to prevent sticking. Lightly flour a large bowl and transfer the dough to it. Cover the bowl with plastic wrap or a damp kitchen towel, set it in a warm spot, and let the dough rise until doubled in size, about 1½ hours.

Punch a bread hole in the middle of the dough and add the currants and candied peel, then bring the dough up over the fruits, enclosing them completely. Turn the dough out onto a freshly floured work surface and knead gently until the fruits are evenly distributed and the dough is once again smooth. Cover and let rest for 10 minutes.

Recipe continues

Lightly butter a large sheet pan. Divide the dough into 12 equal portions and shape each portion into a ball. As the balls are formed, place them, seam side down, on the prepared pan, spacing them evenly apart. Cover them loosely with a damp kitchen towel and leave to rise in a warm spot until puffy, about 1 hour.

Using a very sharp knife, slash a cross in the top of each raised bun. Bake the buns until golden brown, about 15 minutes. Transfer to a wire rack, let cool slightly, and eat hot, or let cool completely on the rack and serve at room temperature. Either way, offer butter at the table for slathering onto the buns.

RECIPE NOTE

Although it goes against the glory of hot cross buns, you can switch the dried currants for other fruits and use different spices and zests (pineapple and ginger with lime zest works well for a twenty-first-century twist). For a more pronounced cross, make a flour-and-water paste and pipe it on top. To embellish the buns with a modern finish (pictured left), make a sugar icing: Combine 1 cup (125 g) confectioners' sugar and ¼ teaspoon orange blossom water or rose water (optional) in a small bowl. Stir in 4–5 teaspoons milk to thin to a good piping consistency, then, using a piping bag fitted with a small plain tip (or a plastic bag with the corner snipped off), pipe the icing onto the cooled buns.

SIMNEL CAKE

Simnel cake is the stuff of legends, most of them entirely unfounded in reality. The name probably comes from the Roman *simla*, which was one of the grades of flour available in ancient Rome. By the Middle Ages, there were references to simnel cake being baked at Easter. By the twentieth century, it had evolved into a light fruitcake with marzipan, the almond paste usually included as both decoration and a layer inside the cake. Different regions had their own versions, however, including one with an outer case of pastry in the shape of a crown. Simnel cakes were generally decorated with Easter-themed decorations, such as chicks and flowers.

SERVES 12–14

INGREDIENTS

FOR THE ALMOND PASTE

2¼ cups (225 g) ground almonds

1 cup plus 2 tablespoons (225 g) superfine sugar

1 egg, lightly whisked

1 teaspoon orange flower water

1 teaspoon fresh lemon juice

1 teaspoon apricot or hazelnut schnapps

FOR THE CAKE

1¾ cups plus 2 tablespoons (225 g) flour, plus more for the work surface

2 teaspoons ground ginger

½ teaspoon ground cinnamon

½ teaspoon baking powder

½ cup plus 2 tablespoons (140 g) butter, at room temperature, plus more for the pan

¾ cup (140 g) superfine sugar

4 eggs

⅓ cup (80 ml) milk

1⅓ cups (225 g) dried currants

¼ lb (115 g) dried apricots, chopped

¼ lb (115 g) mixed candied citrus peel, chopped

1 teaspoon grated lemon zest

1 teaspoon grated orange zest

FOR THE ICING

1 cup (115 g) confectioners' sugar

1 tablespoon water

½ teaspoon orange flower water

Easter decorations of choice, for the top

Preheat the oven to 350°F (180°C). Butter the bottom and sides of an 8-inch (20-cm) round pan, then line the bottom and sides with a double layer of parchment paper and butter the paper generously.

To make the almond paste, combine all the ingredients and mix together until a soft, pliable consistency forms that can be rolled out. Enclose in plastic wrap and refrigerate until ready to use.

To make the cake, in a bowl, mix together the flour, ginger, cinnamon, and baking powder. In a large bowl, using a handheld mixer on medium speed or a wooden spoon, cream together the butter and superfine sugar until smooth and creamy. Add the eggs, one at a time, alternating with the flour mixture in three batches, beginning and ending with the eggs and mixing well after each addition. Beat in the milk until blended. Stir in the currants, apricots, candied citrus peel, and citrus zests.

On a lightly floured work surface, roll out one-third of the almond paste into a round the diameter of the pan. Pour half of the batter into the prepared pan. Carefully lay the almond paste round on top of the batter in the pan, then pour the remaining batter over the almond paste layer and smooth the top.

Bake the cake until a skewer inserted into the center of the top cake layer (not to the marzipan) comes out clean, about 2 hours. Keep an eye on the top, and if it starts to brown too much, cover it loosely with aluminum foil. Let cool in the pan on a wire rack for 10–15 minutes, then turn out onto the rack and peel off the parchment. Turn upright and let cool completely.

When the cake is cool, use a serrated knife to trim off the rounded top to make it level, if needed. Use the rest of the almond paste to decorate the top: roll out a very thin round of the paste the diameter of the cake and lay it on top. Using the remaining paste, make a thick circle around the edge of the cake, forming a sort of bowl in the middle. Use the back of a knife to make cuts all around the circle. Then, using a kitchen torch, brown the top (or slip the cake briefly under a preheated broiler).

To make the icing, mix together the confectioners' sugar, water, and orange flower water in a small bowl until smooth and pourable. Pour the icing into the almond paste circle; it will thicken as it sets. Decorate the icing-lined circle with Easter decorations, such as a bird's nest made of chocolate flakes and filled with chocolate eggs.

RECIPE NOTE

For a shortcut, modern cooks may choose to use store-bought almond paste rather than homemade (18 oz/500 g store-bought paste will be needed). Some versions of this cake suggest baking the cake without the almond layer, splitting the cooled cake horizontally into 2 layers, sandwiching the almond paste between them, and then smoothing off any rough edges and using the rest of the almond paste on top as described.

FOOD FOR THOUGHT

Modern simnel cakes have eleven, twelve, or thirteen marzipan balls on top, said to represent Jesus and some or all of the apostles. This seems to be a 1960s or 1970s development. One of the many legends connected to the cake is a convoluted story that includes a couple called Simon and Nelly (hence Sim-Nel) and the odd notion that the cake was baked by servants to give to their mothers on Mothering Sunday. The holiday was celebrated with pilgrimages to the "mother" church, however, and had nothing to do with actual mothers. And as we see in *Downton*, servants were drawn from all over the country and rarely lived near enough to their families to toddle off and take them cake.

PLUM CAKE

One of the most traditional festive recipes in Britain, rich fruitcake has its roots in medieval great cakes stuffed with dried fruit and spice. The same basic recipe was used for Christmas cake and wedding cake, as well as for birthday and christening cakes. At Downton we see the changing face of wedding cakes, with Edith's a typically late-Victorian affair of three cakes stacked on top of one another, and Mary's, later in the series, given extra height with porcelain columns. Rich fruitcake was used because it was very tough, hence able to support thick layers of icing—and other cakes—without the need for doweling or inedible supports. Christmas cakes were simpler, usually just one large cake covered with icing and an appropriately festive message. In Yorkshire, rich fruitcake is often eaten with a good sharp cheese, such as Wensleydale. This recipe is adapted from *The New Century Cookery Book* by Charles Herman Senn, published in 1901. You will notice there are no actual plums in the cake. The name comes from the seventeenth century, when the word *plum* in this context simply meant dried fruit.

SERVES 10–12

INGREDIENTS

1 cup (225 g) butter, at room temperature, plus more for the pan

1 cup (200 g) superfine sugar

3 eggs

1¾ cups plus 2 tablespoons (225 g) flour

¼ cup (30 g) ground almonds

2 teaspoons ground cinnamon

1 teaspoon ground allspice

1 teaspoon ground mace

1 teaspoon ground ginger

1⅓ cups (225 g) dried currants

1⅓ cups (225 g) golden raisins

⅔ cup (120 g) dark raisins

⅓ cup (about 75 g) chopped mixed candied citrus peel

Grated zest of 2 oranges

Grated zest of 1 lemon

¼ cup (60 ml) brandy

FOR DECORATION (optional)

¼ lb (115 g) naturally colored glacéed cherries

¾ cup (115 g) whole blanched almonds or mixture of almonds and pecans

Preheat a conventional oven to 325°F (165°C) or a convection oven to 275°F (135°C). Butter a 9-inch (23-cm) springform pan with 2-inch (5-cm) sides, line with two or three layers of parchment paper, and butter the top sheet generously.

Using a stand mixer fitted with the paddle attachment, or in a large bowl with a handheld mixer, cream together the butter and sugar on medium speed until smooth and creamy. Add the eggs, one at a time, along with 2 tablespoons of the flour with the first egg to stop the mixture from curdling, beating well after each addition. Increase the speed to high and beat until the mixture is pale and creamy and free of lumps, about 10 minutes.

In a small bowl, stir together the remaining flour, the almonds, cinnamon, allspice, mace, and ginger. Reduce the mixer speed to low and gradually add the flour mixture, beating just until combined. Add the currants, raisins, candied citrus peel, and orange and lemon zests and beat until well mixed. Then, on medium speed, add the brandy and beat until the batter is pale brown and thoroughly mixed, about 5 minutes.

Pour the cake batter into the prepared pan and smooth the top. If desired, decorate the top with circles of the cherries alternating with the almonds.

Wrap the outside of the pan with two or three layers of brown paper and tie them in place with kitchen string. Make a rough lid of a few layers of folded brown paper and place it on top. (You can instead use aluminum foil for wrapping and topping.) Make sure the lid is not touching the batter. It should be sitting loosely above it.

Bake the cake for 2 hours, then remove the lid so the top can brown. Continue baking for about 1 hour longer. The cake is done when a skewer inserted into the center comes out clean.

Remove the brown paper from around the sides of the pan, then unclasp the pan ring and carefully lift it off. Let the cake cool completely on a wire rack before removing it from the parchment and pan base.

RECIPE NOTE

If you wish to decorate the cake Edwardian-style, omit the glacéed cherries and almonds and cover the cake with a thin layer of marzipan, sticking it in place with hot apricot jam (you will need about 2 lb/1 kg marzipan and ¼ cup/70 g apricot jam). Cover the marzipan layer with royal icing (flavored with rose water or orange flower water, if you like), then, using more royal icing and food coloring in various colors, pipe elaborate designs on top (you will need 2 packages of royal icing, each 1 lb/450 g, for icing and decorating the cake). The icing for both wedding cakes and Christmas cakes were often colored as well at the time, and by the 1920s, Christmas cakes were topped with written greetings and jolly festive scenes.

FOOD FOR THOUGHT

This fruitcake is as far removed from the American national joke version as possible. Fruitcake recipes range from quite light to very rich, and this one is somewhere in between. The recipe is flexible. You can vary the fruit according to taste, and dried cherries (never glacéed), stem ginger, cranberries, apricots, and dates all work well. Likewise, cherry brandy, ginger wine, or rum would be great in place of the brandy. If you find the cake is too sweet, reduce the sugar by ¼ cup (50 g) and add the grated zest of an extra lemon.

UPSTAIRS DINNER

DINNER WAS THE MAIN MEAL OF THE DAY, served for the upper classes around 8:00 p.m, and was the focus of the cook's time and attention. While there may have been guests present for lunch, tea, and even breakfast if they were staying with the family, it was always a dinner to which the most prestigious invitations were given, and dinners were the best opportunity for both families and individuals to impress. Ralph Waldo Emerson once commented that in England, trial by dinner, not by jury, was the capital institution.

By the Edwardian period, formal dinners were served *à la russe*, a service style that had gradually superseded the buffet-style service of the previous century. Courses were served in a set order by footmen who offered large plates from the side of each diner. At Downton, each diner helps him- or herself from the plate, and the same with the sauces that accompany many of the dishes. It was not uncommon in upper-class homes to sit down to seven courses, with a choice of two dishes in most courses. Menus tend to be shorter and with more restricted choices at Downton Abbey, however, because, as we later find out, the family is suffering a certain level of financial embarrassment.

After the war, in the 1920s, some houses managed to maintain the prewar habit of serving lengthy, weighty meals, but this was increasingly regarded as both silly and wasteful. Dinners became lighter and slightly quicker, although, as we see at Downton, the centuries-old habit of gentlemen and ladies separating after the meal was often retained, not least for the very practical reason that it gave everyone a chance to go to the loo discreetly.

Meals would sometimes start with hors d'oeuvres (which doubled as canapés for large suppers, for example at balls) but got going properly with soups. Advice books sometimes suggest that ladies should prefer the lighter option, and normally the choice, if there was one, was between a light or clear soup and a darker soup with puréed meat or vegetables. Next would come fish and then the entrées, which at the time meant a fancy savory dish designed to show off the skills of the cook. At this point, there would be a pause or sometimes a sorbet as a palate cleanser.

The most prestigious dish was the roast—always game when it was in season—which in many houses was still cooked on a spit in front of a roaring fire. After this, vegetable entrées were offered, although some of the earlier courses would also have been served with vegetables. Next appeared sweet dishes, called entremets, which concluded the bulk of the menu. The meal ended with dessert, which was intended to cleanse the palate rather than fill you up further. It consisted of fresh fruit and nuts, ices, and sometimes the quintessentially Edwardian British savories, which were punchy little mouthfuls based on things like cheese and anchovies, all highly flavored with spiced relishes.

OYSTERS AU GRATIN

As exquisite as raw oysters are, they were also very popular cooked in the Edwardian era, and a large number of such recipes appear in cookbooks of the time (quite a lot involving Champagne). They were eaten as canapés and hors d'oeuvres and also made an appearance in the savory course at the end of the meal. They had once been so plentiful that they were eaten by everyone, and although they were becoming scarcer, and therefore more expensive, by the twentieth century, they were still eaten frequently. Oysters are on the menu at Edith's wedding breakfast in season 3, and are eventually consumed by the servants at a memorable servants' tea.

SERVES 6

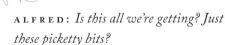

ALFRED: *Is this all we're getting? Just these pickerty bits?*

THOMAS: *Hardly. These are canapés. Alfred, for your first course, some truffled egg on toast perhaps? Some oysters . . . ?*

~ SEASON 3, EPISODE 3

INGREDIENTS

½ cup (120 ml) half-and-half

6 tablespoons (90 ml) dry white wine

4 tablespoons (60 g) butter

1 teaspoon cornstarch

2 anchovy fillets in oil, minced

Generous pinch of cayenne pepper

Grated zest of ½ lemon

24 oysters in the shell, scrubbed

⅔ cup (70 g) dried bread crumbs

1 cup (115 g) grated Parmesan cheese

Chopped fresh flat-leaf parsley, for garnish

Combine the half-and-half, wine, butter, and cornstarch in a small saucepan over medium heat and cook, stirring, until the butter melts and all the ingredients are well mixed and heated through. Add the anchovies, cayenne, and lemon zest, stir well, and bring to a gentle boil over medium-high heat. Boil, stirring constantly, until the sauce thickens, about 2 minutes. Remove from the heat and set aside.

To shuck each oyster, protect your nondominant hand with a folded towel and place the oyster, flat side up, on the towel. Locate the hinge in the pointed end, insert the tip of an oyster knife into the hinge, and turn the knife to break the hinge and loosen the shell. Run the blade along the inside surface of the upper shell, detaching the oyster from the shell, then lift off and discard the top shell. Run the knife along the inside of the rounded bottom shell to detach the oyster, lift out the oyster, and reserve the bottom shell.

Preheat the broiler. Stir together the bread crumbs and Parmesan in a small bowl. Arrange the bottom shells on a large sheet pan. Put a spoonful of the sauce in each bottom shell and lay an oyster on top. Sprinkle the bread crumb mixture evenly over the oysters.

Broil until the cheese is bubbling and the topping is crisp, 3–4 minutes. Serve hot, garnished with the parsley.

RECIPE NOTE

For a simpler and quicker version of the sauce, use a mixture of 1 teaspoon each sweet chile sauce and heavy cream for each oyster.

STUFFED TOMATOES

Always a useful standby, stuffed tomatoes make their appearance in season 4. They were a versatile dish, for they could be served hot or cold, cooked or raw, and stuffed with a wide variety of fillings, depending on what leftovers were on hand or what was deemed suitable for the invited guests. These two recipes are very simple, so it's important to use full-flavored tomatoes, preferably homegrown or from a local farm.

MAKES 6 HOT OR 6 COLD TOMATOES

RECIPE NOTE

You can stuff tomatoes with almost anything (hence the slightly odd but authentic pineapple-mayonnaise mixture featured here). Florence Jack's *The Good Housekeeping Cookery Book*, from which this recipe comes, also suggests cooked stuffings of ham and bread crumbs, mushrooms, scrambled eggs, stewed kidney, and curried rice, and uncooked stuffings of cheese and mayonnaise, apple and celery with salad dressing, and diced cucumber.

INGREDIENTS

FOR HOT STUFFED TOMATOES

6 medium-size tomatoes

3 tablespoons heavy cream

3 tablespoons soft fresh goat cheese

Salt and black pepper

6 quail eggs

Small fresh herb sprigs, for garnish

FOR COLD STUFFED TOMATOES

6 medium-size tomatoes

4 tablespoons shredded fresh or canned pineapple

2 tablespoons chopped toasted hazelnuts

2 tablespoons mayonnaise

Salt and black pepper

Shredded lettuce or spinach, for serving

To make the hot tomatoes, preheat the oven to 325°F (165°C). Using a small, sharp knife, cut out the stem and core from each tomato, then hollow out the inside with a spoon or melon baller.

Mix together the cream and cheese in a small bowl and season with salt and pepper. Divide the mixture evenly among the hollowed-out tomatoes. Make a depression in the center of each filling portion and crack a quail egg into it.

Arrange the tomatoes on a sheet pan and bake until the eggs have set, 7–10 minutes.

To make the cold tomatoes, stem them and hollow them out as for the hot tomatoes. Mix together the pineapple, hazelnuts, and mayonnaise in a small bowl and season with salt and pepper. Divide the mixture evenly among the hollowed-out tomatoes.

Serve both the hot and cold tomatoes on a platter lined with lettuce, which can be cunningly arranged to keep the tomatoes upright. Garnish with the fresh herbs.

CAVIAR CROÛTES

In the world of the canapé, caviar is king. It's salty, fishy, expensive, and interesting looking, all the important elements of an impressive ingredient. It was often served on its own, on a piece of toast, but this recipe elevates it to a new level. It also helps to eke it out a bit, which is always helpful. *Croûtes* like these tend to feature in kitchen scenes at Downton and are useful for using up all that bread we regularly see being sliced by the lower maids. We also see these hors d'oeuvres presented on trays at large events, such as the New Year's ball in the final episode.

MAKES 24 CROÛTES

INGREDIENTS

⅓ cup (30 g) sliced almonds

6–8 slices white bread, each 1 inch (2.5 cm) thick

4 tablespoons (60 g) unsalted butter, melted

1 lemon

3 oz (90 g) caviar

¼ teaspoon paprika

Preheat the oven to 350°F (180°C). Spread the almonds in a single layer on a small sheet pan and toast in the oven, shaking the pan once or twice, until golden brown and fragrant, 4–5 minutes. Pour onto a plate to cool, then break them up roughly. Leave the oven on.

Using a 1½-inch (4-cm) round cutter, cut out 24 circles from the bread slices. Hollow out the center of each bread circle to form a small cup. Brush each bread cup all over with the butter and arrange the cups, amply spaced, in a baking dish.

Bake the cups until golden brown and crispy, about 10 minutes. Let cool completely.

Using a paring knife or zester, pare the zest from the lemon in at least 24 fine strips, then halve and juice the lemon. Combine the caviar, almonds, lemon juice, and paprika in a small bowl and mix together gently.

Just before serving, divide the caviar mixture evenly among the bread cups, piling it up and topping each cup with a curl of lemon zest. Arrange on a platter or tray and serve.

RECIPE NOTE

These canapés are also good topped with a small blob of sour cream, and the almonds can be replaced with hazelnuts or macadamias.

CHICKEN VOL-AU-VENTS

The Downton kitchen table is often laden with vol-au-vents, and it would be groaning were they not supposed to be lighter than air (the name means "fly in the wind"). Chicken is a classic filling, often mixed with mayonnaise or white sauce. This recipe, from Frederick Vine's caterer's manual, is more interesting than many, and has the added advantage of using small amounts of meat that could easily be carved off a roast or set aside from other more substantial dishes.

MAKES ABOUT 24 PASTRIES

RECIPE NOTE

The same basic directions can be applied to making any meat- or vegetable-filled vol-au-vent. Anchovies were phenomenally popular in Edwardian Britain, lauded for their "powerful and unique flavor." They were especially eaten as anchovy paste, spread on bread, and were recommended by one author as a less injurious alternative to a strong brandy and soda as a morning pick-me-up. You can still buy Edwardian-style anchovy paste today under the brand name The Gentleman's Relish, invented in 1828.

INGREDIENTS

¼ lb (115 g) cooked chicken meat (roughly 1 breast)

2 oz (60 g) baked or roasted veal

2 oz (60 g) cooked ham

2 hard-boiled egg yolks

¼ teaspoon cayenne pepper

⅛ teaspoon ground cinnamon

1 anchovy fillet in olive oil, finely minced

6 tablespoons (90 ml) heavy cream

Flour, for the work surface

½ lb (225 g) all-butter puff pastry, thawed according to package directions if frozen

Finely mince the cooked chicken, veal, and ham (using a food processor is fine) and transfer to a bowl. Add the egg yolks, cayenne, cinnamon, anchovy, and cream and mix well. You should have a fairly stiff paste.

Preheat the oven to 425°F (220°C). Line a large sheet pan with parchment paper.

On a lightly floured work surface, roll out the puff pastry a scant ¼ inch (6 mm) thick. Cut out about 24 shapes from the pastry. At Downton, the vol-au-vents are generally round, but you can use a cutter in any shape you like or even cut simple triangles. Lift away the excess pastry. Using a sharp knife or a smaller cutter, cut a lid in the center of each cutout, cutting only halfway down through the layers and leaving the bottom layers intact. (When the pastry puffs up in the oven, the lid you have cut will part company with the surrounding pastry, allowing you to flip the lid out, set it aside, fill the pastries, and replace the lid.)

Arrange the puff pastry cutouts, well spaced, on the prepared pan. Bake until golden brown and fully puffed up, about 10 minutes. Remove from the oven and let cool, then carefully lift off the lid from each pastry.

Fill the pastries with the chicken filling and replace the lids. Serve within a few hours or they will go soggy.

CUCUMBER SOUP

Large houses like Downton relied upon their kitchen gardens to supply most of their fruit and vegetable requirements. With enough money, almost anything could be produced, and in the Victorian era, the rich prided themselves on eating out-of-season produce, forced or retarded through skillful garden management. By the twentieth century, as land rents fell and many aristocrats struggled to maintain their estates, the acres of greenhouses were increasingly left to rot, and the boilers that had once heated the hothouses were abandoned. Some were turned into commercial market gardens, while others simply became less ambitious. But as any gardener knows, vegetable gardens left to their own devices produce a glut of produce, and skilled cooks need recipes to deal with that. The original recipe for this soup appeared in Eliza Acton's *Modern Cookery for Private Families*, one of the best-sellers of the nineteenth century and remaining in print for over sixty years. Cooks who, like Mrs. Patmore, learned their art in the Victorian period would have known it well.

SERVES 6–8 AS A STARTER
OR 4 AS A LIGHT MAIN

INGREDIENTS

4 cucumbers, peeled and sliced 1 inch (2.5 cm) thick

1 shallot, finely diced

2½ cups (600 ml) chicken stock

2 teaspoons salt

½ teaspoon cayenne pepper

1 tablespoon rice flour

1 cup (240 ml) heavy cream

1 bunch fresh flat-leaf parsley, large stems discarded

Combine the cucumbers, shallot, stock, salt, and cayenne in a large saucepan and bring to a boil over high heat. Reduce the heat to a simmer, cover partially, and cook until the cucumbers are tender, about 45 minutes.

Remove from the heat and let cool slightly. Working in batches, transfer to a blender and purée until smooth. Return the soup to the pan and heat over medium-low heat. In a small bowl, stir the rice flour into the cream to dissolve it, and then stir the cream mixture into the soup. Keeping the soup at a gentle simmer, stir it continuously until it thickens, which will take about 10 minutes.

Just before serving, mince the parsley and stir it into the soup. Ladle the soup into bowls and serve hot.

RECIPE NOTE

Cucumbers are rarely served hot today but were popular as a cooked ingredient in the past. They were stuffed, stewed, and, as here, made into soups. The same is true of lettuce. Modern cucumber soups are generally served cold, and this one works as a cold soup as well. This quantity of cayenne makes a fairly mild soup, so taste the soup and add a little more if you like your food a bit spicy.

CONSOMMÉ À LA JARDINIÈRE

Consommés are a true test of a cook's skill, for they must be both absolutely clear and delicately flavored. They take at least a day to make and are easiest done over two days, with the stock made on day one and then clarified on day two. Plain, they were often served to invalids, which is mildly ironic in view of the fact that it's a consommé over which Robert vomits blood when his stomach ulcer bursts in one of the most memorable dining room scenes on *Downton Abbey*.

**SERVES 6 AS A STARTER
OR 4 AS A LIGHT MAIN**

INGREDIENTS

FOR THE STOCK

I chicken carcass, about 2 lb (I kg), or 2 lb (I kg) chicken wings

I tablespoon vegetable oil

I teaspoon salt

2 carrots, cut into chunks

2 ribs celery, cut into chunks

Bouquet garni of 3–4 fresh flat-leaf parsley sprigs, 2–3 fresh thyme sprigs, and I bay leaf, or I bunch fresh savory herb sprigs such as rosemary and sage, tied into a bundle with kitchen string

4 quarts (4 l) water

FOR CLARIFYING

White and shell of I egg

I slice ham, chopped

I teaspoon tomato paste

FOR THE SOUP

4 cups (500–600 g) cut-up assorted fresh vegetables, such as carrots, asparagus, shelled fava beans, and lettuce

Salt and black pepper

FOR THE CROUTONS

4 slices good-quality white bread, each ½ inch thick, cut into ½-inch (12-mm) cubes

2 tablespoons kosher salt

I tablespoon fruity olive oil

I teaspoon dried tarragon

To make the stock, preheat the oven to 425°F (220°C). Put the chicken carcass into a roasting pan and sprinkle with the vegetable oil and salt. Roast until nicely browned, about 30 minutes.

Remove from the oven and, if using the carcass, break it up slightly. Combine the browned chicken, carrots, celery, bouquet garni, and water in a large saucepan and bring to a boil over high heat, skimming off any foam from the surface. Reduce the heat and simmer for I hour.

Scoop out and discard the chicken, vegetables, and bouquet garni and raise the heat to high. Bring to a rolling boil and boil until reduced by about one-third, about 30 minutes. Remove from the heat and strain through a fine-mesh sieve into a large bowl. You should have about 9 cups (2.1 l) stock. Set aside to cool, then cover and refrigerate until cold. You can make the stock up to 4 days in advance and refrigerate it before continuing. It is also an excellent all-purpose stock and can be used as is.

Recipe continues

To clarify the stock, crush the eggshell and white together in a bowl and whisk to a light froth. Add the ham and tomato paste and whisk again. Using a large spoon, lift off the solidified fat from the surface of the cold stock and reserve for another use or discard. Pour the stock into a clean saucepan and stir in the eggshell mixture. Place over medium-low heat and bring very slowly to a boil, stirring regularly. (It should take about 30 minutes.) The egg white mixture will slowly coagulate, taking all the solids with it, and will form a thick, omelet-like layer on top of the stock. At this point, stop stirring and turn the heat down so the liquid is barely simmering. Leave to simmer for another 10 minutes and then remove from the heat.

Using a large slotted spoon, carefully remove the coagulated egg white mixture from the surface of the stock and discard. Then spoon the stock through a fine-mesh sieve lined with a double layer of cheesecloth, a piece of muslin, a kitchen towel, or a jelly bag into a large saucepan. You should have about 8 cups (1.9 l) very clear stock. Reserve any extra stock for another use.

Meanwhile, prepare the vegetables. You can use anything you like, but aim to avoid using more than one type of brassica or allium and try to use as many different colors and types as possible. Anything that needs chopping (for example, zucchini, cucumber, and cauliflower) should be cut into small cubes; anything that needs slicing or cutting into lengths (for example, green beans, asparagus, and baby leeks) should be cut into pieces of similar size; and anything that needs shredding (for example, lettuce) should be cut into thin shreds. If you strive to be utterly purist, you should blanch all the vegetables separately in boiling water for about 2 minutes before adding them to the hot stock and heating them through. (If you cook them in your consommé, it will become slightly cloudy.) Otherwise, simmer them in the stock until just tender and heated through, about 5 minutes.

To make the croutons, preheat the oven to 400°F (200°C). Put the bread cubes into a baking pan, sprinkle with the tarragon, kosher salt, olive oil, and tarragon, and shake the pan vigorously to coat the bread evenly. Spread the cubes in a single layer and toast, shaking the pan after 5–7 minutes, until browned and crisp, 10–15 minutes.

Ladle the soup into bowls and serve piping hot. Offer the croutons at the table for diners to add as they like.

RECIPE NOTE

As involved as the method sounds, this is actually quite a simple soup, plus the consommé without the vegetables can be used as a stock for lots of other soups. You can julienne the vegetables for a julienne soup, or you can add vermicelli to turn it into a noodle soup. A modern alternative to clarifying with egg whites is to freeze the stock in small containers and then put the frozen blocks into a fine-mesh sieve lined with double-thickness cheesecloth or muslin to thaw overnight. It's not as magical that way, however.

PALESTINE SOUP

Downton Abbey starts in the Edwardian era, when meals had become lengthy and food was often very complicated. Cooks prided themselves on their ability to transform anything into a beautiful and tasty dish that often bore little resemblance to the original ingredient. The range of foods eaten, especially vegetables, was greater than today, and there was a particular vogue for root vegetables. This soup, which was ubiquitous on Edwardian Christmas menus in particular, gets its name, Palestine, from the inclusion of what are known in Britain as Jerusalem artichokes (sunchokes), though there is no real link to the actual region.

**SERVES 6 AS A STARTER
OR 4 AS A LIGHT MAIN**

RECIPE NOTE

This soup can be made with other starchy vegetables, such as potatoes, winter squash, parsnips, and, another Edwardian favorite, salsify. You can also vary the seasonings, swapping out the cayenne for curry powder or the parsley for sage, for example.

INGREDIENTS

2 lb (1 kg) Jerusalem artichokes, cut into ½-inch (12-mm) pieces

1 small turnip, peeled and cut into ½-inch (12-mm) pieces

1 yellow onion, chopped

3 ribs celery, chopped

4 cups (950 ml) chicken or veal stock

2 teaspoons cayenne pepper

Scant 1 teaspoon salt

½ teaspoon sugar

Black pepper

½ cup (120 ml) heavy cream

**FOR THE CROUTONS
AND FRIED PARSLEY**

4 thin slices good-quality white bread

1–2 tablespoons unsalted butter, or as needed, for frying

1 small bunch fresh flat-leaf parsley, large stems discarded, finely chopped

Combine the Jerusalem artichokes, turnip, onion, celery, stock, cayenne, salt, sugar, and a little black pepper in a large saucepan and bring to a boil over high heat. Reduce the heat to a simmer and simmer until the vegetables are tender, about 1 hour.

Meanwhile, make the croutons and fried parsley. Using a small biscuit or cookie cutter, cut the bread into small shapes. (Stars, diamonds, and triangles are all suitably Edwardian.) Melt the butter in a frying pan over medium heat until foaming. Add the bread cutouts and fry, turning as needed to color evenly, until golden brown on all sides, 3–5 minutes. Transfer to a bowl. Add the parsley to the same pan and fry over medium heat until just crispy, about 1 minute, adding more butter as needed. Transfer to a separate bowl.

When the soup is ready, remove from the heat and let cool slightly. Working in batches, transfer the soup to a blender and purée until smooth. Return the soup to the pan and heat over medium-low heat, stirring often, until hot. Stir in the cream and heat through.

Ladle the soup into bowls and serve hot, dotted with the croutons and fried parsley, or offer the croutons and parsley on the side for diners to help themselves.

VEGETABLE MARROW AND APRICOT SOUP

One of the characteristics of 1920s cookery is a more varied approach to vegetable cookery. The British had become known for serving vegetables boiled, mashed, or fried, generally with a butter sauce. Recipes from the nineteenth century suggest that if vegetables were served plain, they were habitually overcooked by modern standards, and in many cases were used as purées and garnishes for elaborate meat dishes. Some vegetables resist almost any form of cooking, however, especially when they are past their best. This soup solves the age-old problem of what to do with overgrown zucchini (courgettes), which are known as marrows once that happens and are notoriously watery and tasteless. It can be served hot but is even better cold.

SERVES 6 AS A STARTER

INGREDIENTS

½ lb (225 g) apricots, pitted and roughly chopped

½ lb (225 g) marrow or zucchini, peeled and roughly chopped

2 cups (480 ml) water

2 tablespoons instant tapioca

1 teaspoon sugar

½ teaspoon salt

1 tablespoon brandy

Juice of ½ lemon

¼ teaspoon paprika

Pinch of ground allspice

Combine the apricots, marrow, water, tapioca, sugar, and salt in a saucepan and bring to a gentle simmer over medium-low heat. Reduce the heat to low and cook, stirring occasionally, until the apricots are soft, the marrow is tender, and the tapioca has absorbed the water and the mixture is thickening up, about 30 minutes. Keep an eye on the water level and add more if the mixture starts to burn or stick badly to the bottom of the pan.

Add the brandy, lemon juice, paprika, and allspice, stir well, remove from the heat, and let cool slightly. Working in batches, transfer to a blender and purée until smooth. You can reheat the soup and serve it hot, or you can let it cool, then chill it thoroughly and serve it as a cold soup.

RECIPE NOTE

Spice this soup up with a little peeled and minced fresh ginger and minced chile, or you can trade out the paprika for cinnamon, sweeten the soup a little more, and add dried fruit, which will turn it into a dessert soup. If you don't have a blender or a hand-cranked Mouli (rotary grater), you can always use the Edwardian method, which was to push the solids through a sturdy sieve. Although it is easier than it sounds, it is very repetitive and is a task that would have fallen to the lowest kitchen maid.

MRS. PATMORE: *Not those bowls, Ivy! Chilled soup should be an exquisite mouthful, not a bucket of slop!*

~ SEASON 4, EPISODE 3

SHRIMP CURRY

Downton's connection with India is via Rose's father, Hugh MacClare, the Marquess of Flintshire. In season 4, he is appointed governor of Bombay and moves to India, which at the time was under British rule: in 1877, Queen Victoria was declared empress of India, and in 1887 she had five Indians brought over to act as her personal attendants. British fascination with India went back much further, however, and the first curry recipes appeared in English cookery books in the eighteenth century. By the time *Downton* opens in the Edwardian period, curries were almost as British as fish and chips and were often seen as a way to use up leftovers. This curry from a late-Victorian book can be made with any seafood, though it would originally have been made with shrimp. Using shrimp is a nice nod to Lord Flintshire's nickname, Shrimpie, which he was given after playing the role of a shrimp in his childhood games. For the curry powder, Mrs. Patmore would have had her choice of several different ready-made types, so use one as fiery or as mild as you prefer.

SERVES 4

INGREDIENTS

1 lb (450 g) spinach or other sturdy greens, such as kale or Good-King-Henry, hefty stalks removed

1 small sweet onion, diced

1 tablespoon curry powder

1 teaspoon cayenne pepper

1 teaspoon ground ginger

Kosher salt

1 tablespoon unsalted butter

2 cups (480 ml) full-fat coconut milk

1 lb (450 g) cooked and peeled shrimp

You can cook the spinach in a large pot of boiling water for about 2 minutes, or you can put it in a large saucepan with just the rinsing water clinging to the leaves, cover, and steam over medium heat for about 5 minutes. When it is wilted and tender, drain well, squeeze gently in a kitchen towel to remove the excess moisture, and chop finely.

Sprinkle the onion with the curry powder, cayenne, ginger, and a little salt. Melt the butter in a saucepan over medium-low heat, add the seasoned onion, and cook gently, stirring occasionally, until translucent, about 5 minutes. Add the coconut milk and spinach, raise the heat to medium-high, and bring to a boil, stirring as needed to prevent scorching. Add the shrimp and heat through, then serve right away.

PRINCE OF WALES: *Lady Rose is Lord Flintshire's daughter, Sir.*

KING GEORGE V: *Ah. The Prince of Wales has spoken about your father's hospitality in Bombay.*

ROSE: *He was honoured to entertain His Royal Highness, Your Majesty.*

KING GEORGE V: *The Indian tour was a great success, thanks to Lord Flintshire.*

~ SEASON 4, EPISODE 9

TROUT IN PORT WINE SAUCE

Along with hunting and shooting, fishing is a popular sport for the upper classes at Downton, especially when the family decamps to Scotland for the season 3 Christmas special. Scotland was renowned for the quality of its fishing, which included not just salmon but also trout. Queen Victoria helped to popularize Scotland as a destination for the rich when she bought Balmoral and threw herself into all things tartan, and her successor, Edward VII, retained Balmoral as a royal retreat, ensuring the popularity of the country would not wane. Trout was often gutted and grilled simply over a fire on the riverbank, but it could also be transformed into dishes more suitable for a proper dinner, as here. Cucumber, broccoli, spinach, or cauliflower would make a good accompaniment to this dish.

SERVES 4 AS A STARTER (IF USING FILLETS) OR 2 AS A MAIN

INGREDIENTS

I shallot, minced

2 whole trout, gutted and prepared for cooking, or 4 trout fillets

I cup (240 ml) chicken stock

I cup (240 ml) port, claret, or other full-bodied wine

¼ teaspoon black pepper

¼ teaspoon ground allspice

Pinch of ground cloves

Pinch of salt

2 anchovy fillets in olive oil, finely chopped

1½ teaspoons mushroom ketchup or Worcestershire sauce

I teaspoon fresh lemon juice

2 teaspoons cornstarch

I tablespoon water

Put the shallot in a high-sided frying pan. Lay the trout on top and pour in the stock and port. Add the pepper, allspice, cloves, and salt and bring to a gentle boil over medium-high heat. Reduce to a gentle simmer and cook until the fish flakes when tested with a fork, about 20 minutes for whole trout and 15 minutes if using fillets. Carefully transfer the fish to a plate and keep warm.

Strain the pan sauce through a fine-mesh sieve into a pitcher, wipe the pan clean, and pour the sauce back into the pan. Add the anchovies, mushroom ketchup, and lemon juice, raise the heat to high, bring to a rapid boil, and boil until reduced by half. In a small bowl, dissolve the cornstarch in the water, add to the sauce, and stir constantly until the sauce thickens, 1–2 minutes.

Serve the sauce hot spooned over the fish or on the side.

MATTHEW: *Why don't you come fly fishing tomorrow? We might see a bit more activity? You could bring your evening clothes to change at Duneagle.*

GREGSON: *It's rather an imposition.*

MATTHEW: *But that's what you're here for, isn't it? To get to know us all. Besides, you didn't bring your tails all the way to Scotland to dine in a country pub.*

GREGSON: *No. No, I suppose not.*

~ SEASON 3, EPISODE 9

RECIPE NOTE

Mushroom ketchup was a popular eighteenth-century relish that remained a pantry staple well into the twentieth century. It is not dissimilar to a large number of other sauces, all intended to boost the flavor of gravies and add oomph to a sandwich. Worcestershire sauce and the rather more regional (and obscure) Henderson's Relish are two that survive today, and you can also still buy mushroom ketchup. For substitutes, see page 24, or leave out entirely.

SOLE À LA FLORENTINE

Fish with something green is often seen on the dinner table at Downton. The garnish serves a practical purpose, as it gives the actors something to eat that isn't going to be horrible after several hours under fierce lighting. This was a genuinely popular way to serve fish, and in classic French cuisine, the garnish often dictated the eventual name of the dish. While white fish by itself can be rather bland, overpowering flavors can destroy its subtlety. This recipe, like nearly any recipe called "Florentine," uses spinach for flavor and color. But unlike authentic Italian fish dishes, it contains cheese. It is ideal for people who aren't sure they like fish.

SERVES 4

INGREDIENTS

I cup (240 ml) dry white wine

4 tablespoons (60 g) butter, plus more for the baking dish

4 Dover sole or other firm white fish fillets, each about 6 oz (170 g)

FOR THE SAUCE

4 tablespoons butter

¼ cup (30 g) flour

I cup (240 ml) milk, heated

¼ cup (60 ml) liquid from poaching fish

¼ cup (30 g) grated Gruyère cheese

¼ cup (30 g) grated Parmesan cheese

Ground nutmeg

Black pepper

I lb (450 g) spinach, hefty stems removed

¼ cup (30 g) grated Parmesan cheese

Black pepper

To poach the fish, heat the wine in a large frying pan over medium heat and add 2 tablespoons of the butter. When the butter melts, stir to mix. Add the fish fillets in a single layer, adjust the heat to maintain a gentle simmer, and cook just until the fillets start to flake when prodded with a fork, 4–5 minutes, depending on their thickness. They will finish cooking in the oven. Carefully transfer the fillets to a plate. If you have purchased fillets with the skin attached, let cool until they can be handled, then carefully remove the skin. Reserve ¼ cup (60 ml) of the poaching liquid for making the sauce and discard the remainder or save for another use.

To make the sauce, melt the butter in a saucepan over medium-low heat. Stir in the flour and continue to stir, allowing the mixture to brown slightly without burning, for about 5 minutes. Whisk in the hot milk, little by little. When all the milk is added, whisk in the poaching liquid and continue to whisk until the sauce is smooth and creamy, 3–5 minutes. Add both cheeses and stir until melted. Season to taste with nutmeg and pepper and set aside off the heat.

Rinse the spinach and put it in a large saucepan with just the rinsing water clinging to the leaves. Cover, set over medium heat, and cook until wilted and tender, about 5 minutes. Drain well, squeeze gently in a kitchen towel to remove the excess moisture, and chop roughly. Mix the spinach with the remaining 2 tablespoons butter and season with lots of pepper.

Preheat the broiler. Butter a broiler-proof oven dish just large enough to accommodate the spinach and fish. Spoon the spinach into the dish, spreading it evenly. Arrange the fillets in a single layer on top of the spinach. Pour the sauce over the top, then sprinkle evenly with the Parmesan. Broil until the cheese is browned and bubbling, 3–5 minutes. Serve hot.

RECIPE NOTE

The sauce here also masquerades as sauce Mornay and is very good with eggs, making an easy alternative to hollandaise sauce for eggs Benedict. If you also add spinach, you have eggs Florentine.

TURBOT WITH HOLLANDAISE SAUCE

The turbot kettle, or *turbotière*, was one of the most prestigious pieces of equipment in the country house kitchen. Downton's is usually in the background on a shelf, but it does appear on the kitchen table in a few scenes. Designed specifically for this one fish, it's a large, diamond-shaped copper pan that has a rack, much like a standard fish kettle. Turbot was an expensive fish and was almost always cooked and presented whole, and hollandaise was a classic accompaniment, one that was regularly served at Downton. It's a hollandaise beginning to curdle that Alfred rescues for Ivy in season 3. This recipe, which uses fillets, can be done with any firm white fish, and the sauce is also a traditional accompaniment for salmon. If you do happen to have a *turbotière*, however, a poached whole fish is always impressive. Incidentally, the UK pronunciation of turbot is always with a hard final *t*.

SERVES 4

INGREDIENTS

FOR THE SAUCE

2 tablespoons white wine vinegar

10 black peppercorns

1 fresh tarragon sprig or bay leaf

5 tablespoons (75 g) cold unsalted butter, cut into small cubes

1 egg yolk

1 teaspoon fresh lemon juice

Salt

4 skin-on turbot or other firm white fish fillets, each about 6 oz (170 g)

1 teaspoon salt

4 tablespoons (60 g) unsalted butter

To make the sauce, combine the vinegar, peppercorns, and tarragon in a small saucepan and heat over medium heat until reduced by half, 2–3 minutes. Strain through a fine-mesh sieve and set aside.

Put a cube of the butter in the top pan of a double boiler over (not touching) gently simmering water in the lower pan. (Or rest a heatproof bowl in the rim of a saucepan over simmering water.) Whisk the egg yolk in a small bowl, add it to the melted butter, and whisk together. Then add the remaining butter, a cube at a time, waiting until each cube melts and is whisked into the mixture before adding the next cube. Continue to whisk until all the butter is fully incorporated and the sauce has thickened, then remove from the heat, whisk in the lemon juice, and season to taste with salt. Cover with plastic wrap, pressing it directly against the surface of the sauce to prevent a skin from forming.

Pat the fish fillets dry with paper towels and place them, skin side up, on a plate. Sprinkle the skin side evenly with the salt and let stand for 5 minutes. Select a heavy-bottomed frying pan large enough to accommodate the fillets in a single layer, add 2 tablespoons of the butter, and melt the butter over medium heat. Add the fillets, skin side down, and cook until lightly browned, 3–4 minutes. Turn the fillets over and cook the flesh side for 2 minutes. Flip them back over so they are skin side down and add the remaining 2 tablespoons butter to the pan. When the butter melts, tilt the pan, then use a spoon to collect some of the melted butter and spoon it liberally over the fillets three or four times. At this point, the fillets should be just cooked through.

If the sauce has cooled, reheat it gently over simmering water, whisking constantly. Serve the fish with the sauce on the side.

RECIPE NOTE

You can also poach the fish in a simple mixture of equal parts white wine and water. Should your hollandaise curdle, you can usually save it by removing it from the heat and very, very quickly whisking in 1½ teaspoons ice-cold water. Otherwise you will have to follow Alfred's technique and decant the spoiled sauce into a bowl and start again with a second egg yolk, this time adding the broken sauce rather than just butter.

DAISY: *Oh my god!*

ALFRED: *What's happened?*

DAISY: *It's curdled and it's got to go up in a minute! Oh my Lord!*

~ SEASON 3, EPISODE 5

FISH CREAM

Much drama on *Downton* happens over the fish course, whether it's whole fish with green garnish or delicate little creams such as these. The period in which the series is set is one of great social upheaval, and the battle for women's rights is one of the key themes across all six seasons. From Sybil's cross-class marriage to Edith's championing of women in the workplace when she takes control of Michael Gregson's magazine, we see the impact of the war and changing political discourse on characters whose attitudes evolve over time. The recipe on which this dish is based comes from *The Women's Suffrage Cookery Book*, which was produced to aid the women's suffrage movement and contained recipes contributed by supporters. While hunger strikes and sometimes violent demonstrations were regularly part of the fight, domestic initiatives such as this book were also a fundamental way in which women both funded and publicized their cause. They eventually won equal voting rights in 1928.

SERVES 4 AS A STARTER

INGREDIENTS

⅔ cup (160 ml) milk

Skin-on oily fish fillets, such as mackerel (2 fillets), sardines (6 fillets), or trout (2 fillets)

2 eggs

½ cup (120 ml) heavy cream

2 anchovy fillets in olive oil

¼ teaspoon cayenne pepper

Salt and black pepper

2 tablespoons butter

2 slices good-quality white bread

Preheat the oven to 275°F (135°C).

Pour the milk into a saucepan, add the fish, and heat over medium heat until almost boiling. Reduce the heat to low and cook gently until the fish is cooked through when tested with a fork. It should take only a few minutes. Transfer the fish to a plate, and discard the cooking liquid. Remove the skin and any errant bones from the fish. For the next step, you can use a mortar and pestle, a bowl and the end of a rolling pin, or a blender. Combine the fish, eggs, cream, anchovies, cayenne, and some salt and black pepper in a bowl and beat together until you have a thick cream-like consistency.

Butter four 1-cup (240-ml) ramekins with some of the butter and divide the fish mixture equally among them. Dot any remaining butter on top. Bake until the tops are lightly browned and the interiors are heated through and set, 10–15 minutes.

Meanwhile, trim off the crusts from the bread slices, then cut the slices into narrow strips and toast them.

Serve the ramekins hot with the toast strips on the side.

RECIPE NOTE

If you want more heat, increase the amount of cayenne. If you prefer no heat, replace the cayenne with nutmeg. You can also sprinkle the top of each ramekin with a mixture of dried bread crumbs and grated Parmesan and serve the cream as a gratin.

SALMON MOUSSE

Salmon mousse is one of the few iconic *Downton* dishes. It's referred to a lot, and often at times of stress: Daisy makes one with the new mixer, and Cora makes a point of congratulating her on her success, causing a mild breakdown in Mrs. Patmore, who, despite her dislike of modern gadgets, sneaks in after hours to practice using the machine. It's over a salmon mousse that Harold Levinson half-heartedly woos Madeleine Allsopp in season 4, and it's a salmon mousse that helps Ethel learn to cook in season 3. This version from Escoffier is far simpler and better than many similar recipes of the era, proving exactly why the chef became so highly revered.

**SERVES 8 AS A STARTER
OR 6 AS A MAIN**

INGREDIENTS

1½ teaspoons powdered gelatin or 3 gelatin sheets

1 teaspoon cornstarch

¾ cup (180 ml) chicken or vegetable stock

1 lb (450 g) skin-on salmon fillets

1 cup (240 ml) dry white wine

¼ teaspoon cayenne pepper

Grated zest of ½ lemon

¼ teaspoon salt

1¼ cups (300 ml) heavy cream

Solid vegetable shortening, if using ceramic or glass mold(s)

Spinach, watercress, or other green leaves, for garnish

Crusty bread or crostini, for serving (optional)

Mix the powdered gelatin with 1 tablespoon water in a small bowl or cup and let stand for 1 minute to soften; or if using gelatin sheets, put them in a bowl, add cold water to cover, and let soak until floppy, 5–10 minutes. In a small bowl, dissolve the cornstarch in 1 tablespoon of the stock. Pour the remaining stock into a small saucepan and bring to a boil. Add the cornstarch mixture to the boiling stock and stir until the stock thickens. Remove from the heat, add the softened gelatin, stir until dissolved, and let the stock cool to room temperature. It should be thick and gloopy but still pourable.

Put the salmon and wine in a wide saucepan and add enough cold water to cover the salmon. Bring to a boil over high heat, reduce the heat to medium, and simmer gently until cooked through, 10–12 minutes. Remove from the heat and stir in the gelatin (if using powdered gelatin, first liquefy it by nesting the small bowl of gelatin in a larger bowl of hot water, or heating it in the microwave for 10 seconds). Transfer the fish to a plate and discard the cooking liquid. Remove and discard the skin and any errant bones from the fish.

Put the salmon flesh in a large bowl and flake it with a fork, breaking it into small pieces without mashing it. Add the cooled stock, the cayenne, lemon zest, and salt and mix gently but thoroughly. In a separate bowl, using a whisk or a handheld mixer on medium speed, whip the cream until soft peaks form. Fold the cream into the salmon mixture just until no white streaks remain.

Recipe continues

You can use either one 5-cup (1.2-l) mold or 6–8 individual molds. If using glass or ceramic, grease well with vegetable shortening. If using metal, there is no need to grease, though it is a good idea to line the bottom with parchment paper. Spoon the mousse into the mold(s), packing gently but firmly, then cover with plastic wrap and refrigerate overnight.

The next day, unmold the mousse onto a serving plate, peeling away the parchment if used. Or unmold the small molds onto individual plates. Garnish with the spinach leaves and accompany with bread, if desired.

MRS. PATMORE: *Right, this is a list of what you'll need. I'll come in on Thursday morning and see how you're getting on.*

ETHEL: *Can I really do it? Salmon mousse?*

MRS. PATMORE: *Anyone who has the use of their limbs can make a salmon mousse.*

~ SEASON 3, EPISODE 6

FILETS MIGNONS LILI

Downton Abbey opens with the family receiving the news that the heir to the estate, Patrick Crawley, has died in the *Titanic* disaster of April 1912. This dish appeared on the menu in the first-class dining saloon on the night of the shipwreck. There was also a separate, even more upmarket restaurant run as an independent concession serving food that was more modern and fashionable than that served in the main first-class dining room. This version of the dish is based on one by Auguste Escoffier, the French chef in whose honor the cookery school that Alfred is admitted to in season 4 was founded.

SERVES 4

INGREDIENTS

FOR THE SAUCE DEMI-GLACE

4 tablespoons unsalted butter

¼ cup (30 g) flour

2 cups (480 ml) beef stock

1 tablespoon tomato paste

2 teaspoons sherry or other fortified wine

FOR THE ARTICHOKES

4 globe artichokes or prepared artichoke bottoms

1 lemon, halved, if using whole artichokes

FOR THE POMMES ANNA

4 medium-size waxy potatoes

8–10 tablespoons (115–170 g) lightly salted butter

Salt and white pepper

Unsalted butter, for frying

4 tournedos (small, round cut from end of beef tenderloin)

Salt and black pepper

4 small slices prepared foie gras (optional)

4–8 slices black truffle (optional)

First, make the sauce (this can be done the day before). Melt the butter in a saucepan over low heat. Stir in the flour and cook very gently, stirring, until the mixture starts to brown and smell nutty, 5–7 minutes. Whisk in the stock, a few tablespoons at a time, stirring well after each addition to prevent lumps. When all the stock is added, leave the sauce to simmer, stirring from time to time, until lightly thickened, 10–15 minutes. Add the tomato paste and sherry and cook, stirring occasionally, for 10 minutes longer to blend the flavors. Set aside off the heat.

Next, prepare the fresh whole artichokes, if using. Working with one artichoke at a time, first pull off the outer leaves until you reach the yellow-green cone of tender inner leaves. Cut off the cone just above where it joins the base, then cut off the stem flush with the bottom of the base. With a small spoon, scrape out and discard the hairy choke and any leaf remnants. As you work, rub the cut surfaces with a lemon half to prevent discoloring. Now, with a very sharp, small knife, pare off all the dark green remains of the leaves and the tough skin until you have a pale green artichoke bowl. Squeeze the remaining lemon half into a bowl filled with cold water and plunge the finished artichoke bottom into the lemon water. Repeat with the remaining artichokes, adding them to the lemon water. (You can do this well in advance, leaving the artichoke bottoms in the lemon water until it is time to

Recipe continues

cook them. The dark green leaves that were stripped off can be steamed and eaten.) If using prepared artichoke bottoms, drain them well and pat them dry.

Now, make the pommes Anna. Preheat the oven to 350°F (180°C). Peel the potatoes and slice them as thinly as possible, dropping them into a bowl of cold water as you work to prevent discoloring. Melt 8 tablespoons (115 g) of the butter and use a little of it to butter a small sheet pan and 4 ring molds, each of which should be about the same diameter as the tournedos. Place the rings on the prepared pan. Drain the potato slices, pat them dry, and layer them in the prepared molds, brushing each layer with butter and seasoning every other layer with salt and white pepper. Press the layers down firmly as you go and melt the remaining 2 tablespoons butter if you run short of butter. Each finished stack should be about 1¼ inches (3 cm) high. Pour any remaining butter evenly over the tops. Bake the potatoes until you can pass a knife through them easily, about 15 minutes. Remove from the oven and keep warm.

Meanwhile, if you are using fresh artichoke bottoms, bring a saucepan of water to a boil over high heat. Drain the artichokes, add them to the boiling water, and boil until tender when pierced with a knife. This should take 10–15 minutes, depending on their size. Drain well, pat dry, and reserve. If using prepared bottoms (thawed frozen or canned), they do not need cooking.

To cook the tournedos, melt a knob of butter in a heavy-bottomed frying pan over medium-high heat until it foams and just begins to brown. Season the tournedos with salt and black pepper, then turn down the heat slightly and put the steaks into the pan. Fry them, turning them every 2–3 minutes, until they are cooked to your satisfaction. Tournedos are generally served rare or medium-rare; the timing will depend on their thickness. Leave to rest for 2–3 minutes while you assemble the rest of the dish.

To build the final dish, reheat the sauce until hot and have ready 4 warmed dinner plates. Unmold a portion of the potatoes onto each plate. Top with an artichoke bottom, a slice of foie gras (if using), the cooked steak, and finally the truffle slices (if using). The sauce can be served separately or poured around the base of the potatoes.

RECIPE NOTE

This is quite a stagy dish, typical of high-end French cooking in the Edwardian period. It's not that difficult, but it is time-consuming. To save time, you can buy ready-made sauce demi-glace, or purchase good-quality gravy and add a little sherry and some tomato paste to it. Artichoke bottoms are available both canned and frozen, and either could be used here in place of the fresh. Or you can replace the artichoke bottoms with cooked artichoke hearts and serve them to one side. If you cannot get whole truffles, use truffle pieces, a little truffle oil, or just omit the truffle. If you don't have ring molds for the potatoes, assemble the layers in a shallow square baking pan, bake as directed, and cut into squares to serve. Although the traditional order of elements in the finished dish is as described in the recipe, you can reorder them if you like, as has been done in the photograph to the right, where the pommes Anna and artichoke bottom appear as the crown rather than as the base.

HOW TO HOST
A DOWNTON DINNER

The etiquette of dining at Downton Abbey is a mixture of experience, written guidance, and the needs of shooting a fast-paced drama. Every country house had slightly different habits, but the general outline was the same, and a solid knowledge of how to behave at dinner was drummed into children as soon as they were old enough to eat at a table. Aristocratic dining was invariably slightly at odds with the middle-class rules laid out in etiquette books, and was in a state of constant flux to keep it exclusive to those brought up to it. As one commentator put it, "a manual of etiquette in the possession of a diner is virtually a *pièce de conviction*."

In a modern context, unless you happen to have a substantial waiting staff, preferably in livery, a sideboard with paraphernalia for keeping dishes hot, and guests who all know exactly how to behave, it's wise to slim down the rules and make a nod to Downton without necessarily copying it in its entirety. Even within the scope of the series, etiquette changes subtly, in line with the changing times. However, with the Earl heading the household throughout, the style of dining does not differ as much as it would if, for example, Lady Mary suddenly took charge of the dining table. And the style would have been different again were it set up as the Dowager Countess dined in her heyday.

This section is, therefore, designed to help you tread a path between Edwardian excess and 1920s elegance in your own home and without any Carsons or Thomases to help you out.

SETTING THE TABLE Flowers, and as many as possible, down the middle of the table and on side tables and in empty fireplaces (unless the fire is burning) are key here. By the late Edwardian era, no food would have been present on the table at all, except perhaps a large and beautifully arranged fruit bowl. No jam jars or other late-twentieth-century containers are permitted—instead, vases all the way. Downton has electricity, and small, shaded lights were normal on the table, but many houses preferred candlelight, as it was seen as more flattering and theatrical.

A large, white tablecloth is obligatory, but color was well liked, so lampshades, napery, glasses, and tableware can all be as lavish as you fancy. When it comes to plates, cutlery, and the like, if you don't have anything of the era, plain white is generally a good choice, for it fades nicely into the background. All the cutlery should be laid out before the meal starts, in the order in which it will be needed (that is, soupspoons on the outside, then fish cutlery, and so on), and it was still sometimes the fashion to lay forks and spoons facing down, to show off the family crests. Glasses for every type of wine that will be poured must be provided, plus a tumbler for water.

Written menus were generally provided at the side of each plate, along with a folded napkin (often very elaborately starched into the shape of a tulip, swan, or crown in the Edwardian era and less so in the 1920s), with a bread roll tucked within its folds.

Most advice books point out that too much attention can be spent on the decoration, including the story of a diner who, when asked what he thought, commented merely, "My dear fellow, sell your plate and get a cook."

BEFORE DINNER It's entirely up to you whether to serve predinner cocktails. They are, let's face it, quite exciting. In theory, you should gather in a separate room and progress into dinner in status order, with the host taking the arm of the highest-status woman, the hostess taking the arm of the highest-status man, and everyone paired off neatly (naturally, you'd have equal numbers of men and women in the perfect Downton world). This method can be very fraught unless you all have clear titles, so it may be easier simply to go through to dinner in your own way.

THE MENU If you want to go all out and provide eight courses, do it. Otherwise, a more muted (and manageable) dinner might be soup or fish, entrée or roast, vegetable, and sweet entremets or dessert or savory. For large dinners at Downton, a choice would have been on offer, but at smaller dinners the menu was more often set, so pick your dishes as you desire. Assuming you don't have footmen, you may wish to plate up in the kitchen and give people individual plates, or have one large platter that you put on a side table and either delegate one person to serve or have a slight free-for-all.

DRINK Generally, meals started with sherry with the soup and/or fish, then progressed to hock, with possibly Champagne after the entrée, and a digression into Burgundy or claret, plus port or whisky to end. You may wish to remain partially sober and judge how much drink to offer. One guide advised the aspiring man about town that as the sweet courses drew near, "if you have been drinking claret throughout the meal, either claret or port is excellent to continue on. But if you have been drinking champagne, claret is sour after it, and port and champagne is to some a deadly mixture. Yet another glass of champagne with dessert is often the course which can be pursued with the greatest safety and enjoyment." The drinks were served by a footman, and the bottles or decanters kept on a sideboard.

EATING Reams of words were written on how to eat various foods, from tackling bananas with a knife and fork to maneuvering asparagus with your fingers to the terrifying perils of eating oranges. Attempting to follow Edwardian etiquette from books is not only fraught with issues but also requires vast quantities of cutlery, an iron will, and an amazing memory (or a book on your lap). Even then it would not necessarily be the way they did it at Downton. However, if you do fancy having a crack at it, see pages 260–261 for some recommendations of suitable books for turning your middle-class habits into aristocratic gold.

THE REMOVE Sometimes at Downton you'll hear people talk about a dish called "the remove." The remove was a feature of some versions of the old-fashioned *à la française* dining style, a way of dining that involved anything up to twenty dishes laid on the table at once for each of two courses (plus dessert). There was an order for eating the array—first the soup, next the fish, then the rest—and it wasn't always practical, as the fish got cold while people ate their soup. In the late eighteenth century, the custom developed in which once the soup (at one end of the table) was consumed, it would be "removed" by fish, which might also be "removed" by another dish in its turn, before all of the dishes on the table would then be uncovered and eaten. Over time, the replacement dishes became known as "the remove," and even after the service style changed to the sequential *à la russe* style we see at Downton, the name hung about, now divorced from its original meaning. You can largely ignore this tradition for your own Downton dinner, unless you are desperate to serve something outside your planned menu, in which case just confidently announce it as "the remove" and smile knowingly.

AFTER DINNER Men and women generally separated, the men remaining behind for fifteen minutes or so to drink port and put the world to rights. This habit was in decline by the 1920s, but you should serve coffee and tea. If you are feeling particularly daring and have a piano, then encouraging those who can to perform party pieces would be entirely in keeping.

DUCK WITH APPLES AND CALVADOS

Another of the dishes planned for at Edith's hastily canceled wedding breakfast in season 3, this is a rich and satisfying way to serve duck. The bird was popular at country houses, often served as a result of a good day's shooting, and takes flavor very well. Although this recipe is best with duck, you can also use it with other game birds, as well as with rabbit, squirrel, venison, and, more prosaically, pork.

SERVES 4

MRS. PATMORE: *Right. What's it to be? Lobster, duck, or asparagus?*

ALFRED: *Is there any cheese, Mrs. Patmore?*

~ SEASON 3, EPISODE 3

INGREDIENTS

I whole duck, about 5 lb (2.5 kg)

Salt

2 tablespoons boiling water

FOR THE APPLESAUCE

2 cooking apples, peeled, cored, and roughly chopped

1½ teaspoons firmly packed dark brown sugar

2 tablespoons Calvados or apple brandy

I tablespoon water

2 teaspoons butter

FOR THE GRAVY

I tablespoon quince preserves or red currant jelly

2 tablespoons Madeira

I cup (240 ml) chicken or beef stock

I teaspoon cornstarch

2 teaspoons cold water

Preheat the oven to 450°F (230°C).

Rub the duck all over with salt and put it, breast side up, on a rack in a roasting pan. Roast for 20 minutes. Reduce the temperature to 325°F (165°C) and continue to roast for 1–1¼ hours. Roast duck is generally served pink, so a thermometer inserted into the leg away from bone should register 125°F (52°C), or roast until it registers 160°F (71°C) if you prefer it cooked through.

Meanwhile, make the applesauce. Combine the apples, sugar, Calvados, and water in a saucepan and cook over medium heat, stirring often, until the apples have broken down completely and are fluffy and tender, about 20 minutes. Remove from the heat and stir in the butter. Keep warm.

When the duck is ready, transfer to a platter and let rest for 15 minutes. Add the boiling water to the roasting pan and scrape the bottom to loosen any browned bits, then strain the pan juices through a fine-mesh sieve into a pitcher. Leave to settle and then skim off the fat from the surface. Or, if you have one, use a fat separator to remove the fat.

To make the gravy, combine the preserves, Madeira, and stock in a saucepan and heat over medium heat. Add the strained pan juices and bring the mixture to a boil. In a small bowl, dissolve the cornstarch in the water, stir into the stock mixture, and boil gently, stirring, until the sauce has thickened, 2–3 minutes.

Serve the duck, surrounded by the applesauce, on a warmed platter. Offer the gravy in a sauceboat or pitcher on the side.

DUCK WITH OLIVES

Shooting is a large part of life at Downton Abbey, and wild game would have been served on the dinner table at most country houses. It was often simply roasted and served with gravy or a suitable sauce, but when a large amount was bagged, the kitchen had to be creative with ways to cook it that would not result in guests becoming bored. Popular at the time, this French-influenced dish works with any dark meat.

SERVES 4

RECIPE NOTE

The flour-and-butter method (roux) is the one that would have been used at the time for making the sauce, but you can instead ladle 1 cup (240 ml) of the hot stock into a saucepan over medium heat and thicken it with 1 heaping teaspoon cornstarch or arrowroot dissolved in 1 tablespoon cold water. You can also increase the amount of stock for a thinner sauce. If you'd like, add finely minced shallot or garlic to the lardons when frying them, though alliums were regarded with a certain level of suspicion at the time and thus would not have been regularly included. They were viewed as not entirely suited for polite society, as they led to bad breath and bloating—never good when you're wearing a corset.

INGREDIENTS

I whole duck, about 5 lb (2.5 kg)

3 tablespoons butter

6 oz (170 g) lardons

3 cups (700 ml) beef stock

6 tablespoons (90 ml) dry white wine

1 tablespoon tomato paste

⅓ cup (60 g) pitted black or green olives

Bouquet garni of 3–4 fresh flat-leaf parsley sprigs, 2–3 fresh thyme sprigs, and I bay leaf, or 1 bunch fresh savory herb sprigs such as rosemary and sage, tied into a bundle with kitchen string

Salt and black pepper

¼ cup (30 g) flour

Croutons, for serving

Pat the duck dry with paper towels. Melt I tablespoon of the butter in a wide saucepan over medium heat. Fry the duck on all sides, turning regularly, until the skin is browned and some of the fat has rendered. Transfer the duck to a large plate and pour off the fat from the pan, leaving about I teaspoon in the bottom.

Return the pan to medium-high heat and fry the lardons (bacon cut into strips about I inch/2.5 cm long) until crisp, 3–5 minutes.

Return the duck to the pan, add the stock, wine, tomato paste, olives, and bouquet garni, and season with salt and pepper. Add water just to cover the duck and bring to a boil over high heat. Reduce the heat to a simmer and cook until the duck is tender, 45–60 minutes. It is ready when the legs are just pulling away from the body and a thermometer inserted into the leg away from bone registers 140°–150°F (60°–65°C).

Just before the duck is ready, make the sauce. Melt the remaining 2 tablespoons butter in a saucepan over medium heat, then whisk in the flour until smooth. Reduce the heat to low and stir for 2–3 minutes to cook off the raw flour flavor. Ladle in ¼ cup (60 ml) of the hot stock from the duck, stirring continuously. Gradually add another ¼–½ cup (60–120 ml) hot stock, stirring all the time, and then continue to stir until you have a very thick, smooth sauce. Using a slotted spoon, scoop up the olives from around the duck and add them to the sauce.

If carving at the table, present the duck on a warmed platter garnished with croutons à la Downton. Or serve carved pieces from a warmed platter. Pour the sauce into a warmed bowl and offer it on the side, with a spoon for serving.

PORK CHOPS WITH SAUCE ROBERT

French cuisine had been regarded as the standard to aspire to in Britain since the eighteenth century, and the upper classes ate French food much of the time. The most desirable restaurants served French food, and both they and the aristocracy employed French chefs, invariably men, as their first choice of staff. Menus were also written in French, even when the dishes were rather British, and by the late nineteenth century, the aspiring middle-class hostess, who could barely afford an English woman cook let alone employ a Frenchman, could buy books that helped her to translate English dish names into the more sophisticated-sounding French. Families such as the Crawleys, who were feeling the pinch, found that employing women was significantly cheaper than employing male chefs, but that did not mean the real Mrs. Patmores lacked skills. Indeed, to be cooking for an earl, which was rare for a woman, Mrs. Patmore would almost certainly have trained under a French male chef and be able to turn her hand to classic French sauces such as this one, which was over two hundred years old at the time. You can cook the sauce Espagnole well ahead.

SERVES 4

INGREDIENTS

FOR THE SAUCE ESPAGNOLE

4 tablespoons (60 g) butter

½ shallot, finely chopped

I small turnip, peeled and finely chopped

I small carrot, peeled and finely chopped

2 oz (60 g) veal, chopped

2 oz (60 g) ham or bacon, chopped

3 cups (700 ml) beef stock

⅔ cup (140 g) canned tomatoes, roughly chopped

5 tablespoons (75 ml) claret or similar red wine

2 tablespoons sherry

I tablespoon mushroom ketchup, or Worcestershire sauce, or I teaspoon dried porcini mushrooms soaked in 2 teaspoons boiling water

Bouquet garni of 3–4 fresh flat-leaf parsley sprigs, 2–3 fresh thyme sprigs, and I bay leaf, or I bunch fresh savory herb sprigs such as rosemary and sage, tied into a bundle with kitchen string

6 black peppercorns

2 whole cloves

¼ cup (30 g) flour

FOR THE SAUCE ROBERT

I tablespoon butter

I shallot, finely chopped

I cup (240 ml) sauce Espagnole (above)

6 tablespoons (90 ml) white wine

½–I teaspoon mustard

½ teaspoon sugar

4 bone-in center-cut pork chops

Salt and black pepper

Vegetable oil, for frying

I small bunch fresh flat-leaf parsley, large stems discarded, finely chopped

---

To make the sauce Espagnole, you must first make a stock. Melt I tablespoon of the butter in a saucepan over low heat and cook the shallot, stirring occasionally, until it starts to turn translucent. Add the turnip, carrot, veal, and ham, raise the heat a little, and cook, stirring often, until everything just starts to brown, about 10 minutes. Add the stock, tomatoes, claret, sherry, mushroom ketchup, bouquet garni, peppercorns, and cloves and stir well. Raise the heat to high and bring to a boil, then reduce the heat to medium and simmer for I hour. Strain the stock through a fine-mesh sieve into a pitcher, pushing against the solids with the back of a spoon to extract the maximum amount of flavor and texture.

Recipe continues

Melt the remaining 3 tablespoons butter in a saucepan over medium heat, then whisk in the flour until a smooth, thick roux forms. Reduce the heat to low and continue to stir until the roux is a very light brown, about 5 minutes. Now add the hot stock, a spoonful at a time, to the roux, whisking vigorously after each addition so no lumps develop. When all the stock has been added, continue to cook over low heat, stirring steadily, until you have a creamy, very smooth sauce, about 2 minutes. Remove from the heat. You should have about 2 cups (480 ml). Set aside I cup (240 ml) for the sauce Robert and refrigerate or freeze the remainder for another use.

To make the sauce Robert, melt the butter in a saucepan over medium heat and cook the shallot, stirring occasionally. When it starts to brown, after 3–4 minutes, turn down the heat and add the sauce Espagnole, white wine, the mustard to taste, and the sugar and mix well. Bring to a gentle simmer, then keep warm while you cook the chops.

Season the pork chops on both sides with salt. Heat about 2 tablespoons of oil in a large frying pan over medium-high heat. When the oil is hot, add the chops and cook, turning once, until just cooked through, 2–4 minutes on each side, depending on their thickness. Transfer to a warmed plate, season with pepper, and let rest for 5 minutes before serving. Meanwhile, fry the parsley in the same pan over medium-high heat until crisp, about 30 seconds, adding more oil as needed.

Arrange the chops, edges overlapping, in a line on a warmed platter and sprinkle them with the parsley. Serve the sauce in a sauceboat alongside.

RECIPE NOTE

To serve this recipe in true Edwardian style, the chops should be piled in a circle, bones uppermost, around a bed of mashed potato or other vegetable, with the fried parsley forming a ring around the edge of the plate and the sauce in a sauceboat on the side. Sauce Robert is a compound sauce, meaning it is made up of a few different components. This version is highly simplified but still yields a good result. Kitchens like those at Downton would have had all the elements ready to go all the time, making assembling a sauce like this rather easier than trying to do it all from scratch for one meal. To cook like a true Edwardian, you would need to have ready at least five types of stock, four basic sauces, and a pantry lined with beautiful but niche concoctions, such as mushroom ketchup.

POACHED GAMMON WITH PARSLEY SAUCE

When the pigs arrive in season 4, creating mild havoc as Mary and Charles Blake, in full evening dress, wade in mud to save their lives, it's a moment to savor. The hogs' arrival heralds a new direction for Downton and a determination by Mary to move the estate management into the future, in an effort to keep it financially viable when so many others are going bankrupt. One of the most expensive cuts of a pig was the gammon, made from the back leg. The leg was salted, smoked, and sold whole, to be cooked and served whole or sliced up as ham. Every region had its own recipe and method for curing its hams, and Yorkshire ham, from the county where *Downton Abbey* is set, was reckoned to be some of the best in the world. This recipe calls for an uncooked cured ham that can be served hot or cold. It is one of the staples at Downton not only for dinner but also for lunch, for shooting lunches, and, when a little past its best, for downstairs dinners.

SERVES 10

INGREDIENTS

I uncooked cured boneless ham, about 3 lb (I.4 kg)

½ cup (50 g) dried bread crumbs

2 cups (480 ml) milk

2 bay leaves

I fresh rosemary sprig

8 whole cloves

12 black peppercorns

2 large blades mace or I tablespoon ground mace

2 tablespoons butter

2 tablespoons flour

I large bunch fresh flat-leaf parsley, large stems discarded, finely chopped

Put the ham in a large saucepan, add water to cover generously, and bring to a boil over high heat. Adjust the heat to maintain a gentle boil and cook for 30 minutes per lb/450 g plus an extra 30 minutes, or about 2 hours for a 3-lb (I.4-kg) ham. It is ready if it shows little resistance when pierced with a knife tip. Just before the ham is ready, preheat the oven to 350°F (180°C).

Transfer the cooked ham, fat side up, to a roasting pan. Using a sharp knife, score the fat in a diamond pattern, being careful not to cut into the meat. Sprinkle the fat evenly with the bread crumbs. Bake until the crumbs have browned, about 15 minutes. Remove from the oven and let rest for 15 minutes before serving.

While the ham cooks, make the sauce. Combine the milk, bay leaves, rosemary, cloves, peppercorns, and mace in a saucepan over medium heat and bring almost to a boil. Reduce the heat to low and cook gently, stirring occasionally, for 20 minutes. Do not allow the milk to boil or a skin will form on top. Remove from the heat and let stand for 10 minutes, then strain through a fine-mesh sieve into a pitcher.

Melt the butter in a saucepan over medium heat, then whisk in the flour until a smooth, thick roux forms. Reduce the heat to low and stir for 2–3 minutes to cook off the raw flour flavor. You are making a béchamel sauce, also known as white sauce, so do not allow the butter or the roux to brown or you will end up with a beige sauce. Add the hot milk, a spoonful at a time, to the roux, whisking vigorously after each addition so no lumps develop. You should finish with a thick, smooth sauce. If there are lumps, whisk until they dissolve. Remove from the heat and stir in the parsley.

Transfer the ham to a warmed platter and serve the sauce in a sauceboat or pitcher on the side.

ALFRED: *If that's béchamel, why don't you use parsley or mace?*

MRS. PATMORE: *I do. But I boil it in the milk beforehand. I made it last night.*

JIMMY: *Oh, leave her alone, you big ninnie.*

MRS. PATMORE: *There's nothing wrong with a man who can cook. Some say the best cooks in the world are men.*

~ SEASON 3, EPISODE 7

RECIPE NOTE

Once the ham is done, it can sit in its hot cooking water off the heat for 30–45 minutes without coming to any harm, which makes this quite a good recipe for a busy kitchen. You can also serve the ham cold but with the sauce hot. Leftovers can be used for ham in any of the recipes in this book, or they can be served up with one of the vegetable entremets (pages 173–180) as a light meal.

CHICKEN À LA CRÈME PAPRIKA

The period between 1912 and 1926, when *Downton Abbey* is set, was not only a significant one for social, political, and cultural change, as we see in the series, but also for culinary change. Hilda Leyel, coauthor of *The Gentle Art of Cookery*, founded the Society of Herbalists and was a divorcee, a fellow of the Royal Institution of Great Britain, and a member of the Académie Française, all fairly groundbreaking achievements in the 1920s. Her recipes, in the writing of which she was assisted by Olga Hartley, are fresh, zingy, and make use of ingredients and influences that are markedly different from the flavors of Edwardian Britain. Chicken with an accompanying sauce is a recurring dish at Downton right from the very first episode, in which Daisy nearly garnishes it with salt of sorrel, a poisonous cleaning product.

SERVES 4–6

INGREDIENTS

I whole chicken, about 3 lb (1.4 kg), cut into serving pieces and skin removed

2 teaspoons butter or vegetable oil

I yellow onion, chopped

I teaspoon paprika

½ teaspoon salt

⅔ cup (160 ml) tomato passata mixed with 2 tablespoons water

1¼ cups (300 ml) heavy cream

Lemon wedges, for garnish

Fresh flat-leaf parsley sprigs, for garnish (optional)

Melt the butter in a large, wide saucepan over low heat. Add the onion and and cook, stirring occasionally, until lightly browned and soft, 5–7 minutes. Add the paprika and salt and stir well, then add the tomato passata. Put the chicken pieces into the pan and turn them about to cover them well with the sauce. Bring to a boil, then reduce the heat to a low simmer, cover, and cook until the chicken is cooked through, 45–60 minutes. It is ready when a thermometer inserted into the thickest part of a thigh away from bone registers 165°F (74°C), or when the leg meat is beginning to pull away from the bone. If the pan starts to dry out, add a little water, but be careful not to thin the sauce too much, as it needs to be thick and gooey for the next stage.

Transfer the chicken pieces to a warmed serving plate. Add the cream to the sauce, stir to mix well, and heat through, being careful the sauce does not boil. Strain the sauce through a fine-mesh sieve into a sauceboat.

Garnish the chicken with the lemon wedges and the parsley, if using, and serve the sauce alongside.

RECIPE NOTE

You can vary the spicing by using chile powder, smoked paprika, or even North Africa's popular spice mix *ras el hanout*. The tomato *passata*, sometimes labeled "strained tomatoes," is smooth, liquid puréed tomatoes sold in cartons or bottles. This recipe can also be cooked in a covered baking dish in a 350°F (180°C) oven. If you are short of time, use bone-in chicken thighs and drumsticks or even diced chicken. If using only breast meat, reduce the cooking time by 10–15 minutes, depending on the size of the pieces.

LAMB AND MUTTON

In the past, the meat of sheep was divided into categories according to the age of the animal, though these classifications are not always well defined today. Lamb was always young, eaten from a few weeks old. It was especially associated with Easter, though it was consumed throughout the year. Spring lamb, available in the spring and summer, was from young animals born and reared in the fields, while house lamb was bred in barns for the Christmas market. Meanwhile, hogget was a weaned lamb, and today the label is usually attached to meat from a sheep between one and two years old.

Then there was mutton, one of the most popular meats in the past. Mutton comes from sheep at least two years old. In the Edwardian era, the best mutton was deemed to be between five and eight years old, but many people enjoyed it even older, and ten-year-old mutton was regarded as an epicure's delight. It is more flavorsome than lamb, much more versatile, and tends to have more texture. Like lamb, it can be fatty and was often cooked with sauces that would cut through the richness: Mutton with caper sauce was an iconic Edwardian recipe, but it was also eaten with mint sauce. The offal, especially the heart and kidneys, was generally deviled.

Many of the sheep consumed as mutton were old wool sheep (older sheep start to lose their teeth and are usually killed as soon as they stop being able to feed themselves). Many parts of Britain, especially Yorkshire and the northern counties, were particularly known as wool-producing areas, as their hilly landscapes did not lend themselves to arable crops. They were also home to some of the country's large coal deposits, vital for fueling the mills that processed the wool and wove it into cloth. Towns such as Halifax and Bradford, to the southwest of Downton's rolling landscape, grew rich on the wool trade. However, the invention of man-made fibers and the decline of the British wool industry meant fewer sheep on the hills. Lamb became the meat to aspire to, bred for the purpose of eating, and cheap imports of lamb dealt a final blow to Britain as a mutton-loving nation.

QUAIL AND WATERCRESS

Until the twentieth century, it was common for birds to be served with their feet on, and this is something we see in the Downton kitchen on a number of occasions. One typical dish is quail served with watercress, which appears in both the kitchen and upstairs. Quail were very popular among the aristocracy, as not only were they tasty and delicate but they were also easy to portion out. One bird per person was normal as part of the seven- or eight-course menus that characterized the prewar period, and even after menus were reduced in the aftermath of the war, quail remained a safe choice. They tend to dry out, being small, and this recipe includes an ingenious solution to keep the breasts moist.

SERVES 4 AS A STARTER OR 2 AS A MAIN

RECIPE NOTE

If you want a slightly heavier dish, you can serve the quail with meat gravy. If you don't have access to grapevine leaves, you can use lettuce, kale, or another fairly thin, edible leaf about the size of a grape leaf. Beware of using a highly flavored leaf unless you like the flavor.

INGREDIENTS

4 quail

2 tablespoons butter

Salt and black pepper

4 fresh grapevine leaves

4 slices thick-cut, fairly fatty bacon

FOR THE DRESSING

6 tablespoons (90 ml) olive oil

2 tablespoons white wine vinegar

I teaspoon fresh lemon juice

I teaspoon finely minced shallot

I teaspoon finely minced fresh tarragon

½ teaspoon mustard

¼ teaspoon paprika

FOR THE BREAD CRUMBS

2 teaspoons unsalted butter or olive oil

2 tablespoons fresh bread crumbs

5–6 oz (140–170 g) watercress, for serving

Preheat the oven to 425°F (220°C).

Rub the outside of each quail with ½ teaspoon of the butter and season with salt and pepper. Cover each breast with a grapevine leaf. Cut 4 neat pieces about the size of the breasts from the bacon slices and put a bacon piece on top of each leaf. Truss the quail with kitchen string, making sure the bacon and vine leaf are secure. Distribute the remaining butter evenly among the quail, dotting it over each one.

Place the quail, breast side up, in a small roasting pan. Roast the quail, basting them halfway through cooking with the butter that will have collected on the bottom of the pan, until the vine leaves are brown and crispy on the edges and the juices run clear when pierced at the thigh joint, about 15 minutes. Remove from the oven and let rest for 5 minutes.

Meanwhile, prepare the dressing and bread crumbs. Combine all the dressing ingredients in a small jar, cap tightly, and shake vigorously until the dressing emulsifies. Transfer to a small pitcher. For the bread crumbs, melt the butter in a small frying pan over medium heat, add the crumbs, and fry until browned and crisp, just a few minutes. Pour into a small serving bowl.

To serve, spread the watercress on a large serving plate and arrange the quail on top. Pass the dressing and the bread crumbs at the table for diners to add as they like.

THE PERFECT ROAST

Roast meats were, in many ways, the climax of the meal. The first few courses built up to them and the last few descended down from them. They had been prestigious for many centuries, partly because meat itself was expensive and scarce for most people and partly because it was an inefficient way to cook. Until the late nineteenth century, roasting had only one meaning: cooking meat in front of an open fire. Initially this meant employing someone to sit and turn a spit, as well as baste the meat if required, but in the seventeenth century, automatic spits were invented. This welcome innovation used the draw of the fire to propel the blades of a large fan located just up the chimney, and in turn the fan, through a system of pulleys and cogs, drove the spit. This setup was ubiquitous in country houses until the very end of the nineteenth century, when changing service styles, problems recruiting servants, and the ease of new technology meant that some houses replaced them with ovens. Many houses kept their coal-fired ranges and spits well into the twentieth century, however, arguing that the meat tasted much better cooked that way, and that using an oven was decidedly for the nouveaux riches.

Another point in favor of spit roasting was the high degree of skill it took, both in trussing the meat for the spit and in looking after it as it turned. Large roasts of beef, venison, or mutton were always impressive on the table or sideboard, and smaller animals and birds were instantly recognizable because it was the fashion, until the Great War, to serve them with their head and legs intact. Where possible, the roast course always included game, and if no game was in season, then squab, hare, duck, or quail, which was either exempt from seasonality laws or farmed, was served instead.

Spit roasting did result in better-tasting meat. The meat didn't need resting after cooking and, for birds in particular, it was very practical: the darker meat on the legs and thighs that needs more cooking was closer to the fire as the spit turned, so it would be done at the same time as the breast. However, many country houses did echo Downton and convert their open ranges to more efficient and manageable cast-iron closed ranges, and some even invested in gas. If you happen to have a spit (some grills have one), then celebrate it. If not, assuming you are roasting meat in an electric or gas oven, here's how to make the best of it.

KNOW YOUR MEAT If there are tender parts, such as the saddle on a hare and the breast on a quail, cover them with bacon or parchment paper for half or longer of the cooking time.

KNOW YOUR OVEN Most meats are better off cooked lower and slower than higher and faster, and ovens can vary considerably (and have hot spots).

START WITH A HOT OVEN, THEN GO LOWER AND BASTE Start out at 425°–450°F (220°–230°C) for 30 minutes for larger cuts or 10 minutes for smaller cuts (very small birds don't need this initial heat blast). After that, a good rule is to keep the oven at 300°–325°F (150°–165°C) for 20 minutes per pound (450 g) for well-cooked meat or 10–12 minutes per pound (450 g) for rare meat.

LOVE THE SKIN Rub oil and salt into the skin so it will crisp up. This is especially vital for birds.

USE A THERMOMETER A thermometer is the best way to check for doneness. Meat is generally considered safe to eat when cooked to 165°F (74°C), but this ruins the texture of many meats, so for beef, lamb, and most game, which are generally served rare, go lower. A reading of 125°F (52°C) is usual for rare beef.

REST THE MEAT Allow the meat to rest, uncovered, for 15 minutes for small roasts, 30–40 minutes for large roasts, and 5–10 minutes for small birds.

DON'T WASTE THE PAN JUICES Use the flavorful pan juices to make gravy by first dislodging the browned bits from the pan bottom with boiling water. Then pour the juices into a pitcher or skim off the fat, and finally thicken the defatted juices with cornstarch or arrowroot.

To serve a roast in a suitably Downton style, don't neglect the presentation. By the twentieth century, some of the flamboyance of earlier periods had waned, and because roasting carried its own cachet, presentation was often fairly muted. For small birds, try setting each one on a slightly hollowed-out piece of toast (which will both catch the juices and keep the bird in place) and arrange watercress around it. Larger birds don't need the bread, but watercress still works as a surround. When birds were stuffed, shaping some of the stuffing into balls or ovals and frying or boiling them was a fairly standard garnish. For meat roasts, fried bread crumbs were a typical garnish, and occasionally vegetables, though they got in the way during carving. Fried or minced parsley was another alternative. As we see in *Downton Abbey*, sauces were served separately, usually from a sauceboat armed with a sauce spoon.

MINT SAUCE

Used with lamb and mutton, mint sauce should be a heady mixture of fresh, sharp, and sweet. It keeps for a week in the fridge and is best spread liberally over everything in sight.

MAKES ABOUT 1 CUP (240 ML)

INGREDIENTS

1 large bunch fresh mint, large stems discarded

2 tablespoons white wine vinegar

1 tablespoon superfine sugar dissolved in 1 tablespoon boiling water

Chop the mint very finely, put it in a bowl, and sprinkle with the vinegar. Add the sugar-water mixture and stir well. Serve in a small pitcher with a spoon to ladle it out.

RECIPE NOTE

This is such a simple but flavorful sauce and it freezes well. If you like, for a finer consistency, you can blitz everything in a food processor.

BREAD SAUCE

Bread sauce was the usual accompaniment to roast chicken in the *Downton Abbey* era. Done badly, it's like eating wallpaper paste. Done well, it is very satisfying and rich, though certainly not as sophisticated as a fancy French jus.

MAKES ABOUT 2 CUPS (480 ML)

RECIPE NOTE

White pepper is used here so you don't get unsightly black specks in your sauce. But if you don't mind black specks, by all means use black pepper. If you have only ground mace on hand, use ¼ teaspoon and add it directly to the milk. The sauce is quite rich, so by all means leave out the half-and-half if you prefer.

INGREDIENTS

I cup (40 g) good-quality dense white bread, cut into I-inch (2.5-cm) cubes

Boiling water, to cover

½ very small shallot

2 blades mace

1¼ cups (300 ml) milk

Generous pinch of salt

White pepper

2 tablespoons half-and-half

Put the bread in a heatproof bowl and pour in boiling water to cover. Let soak for 5–10 minutes. Remove the bread and gently squeeze out as much of the moisture as you can.

Meanwhile, put the shallot and mace blades into a tea infuser (or tie them in a square of cheesecloth). Pour the milk into a small saucepan, add the tea infuser, and heat over medium heat to just below boiling. Remove from the heat and let steep for 10 minutes.

Remove the tea infuser from the milk. Add the bread and salt, season with pepper, and mash the bread until it has fully disintegrated in the milk. Then, using a spoon, beat the sauce until it is thick, creamy, and free of lumps.

Just before serving, stir in the half-and-half, stir through, taste and adjust the seasoning, and heat gently just until hot.

"For chicken there is nothing to beat the old bread sauce if well made, but let us rather eat a French salad with our chicken than face the lumpy stodginess so often served!"

—ALICE MARTINEAU, *CAVIARE TO CANDY* (1927)

YORKSHIRE PUDDINGS

The ubiquitous accompaniment to roast beef, Yorkshire puddings started life in the seventeenth century as so-called fire puddings, batter puddings baked in a large dish in front of the fire and under the roasting meat (back then mutton as often as beef). The puddings baked and rose happily while also incorporating all the drippings from the roast. Cheap to make, in poorer families they were a good way to stretch the more expensive meat, often filling up hungry stomachs even before the meat was served. They were first called Yorkshire puddings in the eighteenth century and remain incredibly popular across the country, regardless of class. This recipe comes from a 1904 French cookbook, *La Cuisine et pâtisserie anglaise et américaine* by Alfred Suzanne. If you're making a roast, be sure to use the pan drippings.

SERVES 6–12

INGREDIENTS

---

4 eggs

½ cup (120 ml) milk

¼ cup (60 ml) plus 3 tablespoons water

1 cup (115 g) flour

¼ teaspoon salt

½ teaspoon white wine vinegar

2 tablespoons pan drippings or lard

Crack the eggs into a bowl and whisk until frothy, then whisk in the milk and water until well blended. Whisk in the flour and salt until smooth and pale yellow. Whisk in the vinegar. Let rest at room temperature for 30 minutes.

Put ½ teaspoon of the pan drippings or lard in the bottom of each of 12 standard muffin cups (about 2½ inches/6 cm in diameter), or drizzle the pan drippings across the bottom of a 9 x 12-inch (23 x 30-cm) baking pan. Put the muffin or baking pan into the oven and preheat the oven to 425°F (220°C).

When the oven reaches temperature, remove the pan and quickly brush the pan drippings over the bottom and up the sides of the cups or pan. Pour the batter into the hot cups, dividing it evenly, or into the hot pan. Immediately return the pan to the oven and bake until the batter has puffed up (always lopsidedly, which is part of the joy) and the pudding is brown all over, about 20 minutes. Serve hot.

RECIPE NOTE

Unlike soufflés, these puddings will keep their structure when they come out of the oven, and they can be refrigerated or frozen and reheated in the oven when needed. When cold, they are also good sliced and fried in a little more pan drippings or lard.

ASPARAGUS CUPS

The roots of this recipe lie in the eighteenth century, and variations on it appeared in books until the 1930s. The cups were often made of simple bread rolls or occasionally pastry, and the custard could be plain or flavored. Ivy's first solo dish is pastry and asparagus, and asparagus appears in many different guises throughout *Downton Abbey*, including in the first episode, where it's made into a showstopping crown. The cup here uses brioche dough, which was very popular in France but has English equivalents in various fortified breads and buns. It is less rich than a modern brioche. These cups can be served hot or cold, so you can make them a day ahead. One cup per diner is enough if serving a seven-course meal. Otherwise, two cups per diner make a good starter. They are also ideal for serving with a slice of cold ham for a light lunch. Start the brioche the day before you plan to serve the cups. If you don't chill it overnight, it will be challenging to handle.

MAKES 12 CUPS

INGREDIENTS

FOR THE BRIOCHE

½ teaspoon active dry yeast

3 tablespoons lukewarm water

1¾ cups (210 g) plus 2 tablespoons flour, plus more for shaping the dough

1 tablespoon superfine sugar

Pinch of salt

3 eggs

½ cup (115 g) butter, cut into bits, plus more for the muffin cups

5 tablespoons (75 ml) milk

FOR THE FILLING

1 teaspoon cornstarch

1 cup (240 ml) milk

2 egg yolks

¼ teaspoon ground nutmeg

Black pepper

½ cup (60 g) grated Parmesan cheese

48–60 asparagus spears (3–4 lb/1.4–1.8 kg)

1 tablespoon butter, cut into 4 pieces, at room temperature

In a bowl, combine the yeast, water, and the 2 tablespoons flour and mix briefly to make a sponge. Cover with plastic wrap or a damp kitchen towel and set aside in a warm spot for 1–2 hours.

Add the remaining flour, the sugar, and the salt to the sponge and mix well. Add the eggs, one at a time, beating well after each addition, then continue to beat for 5 minutes, scraping down the sides of the bowl occasionally to ensure all the flour is incorporated. At the same time, combine the butter and milk in a small saucepan and heat over low heat just until the butter melts. Remove from the heat, let cool for 1–2 minutes, and then gradually beat the milk-butter mixture into the dough. Continue to beat the dough until very smooth, about 15 minutes. You can do this by hand if you are vigorous (or have a willing kitchen maid), but it's a lot easier in a stand mixer fitted with the dough hook. Scrape down the sides of the bowl with a rubber spatula or dough scraper to ensure the batter is in a single mass. Cover the bowl with plastic wrap or a damp kitchen towel, set aside in a warm spot, and let the dough rise until puffed and nearly doubled in size, 3–4 hours. Chill the dough overnight so the butter will harden, which will make the dough easier to handle.

Recipe continues

The next day, preheat the oven to 350°F (180°C). Butter 12 standard muffin cups (about 2½ inches/6 cm in diameter). Using lightly floured hands, pinch off 2-inch (5-cm) pieces of dough and loosely form each piece into a ball. Place a ball into each of the prepared cups.

Bake the brioche cups until cooked through, risen, and lightly browned, about 20 minutes. A thermometer inserted into the center of a brioche should register about 200°F (95°C). Transfer the pan to a wire rack. When the brioche cups are cool enough to handle, run the blade of a small, sharp knife along their edges to release them, then let the cups cool completely on the rack. You can bake the brioche cups up to a day ahead, store them in an airtight container at room temperature, and fill them the next day.

To make the filling, in a heavy-bottomed saucepan, whisk the cornstarch into the milk until dissolved, then whisk in the egg yolks, nutmeg, and a little pepper, mixing well. Place the pan over medium-low heat and cook, stirring often, just until the mixture comes to a boil. If it heats too quickly, the finished custard won't have a velvety texture. Once it reaches a boil, stir in the cheese, reduce the heat to low, and simmer gently, stirring continuously, until the mixture is thick enough to coat the back of a spoon, about 5 minutes. Remove from the heat.

Trim the asparagus spears so they are 1–2 inches (2.5–5 cm) taller than the brioche cups. Steam or boil them briefly, just until crisp-tender. Drain well, then transfer the hot asparagus to a bowl and toss with the butter to coat. Set aside to cool.

Preheat the oven to 375°F (190°C). Line a sheet pan with parchment paper. Cut a hole in the top of each brioche cup about 1 inch (2.5 cm) in diameter (larger if your spears are thick, smaller if they are thin). Using your fingers or a small spoon, hollow out the cups, making sure you leave enough crumb so the custard won't leak out when you fill the cups. Spoon 2 tablespoons custard into each cup and then poke 4 or 5 trimmed asparagus spears, tip up, through the hole and into the custard. The spears should stand upright, as if they are growing out of the top. Arrange the brioche cups on the prepared pan.

Bake until the brioche cups are heated through and the tops of the spears are very lightly browned, 5–10 minutes. Serve hot.

RECIPE NOTE

Normally if you boil custard, the egg yolks will curdle and you'll have to start again. Adding cornstarch prevents the curdling, and you can give the mixture a good boil, meaning it will thicken up nicely without splitting. You can use nearly any cheese or a different spice for the filling. Goat cheese is a solid choice, and you could add finely chopped sun-dried tomatoes for a contemporary twist. Don't throw out the brioche crumb scooped from the cups. It can be used for recipes calling for fresh bread crumbs, such as the Treacle Tart on page 229.

ARTICHOKE AND ASPARAGUS SALAD

The 1920s brought a significant change in women's fashion. While corsets and body-shaping garments were by no means discarded completely, the prevailing shape was less sculpted and more apparently natural. Slender boyish figures were favored, and the new flapper-style dresses with their dropped waists and casual necklines meant that a few daring women with exactly the right kind of body were able to wear less heavily boned undergarments. Others found that the need to flatten one's bust and disguise protruding stomachs took just as much effort, but with more strong elastic and slightly less whalebone than previously. Additionally, calorie-controlled diets appeared on the scene, including the Hollywood diet, which largely revolved around coffee and grapefruit. Salads became popular, and authors of cookbooks promoted new ways with vegetables. This very simple salad is typical of the era.

SERVES 4

INGREDIENTS

6 tablespoons (90 ml) heavy cream

Zest (in long, fine strips) and juice of 2 lemons

2 tablespoons ground almonds

Salt and black pepper

12 well-drained canned or jarred globe artichoke bottoms or hearts, halved

24 asparagus spears, trimmed, cooked, and cut into 1-inch (2.5-cm) pieces

2 tablespoons sliced almonds, toasted (optional)

Stir together the cream, lemon juice, and ground almonds in a small bowl. Season well with salt and pepper.

Combine the artichokes and asparagus in a serving bowl. Add the cream mixture and mix gently to coat. Sprinkle with the sliced almonds, if using, and lemon zest and serve.

NAVY BEANS WITH MAÎTRE D'HÔTEL SAUCE

The remarkably simple maître d'hôtel sauce was ubiquitous with plain vegetables and beans from the Victorian era onward. Butter, parsley, and lemon juice were some of the most common ingredients in cookery at this time, and country house kitchens like that at Downton regularly went through anything between three and fifteen pounds (1.4 and 6.8 kilograms) of butter a week (more at Christmas). Parsley was used as a green herb and fried as a garnish, and lemons were used both for flavor and in their practical role as an acid that helped stabilize egg foams (and clean copper).

SERVES 4

INGREDIENTS

2 cans (14 oz/400 g each) navy (haricot) beans, rinsed and drained

4 tablespoons (60 g) butter

Juice of 1 lemon

¼ teaspoon cayenne pepper

Salt and black pepper

1 large bunch fresh flat-leaf parsley, large stems discarded, minced

Put the beans into a saucepan, add water just to cover, and bring to a boil over medium-high heat. Boil until heated through, 2–3 minutes.

Meanwhile, in a second saucepan, melt the butter over medium heat. Add the lemon juice and cayenne, season with salt and black pepper, and whisk thoroughly. Stir in the parsley.

Drain the beans, add them to the sauce, and mix gently to coat. Serve hot.

RECIPE NOTE

You can substitute a fruity olive oil for the butter, in which case there is no need to heat the sauce. If you don't like the spiciness of cayenne, leave it out. The sauce also works with other beans and lentils, green vegetables, potatoes, pasta, and starchy roots such as celery root.

CHAMPAGNE JELLY

No Downton dinner would be complete without some form of molded jelly or cream, and the one featured here is one of the simplest and yet most effective. It was served at Edward VII's coronation banquet in 1902, and makes any dinner into a celebration. Champagne itself appears regularly at Downton, most obviously on occasions such as New Year's and at the numerous weddings, but it is also the drink of choice at a number of parties and at London nightclubs. Edith quaffs it with Michael Gregson and then later with Bertie Pelham, in season 6, when he realizes that he wants to marry her despite her illegitimate child and sets out to win her back over dinner at the Ritz.

SERVES 6

IVY: *Well, what do you want?*

JIMMY: *To have a good time. To see the world. To meet beautiful women and spend money and drink Champagne.*

IVY: *You can't make a career out of that.*

JIMMY: *Some people do. I want a life that's fun.*

~ SEASON 4, EPISODE 4

INGREDIENTS

1 bottle (750 ml) Champagne or other sparkling wine

2 envelopes (about 5 teaspoons) powdered gelatin or 8 gelatin sheets

2 tablespoons water

½ cup plus 1 tablespoon (115 g) sugar

Berries and/or edible flowers (optional)

Fresh mint leaves, for garnish

Put the Champagne bottle in the freezer 30 minutes before you start the recipe. This step ensures the bubbles will stay in the final jelly. In a small bowl, mix the gelatin with the water and let stand until softened, about 2 minutes. (If using gelatin sheets, put the sheets in a bowl, add cold water to cover, and let soak until floppy, 5–10 minutes.)

Open the Champagne and pour ½ cup (120 ml) into a small saucepan. Return the Champagne to the freezer if you can stand the bottle upright. If not, put the bottle in the fridge. Add the sugar to the saucepan, place over medium heat, and heat, stirring, until the sugar dissolves. Remove from the heat. Liquefy the powdered gelatin by setting the small bowl of gelatin in a larger bowl of hot water (or microwaving the gelatin on high for 5 seconds). Stir the softened gelatin into the Champagne mixture and stir until dissolved. Strain the mixture through a fine-mesh sieve into a bowl or pitcher and let cool to room temperature.

Add 2 cups (480 ml) of the chilled Champagne to the cooled gelatin mixture and stir well. If adding embellishments to the gelatin, pour half of the gelatin mixture into a 2½-cup (600-ml) mold and refrigerate until almost set, 30–45 minutes; arrange the embellishments on top, then add the remaining gelatin mixture. If serving the jelly without embellishments, pour all of the gelatin mixture into the mold. Cover the filled mold and refrigerate until fully set, at least 8 hours or up to 1 day. (If the time of day is right, you can sip the remaining Champagne.)

To serve, fill a bowl with hot water. Dip the bottom of the mold into the hot water for a few seconds to loosen the jelly from the mold, then unmold the jelly onto a serving plate. Garnish with the mint.

SYLLABUB

Syllabubs first appeared in cookery books in the seventeenth century and remained popular until the end of the twentieth century. Many early recipes call for the cook to mix alcohol and sugar and then milk a cow directly into the mixture. As amusing (and bonkers) as this sounds, it's unlikely it was actually done (much), for a whisk does the job just as well. These early syllabubs were made by whisking thin cream to a froth like bath bubbles, which was then dried out and served floating on the liquid that drained from it. By the late nineteenth century, the early versions were being eclipsed by the kind of syllabub featured here, originally known as "everlasting syllabub," which was simpler, especially if the cook didn't have easy access to a cowshed.

SERVES 4–6

INGREDIENTS

1 cup (240 ml) heavy cream

3 tablespoons superfine sugar

6 tablespoons (90 ml) dessert wine, such as Sauternes

Grated zest and juice of 1 lemon

Juice of 1 small orange

Whisk together the cream and sugar in a bowl until the sugar dissolves. Add the wine, lemon zest and juice, and orange juice and whisk by hand or with a handheld mixer on medium speed until soft peaks form and the mixture is almost at piping consistency.

Spoon the syllabub into small glasses, cover, and chill for 1 hour before serving.

RECIPE NOTE

You can vary the alcohol, as long as it has a fairly high sugar content. Sherry, ginger wine, port, and flavored liqueurs based on brandy or whiskey will all work.

MRS. PATMORE: *What about the syllabubs?*

DAISY: *The orange peel and brandy mix is cooling in the larder. I'll whip the cream during the first course.*

~ SEASON 4, EPISODE 3

BANANAS AU CAFÉ

Bananas were a relatively new fruit in Britain in the Edwardian period. Although the earliest evidence of them is from a Tudor rubbish pit in London, they remained a novelty for most people until the late nineteenth century. Most modern bananas come from a type bred in the 1830s at Chatsworth House and named Cavendish after the estate's resident, William Cavendish, the sixth Duke of Devonshire; today, the stately home is still occupied by a Cavendish, the twelfth Duke of Devonshire. Aristocrats like those portrayed in *Downton Abbey* knew of and enjoyed exotic fruit far before recipes using them appeared in books. This dish is a classic combination of coffee and bananas, with an added 1920s touch in the shape of the rice-based sauce.

SERVES 6–8

INGREDIENTS

6 bananas, peeled

2 tablespoons firmly packed brown sugar

3 tablespoons curaçao

2 cups (480 ml) milk

⅓ cup (60 g) rice flour

4½ tablespoons (60 g) granulated sugar

½ cup (120 ml) very strong brewed coffee

Cut each banana in half crosswise and then cut each half lengthwise into 4 equal pieces, for a total of 8 pieces from each banana. Put all the banana pieces in a shallow dish and sprinkle evenly with about half of the brown sugar and all the curaçao. Let steep for 1 hour.

Combine the milk, rice flour, and granulated sugar in a bowl and whisk together until the flour and sugar are dissolved. Stir in the coffee and pour the mixture into a saucepan. Bring to a boil over medium-high heat, stirring occasionally. Reduce the heat to medium-low and simmer, stirring often, until the sauce is thick and gloopy, 3–4 minutes. Be careful, as it tends to splatter. Remove from the heat and let cool before serving.

Make alternating layers of the sauce and the bananas in a large glass dish (or individual glasses), finishing with a layer of the sauce. Just before serving, sprinkle the top evenly with the remaining brown sugar and melt and caramelize the sugar with a kitchen torch.

RECIPE NOTE

You can swap out the brown sugar on the bananas for dark chocolate flakes, and add chocolate to the rice sauce for a chocolate-coffee version of this dish. You can also use another liqueur or spirit, such as bourbon, rum, or brandy, in place of the curaçao. If you don't have a kitchen torch, brown the top under the broiler, making sure you use a broiler-proof glass dish.

CHOCOLATE AND VANILLA STRIPED BLANCMANGE

In the early twentieth century, blancmange gained an unfair reputation as stodgy nursery food, pushing it down the social scale. Before that, however, and in various guises, it was regarded as a light and easily digestible entremets. Dinners at Downton frequently include some form of molded cream, and this version, which is set with cornstarch rather than gelatin, is a very easy way to replicate one. The recipe is a twist on one that was widely circulated in late-Victorian Britain, printed onto ceramic molds as a rather cunning form of advertising by the Scottish firm Brown and Polson. The molds continued to be produced until the mid-twentieth century, by which time blancmange could also be bought ready-made in cans.

SERVES 6–8

RECIPE NOTE

For a plainer version, more suited to the servants' hall than upstairs, leave out the vanilla and chocolate, don't divide the mixture, and put in less sugar. This blancmange is very bland and is designed to be eaten with jam, marmalade, or fruit compote.

INGREDIENTS

5 cups (1.2 l) milk

½ cup plus 2 tablespoons (80 g) cornstarch

½ cup (125 g) sugar

⅛ teaspoon salt

1 tablespoon pure vanilla extract

2 tablespoons Dutch-process cocoa powder

Marmalade, for serving (optional)

Whisk together 1 cup (240 ml) of the milk, the cornstarch, sugar, and salt in a small bowl until the dry ingredients are dissolved. Warm the remaining milk in a small saucepan over medium-low heat; do not allow to boil. Whisk the milk-cornstarch mixture into the warm milk and cook, whisking almost constantly and not allowing the mixture to boil, until the raw cornstarch flavor disappears and the mixture thickens, about 15 minutes.

Remove from the heat and let cool for 20 minutes, whisking occasionally to speed cooling and to prevent a skin from forming. (You should have about 5 cups/1.2 l.) Stir in the vanilla. For the chocolate portion, pour half of the mixture into a bowl. Scoop out ½ cup (120 ml) from the bowl into a cup, add the cocoa powder and stir until dissolved, then return the chocolate mixture to the bowl and mix well. Let cool just until thickened.

Fill a large bowl two-thirds full with crushed ice, make a hollow in the center, and place a 5-cup (1.2-l) glass or ceramic mold in the hollow (if you don't have a mold, a bowl is fine). Fill the mold with the vanilla and chocolate mixtures, pouring in first one color and then the other and whisking the remaining custard until smooth before each new addition to make a total of 4–6 layers in alternating colors. Smooth each layer with the back of a spoon or a rubber spatula and pause for a minute or two for the custard to cool and thicken after applying each layer, but not much longer or the layers will slide apart when you unmold the blancmange. Smooth the top layer, cover the mold, and refrigerate until set, at least 4 hours or up to 1 day.

Place a serving plate over the mold, then invert the mold and plate together. Give the mold a good shake, and you'll hear a damp thud that indicates the blancmange has come loose. Lift off the mold, spoon into bowls, and serve with marmalade, if desired.

THE QUEEN OF TRIFLES

Trifles are, as the author of this recipe states, "exceptionally English dishes." They can seem incoherent, using everything from sponge cake to Jell-O to fruit in all of its fresh and preserved forms. At their worst, they are a horrid concoction of soggy cake, bland fruit, and powdery custard. At their best, they are sublime. This one uses many elements that appear in the background of kitchen scenes at Downton: whipped cream, jam, preserved fruits, and some of the many eggs always ready for use in a rack on the kitchen table. It should be served in a glass dish so the layers are visible.

SERVES 8–10

FOOD FOR THOUGHT

Trifle first appeared in cookery books in the sixteenth century, but it wasn't until the 1750s that it started to take on the form it has today. By the early twentieth century, a bewildering number of recipes for trifle were in print, and this is one of thirteen trifles in *The Encyclopaedia of Practical Cookery* alone. Unusually, the book also includes two savory versions, one with lobster and one with veal.

INGREDIENTS

¼ lb (115 g) ladyfingers

¼ cup (60 ml) brandy

1 cup (320 g) apple jelly

¼ lb (115 g) mixed crystallized fruit (such as ginger, pineapple, and cherries), finely chopped

¼ lb (115 g) small almond macaroons

½ cup plus 2 tablespoons (150 ml) port or sherry

1 teaspoon powdered gelatin or 2 gelatin sheets

2 teaspoons cornstarch

1¼ cups (300 ml) milk

2 egg yolks

6 tablespoons (90 g) superfine sugar

2 teaspoons rose water

1 cup plus 2 tablespoons (115 g) ground almonds

2½ cups (600 ml) heavy cream

FOR DECORATION

Slivered blanched almonds

Mixed crystallized fruit as above, cut into small cubes

Layer the ladyfingers across the bottom of a 3-quart (3-l) glass trifle bowl (or other large glass bowl). Drizzle the brandy, a spoonful at a time, evenly on the ladyfingers, and then spread a thin layer of the jelly (about ¼ cup/80 g) on top. Next, layer the fruit on top, followed by the macaroons. Drizzle the port, a spoonful at a time, evenly on the macaroons. Cover these first 4, booze-soaked layers with the rest of the jelly and set aside for an hour or two to steep.

Meanwhile, make a custard. Mix the powdered gelatin with 2 tablespoons water in a small bowl and let stand for 2 minutes to soften; if using the gelatin sheets, place them in a bowl, add cold water to cover, and let soak until floppy, 5–10 minutes. In a bowl, whisk the cornstarch into the milk until dissolved, then whisk in the egg yolks, 4 tablespoons (60 g) of the sugar, and the rose water until well mixed. Pour the mixture into a saucepan and heat gently over medium-low heat, stirring often, just until it starts to thicken. It should be the consistency of heavy cream. Add the softened gelatin. (If using powdered gelatin, first liquefy it by nesting the small bowl of gelatin in a larger bowl of hot water, or heating it in the microwave for 5 seconds.) Stir until the gelatin is dissolved. Do not allow the mixture to boil. Remove from the heat and stir in the ground almonds. Let cool completely before starting the next step.

You can prepare the recipe up to this point the day before you plan to serve the trifle and then finish the trifle the next day. Because you will refrigerate the custard overnight, you will need to melt it slightly before proceeding. You can do this by resting the bowl of custard in a bowl of hot water. It should be at room temperature and gloopy, rather than set, for the next step.

To finish assembling the trifle, spoon the custard on top of the booze-soaked layers, ensuring that it forms an even layer. In a bowl, using a whisk or a handheld mixer on medium speed, whip the cream with the remaining 2 tablespoons sugar until it is a good piping consistency. Transfer the whipped cream to a piping bag fitted with a star tip and pipe the cream attractively on top of the trifle. If not serving immediately, cover and chill thoroughly.

Just before serving, decorate the trifle with slivered almonds and crystallized fruit.

Trifles are infinitely variable. You can use whatever crystallized fruit you desire, and the same with the jam. Just make sure they go together. Likewise, any fortified wine can be used in place of the port or sherry, and you can swap in different nuts for the almonds. The decoration suggested here is fairly muted, fitting for an upper-class dinner. Cherries cut into flower shapes and candied angelica leaves were another popular decoration at the time. You can also use fresh or candied edible flowers, such as borage blossoms, nasturtiums, violets, and pansies.

RASPBERRY MERINGUE

Another firm favorite for the sweet course at Downton is meringue with fruit, generally raspberries. It's served instead of the desired apple charlotte when Mrs. Patmore refuses to change her menu in season 1, and it's on the table when Robert first starts to fall for Jane Moorsum, a housemaid, in season 2. It's a fairly simple recipe, ideal for country house kitchens, as its various components can be made in advance and the dish plated up with a flourish as required. Filled meringues of this type were also sometimes called pavlovas, after the Russian ballerina Anna Pavlova, who toured New Zealand and Australia in the 1920s and, like Dame Nellie Melba, gave her name to a delicious dessert.

SERVES 4–6

RECIPE NOTE

If it goes a bit wrong and the meringue nests break or don't harden evenly, simply break them up roughly and mix them with the whipped cream, the raspberry purée, and a few whole raspberries and call it a Downton mess (if you use strawberries, it's the classic Eton mess, named for the school to which most aristocratic boys were sent at the time). You can replace the raspberries with strawberries, blackberries, blueberries, gooseberries, or plums (the latter two need to be simmered with a little water to soften before you purée them). The fool is also good on its own, served in glasses on a summer day.

INGREDIENTS

FOR THE MERINGUE
2 egg whites
I teaspoon fresh lemon juice
½ cup plus I tablespoon (II5 g) superfine sugar

FOR THE FOOL
½ lb (225 g) raspberries, plus more for decorating
½ cup plus 2 tablespoons (150 ml) heavy cream
¼ cup (55 g) superfine sugar
Confectioners' sugar, if needed

To make the meringue, preheat the oven to 200°F (95°C). Line a sheet pan with parchment paper.

Using a whisk or a handheld mixer on medium speed, beat together the egg whites and lemon juice in a bowl until soft peaks form, increasing the mixer speed to medium-high once the whites are foamy and begin to thicken. Beating constantly, add the superfine sugar, a little at a time, and beat until stiff peaks form. Transfer the mixture to a piping bag fitted with a large star tip. Pipe 6 meringue nests each 2–3 inches (5–7.5 cm) in diameter— first outlining them, then filling the centers, and finally building up the sides—and some small stars for garnish on the prepared pan.

Bake the meringues for 2–2½ hours. They should be crisp to the touch and lift off the parchment easily. Let cool completely.

To make the fool, purée the raspberries in a food processor or blender, then pass the purée through a fine-mesh sieve to remove the seeds, or use a food mill, which will extract the seeds as it purées. (Removing the seeds is optional but would have been done in houses like Downton.) Combine the cream and superfine sugar in a bowl and, using a whisk or a handheld mixer on medium speed, whip together until soft peaks form. Gently fold in the raspberry purée just until no white streaks remain. Taste and adjust with confectioners' sugar if you prefer it sweeter. The fool should be fairly tart, however, to contrast with the meringue.

Both the meringues and the fool can be made a day in advance. Store the meringues in an airtight container at room temperature and the fool tightly covered in the fridge. When you are ready to serve, fill the meringue nests with the fool and top with the small meringues. Serve with raspberries alongside.

PEACHES MELBA

Among the reasons Auguste Escoffier is still widely regarded as one of the key figures in Western cuisine are his simplification of late Victorian cookery and his introduction of fresh, zingy combinations. He invented this recipe, deservedly a classic, in honor of Nellie Melba, an Australian opera singer who was the toast of Europe in the *Downton* era. It was designed for restaurant service—the components could be made in advance and assembled as needed—and is ideal for a Downton dinner, as it is both practical and delicious. Dame Nellie herself makes an appearance in season 4, where she bonds with Robert over the wine and performs after dinner at a private concert.

SERVES 4

FOOD FOR THOUGHT

Nellie Melba was born Helen Porter Mitchell in Melbourne, Australia, and took the name Melba from her hometown. She was not only a brilliant singer but was also committed to social work, and was made a dame in 1918 for her fund-raising work during the Great War. Escoffier was a huge fan and, along with peaches Melba, he honored her with toast Melba and Melba sauce.

INGREDIENTS

4 large ripe peaches
2 cups (480 ml) water
1 cup (200 g) superfine sugar
½ teaspoon pure vanilla extract

FOR THE SAUCE

1 cup (115 g) raspberries
1 tablespoon confectioners' sugar
Juice of ½ lemon

4 generous scoops good-quality vanilla ice cream

Have ready a large bowl of ice water. Halve and pit the peaches. Pour the 2 cups (480 ml) water into a saucepan large enough to hold all the peach halves in a single layer and bring to a boil over high heat. Add the peaches, skin side down, to the boiling water and boil just until the skins begin to loosen, 2–3 minutes. Using a slotted spoon, transfer the peaches to the ice water to stop the cooking, reserving the water in the pan. Peel the peach halves (the skins should come off easily, thanks to the brief boil) and set them aside.

Add the superfine sugar and vanilla to the water in the pan and bring back to a boil, stirring to dissolve the sugar. Add the peach halves, reduce the heat to a simmer, and poach, turning the peaches once, until tender when pierced with a knife, 3–4 minutes on each side. Remove from the heat, cover the pan, and leave the peaches to steep for at least 30 minutes before serving. They can be kept in the syrup in the fridge for up to a couple of days.

To make the sauce, combine the raspberries, confectioners' sugar, and lemon juice in a food processor or blender and process until puréed, then strain through a fine-mesh sieve into a bowl to remove the seeds. Whisk to form a slightly frothy sauce. The sauce will also keep happily in the fridge for a couple of days.

Use individual bowls or glass dishes for serving. Put a scoop of vanilla ice cream at the bottom, top with 2 peach halves, and finish with a generous spoonful of raspberry sauce. Serve immediately.

PEAR CHARLOTTE

Charlottes have a long history and were probably named after Queen Charlotte, the wife of George III. They can be made with any fruit suitable for stewing, though they are usually made with apple or pear. Modern versions tend to be served cold, but they were hot dishes in the past. It's because of an apple charlotte, Sir Anthony Strallan's favorite dish, that we first get an inkling of Mrs. Patmore's eye problems in season 1, when she refuses to make what, for her, is an unfamiliar recipe because she knows she won't be able to read it properly. This version comes from *The Modern Cook*, written by a one-time cook to Queen Victoria. (He was almost certainly sacked, but that didn't stop him using it to sell books.)

SERVES 4-6

INGREDIENTS

4 pears

Peel (in strips) and juice of ½ lemon

2 cups (480 ml) water

¾ cup plus 2 tablespoons (170 g) sugar

¼ teaspoon ground cinnamon

4 tablespoons (60 g) unsalted butter, plus more for the mold

7–8 slices white bread, about ¼ inch (6 mm) thick, crusts removed

6 tablespoons (115 g) plum or damson jam

¼ cup (80 g) honey mixed with 2 teaspoons orange flower water, for serving

Peel, quarter, and core the pears, then toss them with the lemon juice in a bowl. Combine the water and sugar in a saucepan and bring to a boil over medium-high heat, stirring to dissolve the sugar. Add the lemon peel and cinnamon and finally add the pears. Reduce the heat to a simmer and cook until the pears are just tender when pierced with a knife, about 10 minutes. Remove from the heat and set aside in the cooking liquid.

Preheat the oven to 350°F (180°C). If you have a charlotte mold (a straight-sided, bucket-shaped pan) about 5 inches (13 cm) in diameter and 3 inches (7.5 cm) deep, use it. Otherwise, use a 2½-cup (600-ml) pudding mold or small ovenproof pie dish. Butter the bottom and sides generously, then line the bottom with parchment paper and butter the parchment. Cut out a piece of parchment the diameter of the top of the mold, butter one side, and set aside.

Cut your bread slices to fit the mold. You will need a round piece for the bottom and several tapered or straight slices for the sides. Melt the butter in a small saucepan on the stove top, brush each bread slice well on both sides with butter, and then line the mold with the bread, overlapping the pieces slightly at the edges. Cut a piece or pieces for the top, brush on both sides with melted butter, and set to one side while you fill the mold.

Warm the jam in a small saucepan on the stove top just until slightly warmed and fluid. Drain the pears and mix them with the warm jam, coating evenly. Arrange the pears in the prepared mold, then put the reserved bread piece(s) on top. Press down firmly on the bread, sealing it to the bread lining the sides, and top with the reserved parchment round, buttered side down.

Put an ovenproof saucer or plate on top of the mold, then top the saucer with an ovenproof weight. (If you don't have old-fashioned metal weights, a heavy stone will do.) Put the mold on a sheet pan and transfer to the oven. Bake until golden brown (peek under the parchment), about 30 minutes.

Remove the charlotte from the oven, take off the weight and saucer, and peel off the parchment from the top. Carefully slide a knife around the inside edge of the mold to loosen the charlotte sides, then invert a serving plate on top of the mold and invert the mold and plate together. Lift off the mold and peel off the parchment.

Serve hot, with the honey–orange flower sauce drizzled over the top.

RECIPE NOTE

You can easily make this into an apple charlotte by replacing the pears with good, firm eating apples. Likewise, the jam can be traded out for another flavor; a ginger jam works well. You can also replace the honey sauce with heavy cream or a custard sauce.

MRS. HUGHES: *There's nothing here that looks very complicated. Apples, lemons, butter . . .*

MRS. PATMORE: *I cannot work from a new receipt at a moment's notice!*

DAISY: *But I can read it to you, if that's the problem.*

MRS. PATMORE: *Problem? Who mentioned a problem? How dare you say such a thing in front of her Ladyship!*

CORA: *(who has had enough) Very well. We'll try it another time, when you've had longer to prepare. We'll stay with the raspberry meringue.*

~ SEASON 1, EPISODE 5

CHARLOTTE RUSSE

Another of *Downton's* iconic dishes, charlotte russe is a cold, set sweet dish, with a mixture of Bavarian cream and jelly ringed with sponge finger biscuits. It's related to trifle, but while trifle is a very English dish, this is very French, and was invented by Chef Antonin Carême in the early nineteenth century. It appears at Downton a lot, sometimes unmentioned but lurking distinctively in the background and at other times brought to the fore. It's one of the dishes cooked by Ethel for Isobel's ladies' luncheon, where she presents it herself, interrupting a showdown between Robert and his wife, daughters, and mother. Mrs. Patmore and Daisy would have made the ladyfinger biscuits in advance. Modern cooks looking for a shortcut may choose to substitute store-bought ladyfingers.

SERVES 6–8

INGREDIENTS

FOR THE LADYFINGERS

½ cup (100 g) plus 2 tablespoons superfine sugar

2 eggs

1 cup plus 3 tablespoons (140 g) flour

¼ teaspoon baking powder

½ teaspoon ground cinnamon

FOR THE STRAWBERRY JELLY

2 cups (285 g) strawberries, stemmed and halved lengthwise

2–4 tablespoons granulated sugar, depending upon the sweetness of the strawberries

Juice of ½ lemon

⅔ cup (160 ml) water

1½ teaspoons powdered gelatin or 2 gelatin sheets

FOR THE BAVARIAN CREAM

2 tablespoons water

4 egg yolks

⅓ cup (140 g) granulated sugar

¾ cup (180 ml) milk

½ teaspoon pure vanilla extract

1 envelope (about 2½ teaspoons) powdered gelatin or 5 gelatin sheets

1¼ cups (300 ml) heavy cream

FOR GARNISH

10–12 large firm strawberries

2 teaspoons granulated sugar, preferably vanilla sugar

Other fruits or edible flowers as desired (optional)

To make the ladyfingers, put ½ cup (100 g) of the superfine sugar and the eggs into a heatproof bowl (preferably metal). Rest the bowl over a pan of barely simmering water and whisk until the mixture is light and foamy and warmed through. Remove from the heat and continue whisking until the mixture is cold, 10–15 minutes. Fold the flour, baking powder, and cinnamon into the cold yolk mixture just until fully incorporated.

Preheat the oven to 375°F (190°C). Line a sheet pan with parchment paper. Transfer the ladyfinger mixture to a piping bag fitted with a large plain tip and pipe lengths of the mixture onto the prepared pan, making sure they are about ¾ inch (2 cm) longer than the height of the mold you will be using. Sprinkle the lengths evenly with the remaining 2 tablespoons superfine sugar.

Bake the ladyfingers until they are lightly browned and cooked through, about 5 minutes. Let cool on the pan on a wire rack, then carefully lift them off the parchment and set aside.

Recipe continues

To make the jelly, combine the strawberries, granulated sugar, lemon juice, and water in a saucepan and bring to a boil over high heat. Use a masher or the back of a wooden spoon to crush the strawberries slightly, helping them to yield their juice. Remove from the heat and let steep for 2 hours.

Strain the strawberry mixture through a wire-mesh sieve lined with a double thickness of cheesecloth placed over a bowl or pitcher. Don't force the mixture through the sieve or the jelly will be cloudy. Let gravity do the work. Measure the strawberry juice, add water as needed to total about 1 cup (240 ml), and set aside for the strawberry jelly. Reserve the strawberries for another use, or purée and then strain them to make a sauce for the cream.

To make the Bavarian cream, in a bowl, briefly beat the water and egg yolks with a wire whisk or an electric mixer. Gradually beat in the granulated sugar, whisking constantly or beating with the electric mixer on medium speed, until the mixture is thick, pale yellow, and drops from the beaters in a thick ribbon when they are lifted from the bowl, about 3 minutes.

In a small saucepan over medium heat, warm the milk just until bubbles appear at the edge of the pan. Slowly pour the hot milk into the eggs, whisking constantly just until combined. Return the egg-milk mixture to the saucepan and cook over low heat, stirring constantly, until the mixture thickens into a custard thick enough to coat a spoon. (Do not allow to boil or the eggs will curdle.) Pour the custard through a strainer into a bowl. Stir in the vanilla. Mix the powdered gelatin with 2 tablespoons water in a small bowl and let stand for 2 minutes to soften; if using the gelatin sheets, place them in a bowl, add cold water to cover, and let soak until floppy, 5–10 minutes.

Add the softened gelatin. (If using powdered gelatin, first liquefy it by nesting the small bowl of gelatin in a larger bowl of hot water, or heating it in the microwave for 5 seconds.) Stir until the gelatin is dissolved.

Prepare an ice water bath by filling a large bowl halfway with ice and water. Place the bowl with the custard over the ice water bath and stir often until cooled to room temperature, about 15 minutes. Using a wire whisk or electric mixer, beat the cream to soft peaks and fold into the cooled custard mixture.

Recipe card from the set of *Downton Abbey*

RECIPE NOTE

If you are pressed for time, the ladyfingers, as suggested in the headnote, can be replaced by store-bought ladyfingers. Any leftover ladyfingers are excellent on their own and also make a good base for trifle. The Downton kitchen is equipped with copper egg bowls, which are not only great for whisking eggs but are also ideal for heating eggs and sugar over water, as here. If you don't have a copper bowl handy, any metal bowl will do, or even a heatproof glass one (though it will take longer to heat up). You can easily vary the flavorings in this charlotte, using a different fruit jelly or flavored cream or changing the spice in the ladyfingers.

For the garnish, stem the strawberries, then slice them lengthwise thickly but evenly. Transfer to a bowl, sprinkle with the granulated sugar, and toss gently. Cover and leave for 2 hours.

Remove the bottom from a 6- or 7-inch (15- or 18-cm) round springform pan and put the pan ring on the plate on which you plan to serve the charlotte. Cut one end off of each ladyfinger so they all have a nice flat end and are the same height. Use them to line the pan ring, standing them up vertically with the rounded end at the top. They will be slightly squishy, so you can press them into one another to keep them in place.

Carefully spoon the custard into the ladyfinger-lined ring and spread it out gently with the back of a spoon to secure the ladyfingers in place. Put the mold in the fridge for 30–45 minutes to set the custard more firmly.

Meanwhile, finish preparing the jelly: Mix the powdered gelatin with 2 tablespoons water in a small bowl and let stand for 2 minutes to soften; if using the gelatin sheets, place them in a bowl, add cold water to cover, and let soak until floppy, 5–10 minutes. Stir the liquefied gelatin into the strawberry juice. (If using powdered gelatin, first liquefy it by nesting the small bowl of gelatin in a larger bowl of hot water, or heating it in the microwave for 5 seconds.) Stir until the gelatin is dissolved. Prepare another ice water bath in a large bowl. Nestle the bowl with the strawberry jelly in the ice water bath and stir often until thickened, about 15 minutes. Pour the jelly over the chilled custard. Cover the charlotte and chill for 1–2 hours.

Unclip the springform pan ring and carefully lift it off. The ladyfingers will probably attempt to collapse slowly, which is why charlottes are often served, including at Downton, with a natty ribbon tied around their middle. It's a very good idea to have a ribbon handy, especially if you are unmolding this more than a few minutes before serving. Tie the ribbon securely round the middle and then arrange the sliced strawberries on top. You can add other fresh fruit, edible flowers, or candied fruit as you prefer.

ROBERT: *We're leaving.*

ETHEL: *Is this because of me, my lord?*

CORA: *No, it is because of his Lordship. And we are not leaving. It's a Charlotte Russe? How delicious.*

ETHEL: *I hope it's tasty, m'lady. Mrs. Patmore gave me some help.*

CORA: *I'm glad to know Mrs. Patmore has a good heart and does not judge.*

ROBERT: *Is anyone coming?*

VIOLET: *It seems a shame to miss such a good pudding.*

~ SEASON 3, EPISODE 6

GINGER SOUFFLÉ

There are lots of soufflés served at Downton Abbey, some savory and others sweet. They were notoriously difficult to make, especially in slightly unpredictable ovens, and were regarded as a test of a cook's skill. In many ways, however, the skill lies in getting them to the table before they deflate, and their eventual success depended as much on good communication among the footmen in the dining room and the cooks in the kitchen as it did on the cooking itself. Soufflés rely on extremely well-whisked eggs, and without such modern conveniences as electric egg whisks, they were a good workout for the lower maids tasked with whisking the eggs to a suitable degree. No wonder Daisy takes to the new mixer so rapidly in season 4.

SERVES 6

RECIPE NOTE

Timings are crucial here, but soufflés are not quite as time critical as they sometimes seem. They can be put back in the oven if things fall apart and they will rise again, though not as well as the first time round. You can also make the mix in advance, preparing it up to the point at which it goes into the oven, and it will keep in the fridge for several hours until you are ready to bake it.

INGREDIENTS

4 tablespoons (60 g) unsalted butter, plus more for the soufflé dish

4 tablespoons (50 g) superfine sugar, plus more for the soufflé dish

1¼ cups (300 ml) milk

3 tablespoons very finely chopped stem ginger in syrup, or 3 tablespoons very finely chopped crystallized ginger softened in 3 tablespoons hot water

1 teaspoon ground ginger

¼ cup (20 g) flour

4 egg yolks

Grated zest and juice of ½ lemon

6 egg whites

FOR THE SAUCE

Grated zest and juice of ½ lemon

2 egg yolks

2 tablespoons syrup from stem ginger, or 2 tablespoons simple syrup warmed with 3 thick slices peeled fresh ginger and allowed to steep for 1 hour

1 tablespoon warm water, or as needed

Butter a soufflé dish about 8 inches (20 cm) in diameter and 3½ inches (9 cm) deep or other straight-sided dish of equal size. Sprinkle with sugar, coating evenly and tapping out the excess.

Cut a sheet of parchment paper 13 inches (33 cm) long, then cut the sheet in half lengthwise. Fold half of the sheet in half lengthwise, wrap it around the rim of the soufflé dish to form a collar that rises 2–3 inches (5–7 cm) above the rim, and secure in place with kitchen string. Save the remaining half for another use. Position a rack in the lower third of the oven and preheat the oven to 400°F (200°C).

In a small saucepan, combine the milk, sugar, stem ginger, and ground ginger. Warm over medium heat until small bubbles appear along the edge of the pan. Meanwhile, in another small saucepan, melt the butter over medium-low heat. Add the flour and cook, stirring constantly, for 2 minutes. Whisk in the hot milk mixture and cook, stirring often, until thickened. Reduce the heat to low and whisk in the egg yolks, one at a time, whisking well after each addition. Remove from the heat and let cool, whisking often to speed the cooling process. Stir in the lemon zest.

Combine the egg whites and lemon juice in a large bowl and whisk by hand or with a handheld mixer on medium-high speed until stiff peaks form. Fold about one-third of the egg whites into the cooled ginger mixture to lighten it, then fold in the remaining whites just until no white streaks remain.

Pour the mixture into the prepared soufflé dish and level the top with a spatula or the back of a spoon. Bake the soufflé on the bottom rack of the oven until risen and golden brown, 25–30 minutes.

While the soufflé bakes, prepare the sauce. Combine all the ingredients in the top pan of a double boiler set over (not touching) gently simmering water in the lower pan. (Or rest a heatproof bowl in the rim of a saucepan over simmering water.) Whisk vigorously as the mixture heats, and continue to whisk until frothy and thoroughly blended. Whisk in additional water, 1 teaspoon at a time, if needed to achieve the correct consistency.

Serve the soufflé immediately from the oven, with the sauce in a warmed serving bowl alongside.

MRS. PATMORE: *But why would we need it?*

DAISY: *It's a mixer. It beats eggs and whips cream and all sorts.*

MRS. PATMORE: *But you and Ivy do that.*

DAISY: *And we'd be glad not to, thank you very much.*

~ SEASON 4, EPISODE 1

CRÊPES SUZETTE

One of the most iconic recipes of the twentieth century, crêpes Suzette became something of a cliché in Britain in the 1960s. It's a shame, for the dish is fabulous in its original incarnation. Characteristically simple yet packed with flavor, it's typical of the streamlined haute cuisine practiced by Escoffier, who at the time of *Downton* was chef de cuisine at the Ritz in London. Mrs. Patmore cooks the crêpes for Lavinia Swire's first visit to Downton in season 2, when rationing was still in force. Houses like Downton often grew their own citrus fruit, however, escaping the food shortages that affected the wider population during the Great War.

SERVES 4

> ## RECIPE NOTE
>
> The original recipe does not call for the crêpes to be flambéed, and there is no need to do so. However, if you desperately want to flambé them, remember to heat the curaçao before you ignite it. You can substitute oranges for the mandarin oranges, but they are less subtle. Likewise, you can use brandy or Calvados instead of the curaçao.

INGREDIENTS

FOR THE CRÊPES

1 cup plus 2 tablespoons (130 g) flour

¼ cup (50 g) superfine sugar

Pinch of salt

3 eggs

1¾ cups (425 ml) milk

2 teaspoons curaçao

Grated zest of 1 orange

2 teaspoons butter

FOR THE FILLING

5 tablespoons (70 g) unsalted butter

1 tablespoon superfine sugar

Juice of 6 mandarin oranges

Grated zest of 3 mandarin oranges

3 tablespoons curaçao

To make the crêpe batter, combine the flour, sugar, salt, eggs, milk, curaçao, and orange zest in a bowl and whisk together until well mixed. Cover and set aside for 20 minutes.

To cook the crêpes, put a large heatproof plate in the oven and preheat the oven to 200°F (95°C). Melt ½ teaspoon of the butter in an 11-inch (28-cm) crêpe pan (or frying pan) over medium-high heat until it foams. Add a ladleful of about ¼ cup (60 ml) of the batter and quickly tilt and swirl the pan to coat the entire bottom evenly. Cook, shaking the pan from time to time, until the batter looks set, about 1 minute. Carefully flip the crêpe over and cook until the second side is set and lightly browned, about 45 seconds. Transfer to the hot plate and keep warm in the oven while you cook 3 more crêpes.

To make the filling, combine all the filling ingredients in a heavy-bottomed pan and bring to a boil over medium-high heat, stirring occasionally. Boil until reduced to a thick syrup the consistency of heavy cream, 1–2 minutes. As soon as it browns and starts to caramelize, quickly remove it from the heat.

To serve, spread each crêpe with a thick layer of the filling and then either roll it up or fold it into quarters. Serve hot on individual dessert plates.

BANANA CREAM ICE

Agnes Marshall was a late-nineteenth-century entrepreneur extraordinaire. Trained (probably) in Paris and Vienna, she set up a cookery school in her own name and ran it successfully for many years (the married women's property act had just come into force, allowing women to hold property independent of their husbands). Marshall wrote four cookery books, publicizing them through nationwide live cookery tours, and also held patents for a number of culinary gadgets. Her recipes are variable in quality and ease of execution, especially to a modern eye, except for *The Book of Ices*, her first book. It's a glorious collection of Victorian flavors for both water- and cream-based ices, the variety of which puts most modern ice cream books to shame. This recipe is fabulous and has all the qualities of a Downton-style dessert: it is light, simple, yet full of flavor.

MAKES 1½ QUARTS (1.4 L)

INGREDIENTS

6 ripe bananas

Juice of 2 lemons

¼ cup (60 ml) curaçao

2½ cups (600 ml) heavy cream

½ cup (100 g) superfine sugar

Peel the bananas and purée with a masher in a bowl, or purée in a blender and transfer to a bowl. Add the lemon juice and curaçao and mix well. In a large bowl, whisk together the cream and sugar until it is half-whipped. It should be quite thick but not yet at piping consistency. Fold in the bananas just until combined.

Freeze the mixture in an ice cream maker according to the manufacturer's instructions. Transfer to an airtight container and store in the freezer until serving.

RECIPE NOTE

To make ice cream without an ice cream maker, you will need a metal container with a tight-fitting lid (a tea caddy works well). Choose a container large enough to allow for the expansion of the liquid ice cream mixture once the mixture freezes and for easy stirring. Fill a big plastic bowl or bucket two-thirds full with crushed ice. Add a cupful (about 300 g) of cheap table salt, pouring it all over the ice and then mixing it in well. Pour the ice cream mixture into the metal container and then immediately nest the container in the ice, making sure the ice sits about 1 inch (2.5 cm) below the lid. Every 10 to 15 minutes, use a sturdy spoon to scrape the solidifying ice cream from the sides of the container and stir it in vigorously. You will have ice cream at a good eating consistency in about 1 hour. If you want to see how well the ice and salt work, stick a thermometer into the ice-salt mixture; it should read well under 15°F (-9°C), which is the average temperature of a domestic freezer. This method works much better than putting the mixture in the freezer and stirring it every so often because you aren't constantly opening the freezer door, which raises the temperature, and you are less likely to forget to stir!

CHEESE BOUCHÉES

Cheese was a firm favorite for the after-dinner savory and was transformed into a wide range of small bites, from custards to straws to everything in between. Like hors d'oeuvres, they were intended to refresh the palate and appealed to diners who did not have a sweet tooth. Cheese, when served, was eaten after the sweet entremets, ostensibly to prepare the palate for the dessert wines, which were followed by a simple dessert of fruit, nuts, and ices. The rise of the savory was an ingenious solution to curb the length of the meal but still satisfy those who preferred a salty hit to a sweet one—or wanted both. Serving savories was also more elegant than cutting slices from large blocks of cheese, an important concern at formal dinners. These little cheesy bites are typical of the period. We see Alfred making a similar recipe in season 4, when Mrs. Patmore is helping him prepare for culinary school.

MAKES ABOUT 20 BOUCHÉES

DAISY: *Alfred's making tarts with an egg and cheese filling.*

MRS. PATMORE: *Ah. Bouchées de fromage. They could be tonight's savory.*

~ SEASON 4, EPISODE 5

FOR THE PASTRY

1⅓ cups (170 g) flour, plus more for the work surface

6 tablespoons (90 g) cold butter, cut into small cubes

4–5 tablespoons ice-cold water

FOR THE FILLING

1 egg

¼ cup (30 g) grated sharp Cheddar cheese

¼ cup (30 g) grated Parmesan cheese

1 tablespoon butter, melted and cooled

Pinch of cayenne pepper (optional)

Salt and black pepper

Milk, for sealing and brushing

To make the pastry, put the flour in a bowl, scatter the butter cubes over the top, and work the butter into the flour with a pastry blender or your fingertips just until the mixture is the consistency of bread crumbs. Add just enough of the water, stirring and tossing it with the flour mixture as you do, until the dough comes together in a rough mass. Shape into a ball, wrap in plastic wrap, and refrigerate for 20–30 minutes.

To make the filling, whisk the egg in a bowl just until blended. Add both cheeses, the butter, cayenne (if using), and a little salt and black pepper and mix well.

Preheat the oven to 400°F (200°C). Line a large sheet pan with parchment paper.

Divide the dough in half. Cover and refrigerate half. On a lightly floured work surface, roll out the other half into a round about 1/16 inch (2 mm) thick. Using a 3½-inch (9-cm) round cutter, cut out as many circles as possible. To shape each pastry, put about ¾ teaspoon of the filling on half of the circle, leaving the edge uncovered. Brush the entire edge of the circle with milk, then fold the uncovered half over the filling to form a half-moon, pressing the edges to seal. Now bring the two corners together and press them together, sealing well (like shaping tortellini). Transfer the filled pastries to the prepared pan and refrigerate while you roll out, fill, and shape the remaining dough. Arrange all the filled pastries on the pan. Lightly brush the tops with milk.

Bake until golden brown, 22–24 minutes. Serve warm (let cool slightly on the pan on a wire rack) or at room temperature.

RECIPE NOTE

You can pep up the filling with Worcestershire sauce, or make the pastries even more savory with a little anchovy paste. Any leftover filling is also good baked in a buttered ovenproof dish, in which case you could call it a cheese ramekin, another type of Edwardian savory.

DEVILED KIDNEYS

Kidneys and liver, generally served with spice and lots of salt, were common elements of the savory course (they were also popular for breakfast). Cooked this way, with cayenne, mustard, chile, or curry, they were intensely savory and reflected the flavors in other deviled dishes (such as the biscuits on page 41 in the breakfast section). Offal has gained a modern reputation as inferior to muscle meats, but in the past it was simply regarded as another type of ingredient. It does tend to spoil more quickly than other cuts, so if you kept a pig, as many working-class people did, when it was butchered you'd be more likely to eat the offal than the ham, which could be salted and sold. This was one reason offal gained a reputation as a poor person's dish. During the Second World War, offal wasn't rationed, and when the war ended, there was a move away from offal and back to steak, and eating organs has been in decline ever since. At Downton, kidneys are often served for the savory, including during Martha Levinson's visit in season 3.

SERVES 4

INGREDIENTS

2 pig or 4 sheep kidneys

2 teaspoons kosher salt

Scant 1 teaspoon cayenne pepper

2 tablespoons unsalted butter

2 tablespoons minced fresh flat-leaf parsley

¼ cup (60 ml) dry white wine

2 teaspoons mushroom ketchup or Worcestershire sauce

Small toasts, for serving

Using a very sharp knife, slice the kidneys as thinly as you can (you may also need to remove the tough lump in the middle if your butcher has not already done that). Sprinkle the slices on both sides with the salt and cayenne.

Melt the butter in a frying pan over high heat until it foams. Add the kidney slices and fry, turning often, until the last point of pink is just disappearing from the middle of each slice, 5–10 minutes. Add the parsley and stir well. Using a slotted spoon, transfer the kidneys to a warmed serving plate.

Add the wine and mushroom ketchup to the pan and deglaze it, scraping up all the scraps of sticky goodness and keeping the heat high so the liquid reduces to a thick jus. Pour this over the kidneys and serve piping hot, with little toasts to mop up the juices.

MRS. PATMORE: *Oh, she ate it then. I'm never sure about Americans and offal.*

~ **SEASON 3, EPISODE 2**

MARMALADE WATER ICE

Water ices, or sorbets, as we now know them, were very useful as part of the dessert course. Not only did they cleanse the palate, which was the main point of dessert, but they could also be made of an almost infinite variety of ingredients and, because they set more solidly than cream-based ices, they could be molded into any number of shapes. By the Edwardian period, a dizzying range of molds for ices was available: everything from fish to fruit, from winged doves to floral baskets. With judicious use of food coloring and a great deal of skill, the results could be breathtaking. This is one of the simple recipes for water ice, but one of the most effective.

MAKES ABOUT 1 QUART (950 ML)

INGREDIENTS

I cup (320 g) orange marmalade
Juice of I lemon

2½ cups (600 ml) water

Mix together all the ingredients in a bowl. If the marmalade is fairly solid, heat it in the water in a saucepan on the stove top to dissolve it fully, then add the lemon juice and leave to cool completely.

Freeze the mixture in an ice cream maker according to the manufacturer's instructions, or use the Edwardian trick of a lidded metal container set in a bowl of crushed ice and lots of salt (see Recipe Note on page 203). Transfer to an airtight container and store in the freezer until serving.

RECIPE NOTE

You can use any jam or jelly for this recipe. The glory of it is that the balance of sugar and fruit in the preserves is perfect. It also molds especially well, in which case make it as directed, then paddle it into a mold with a spoon and put the mold in the freezer to set properly. The mixture can be made into ice pops or lollies, too.

MRS. PATMORE: *Daisy! I said ices, not iced cakes! Now, unclog your ears and get these to William before they turn into soup!*

~ SEASON 1, EPISODE 7

PUNCH ROMAINE

This punch dates back to the late eighteenth century and was a spin on the alcoholic punches often served at the end of a meal, after the ladies had departed for the drawing room. It was very common at gentlemen's clubs, and satires of the time lampooned the English habit of getting too drunk to stand up and missing the chamber pot. In the more staid atmosphere of the late nineteenth century, large bowls of punch continued to be popular for parties, but iced punches evolved both as a pick-me-up at balls and as a refreshing palate cleanser after dinner. This one is best known for being served in the first-class dining saloon on the last night of the *Titanic*'s ill-fated voyage, the news of whose sinking opens *Downton Abbey*. Simpler versions were around, but this one, from Escoffier, is sublime.

SERVES 6–8

INGREDIENTS

¼ cup (50 g) sugar

I egg white

1¾ cups (425 ml) Champagne or other sparkling wine, chilled

¼ cup (60 ml) simple syrup, see Recipe Note

Grated zest and juice of I orange

Juice of 2 small lemons

¼ cup (60 ml) rum

Start by making an Italian meringue. Put the sugar into a small, heavy-bottomed saucepan and add just enough water (about ¼ cup/60 ml) to moisten it. Heat over high heat without stirring, brushing down the sides of the pan with a brush dipped in cold water to remove any sugar crystals, until the sugar syrup registers 240°F (116°C) on a candy thermometer (soft-ball stage).

Meanwhile, in a bowl, whisk the egg white by hand or with a handheld mixer on medium speed until soft peaks form. When the sugar syrup reaches the desired temperature, slowly pour it into the egg white while whisking continuously, increasing the speed to high if using a mixer. (This step is much easier if you use a mixer.) Continue whisking until soft peaks form again, about 5 minutes.

In a bowl, stir together the Champagne, simple syrup, orange zest and juice, and lemon juice. Fold in the Italian meringue just until fully mixed, then freeze the mixture in an ice cream maker according to the manufacturer's instructions. The punch won't freeze completely, but it should be well mixed and relatively solid. Transfer to an airtight container and place in the freezer for 3 hours to harden further before serving.

To serve, scoop into individual glasses and pour an equal amount of the rum over each serving.

RECIPE NOTE

You can also serve the rum in a small pitcher and allow everyone to pour his or her own. The mixture never quite freezes because of the level of sugar, so it remains a sticky, velvety, soft-scoop kind of dessert. To make the simple syrup, bring equal parts sugar and water to a boil, stir until the sugar dissolves, and then let cool before serving.

DAISY

*Right. The first course is ready to go up.
The soufflé mix is done for the savoury and I'll
make a béchamel for the cauliflower.*

MRS. PATMORE

*Thank God for you Daisy. I've never
known your true value 'til now.*

~ SEASON 4, EPISODE 9

DOWNSTAIRS

FOOD FOR THE SERVANTS WAS ALWAYS MUCH PLAINER THAN WHAT was served to the family, but that did not mean it was inferior. An indoor servant at a country house in the Edwardian era could expect to eat around a pound (450 grams) of meat a day, bulked out with plenty of vegetables and carbohydrates, the latter in the form of not only the ubiquitous bread but also pasta, tapioca, and rice pudding. The time-consuming sauces and molded dishes of upstairs weren't present, but the range of food was nevertheless impressive, if sometimes monotonous in its flavors. Servants at the time reported that the weekly menus rarely varied, except by season in terms of the vegetables.

The daily pattern was dictated by both the needs of the working day and the desire to impose status upon servants by their employers. Kitchen maids, housemaids, and footmen all had to be early risers, to make sure that fires were lit, clothes laid out and shoes shined, and breakfast started well before the family woke up. Breakfast below stairs generally took place once its consumers had been up for a few hours, and for the footmen who attended to breakfast upstairs, as soon as it was over. It tended to be a rather snatched meal for everyone. Dinner took place around two o'clock in the afternoon, once the family luncheon was over. The timing was a deliberate reminder to servants that they were lower status, for the upper classes ate dinner in the evening. It was, like the upstairs dinner, the main meal of the day, and the only one that the majority of staff would attend (always with an ear out for a bell demanding their presence, of course). Tea would be around four o'clock, timed so the upstairs tea could take place just after it, and supper was a final chance to grab some food before bed, the two both being informal meals and frequently eaten between jobs.

Four substantial meals a day may seem a large amount to modern eyes, but the life of a domestic servant was extremely physical, even with the advent of electric egg whisks and refrigeration. The school-leaving age at the time was thirteen, and many servants started work at that age. Letters and diaries from the era frequently include young maids at their first job crying themselves to sleep, not through misery but through sheer exhaustion. Downton's servants are all slightly older than this, which was normal in country houses, who rarely took on completely inexperienced staff if they could help it. They were used to the pace and didn't crack under the pressure.

Status was strictly enforced at mealtimes, which we see at Downton in both the seating arrangements and the scrambling to rise whenever a higher-status servant or, more alarmingly, a family member enters the servants' hall. At many houses, the upper servants—cook, butler, housekeeper, governesses and tutors, valets and ladies' maids—ate with the lower servants for the first course of dinner and then decamped to the housekeeper's room for the sweet course. They also had the best pickings of any leftovers from the family dinner that could not be reused in some way.

The lowest servant, in large houses usually a steward's room boy who was employed to do the most menial tasks while being slowly trained up as a footman, served the other staff at their table. At Downton, this often falls to Daisy or, when she is promoted, to Ivy. It was yet another way of ensuring that everyone knew exactly where they fitted in, quite literally knowing their place.

DOWNSTAIRS DINNER

DINNER DOWNSTAIRS WAS, AS UPSTAIRS, THE main meal of the day, made up of the most substantial dishes and served with a degree of formality. At Downton we often see the servants' dinner in progress, presided over by the most senior servant, Mr. Carson, the butler. Staff were expected to exhibit good table manners, and conversations were, as they often are at Downton, censored by the upper staff if they were deemed to be unsuitable topics for the dinner table.

Servants' dinners consisted of only two courses, unlike the seven-course extravaganzas upstairs. At Downton, as with many houses, they are served in the old-fashioned manner, with many dishes put on the table at once. Service was not a free-for-all, however, not least because several of those present could be expected to serve at the upstairs table and would have learned some of their skills downstairs. This included both footmen and, on less formal occasions such as luncheons, housemaids.

The food was plain but plentiful. Large cuts of poached meat were a standard fixture in most servants' halls, along with a range of stews and casseroles, which often made their appearance every week on a fixed day. Sundays generally involved a roasted meat, though very rarely was it chicken or game, as these were expensive and prestigious. Rabbit, considered a pest, was common, as was pork, which was cheap, and the less tender cuts of mutton and beef. Unlike upstairs, where serving out-of-season vegetables was deemed desirable to show off the skills of the gardeners, downstairs the vegetables were more seasonal and tended to be served simply boiled and then dressed with butter. Lots of bread, potatoes, and, especially by the 1920s, dishes such as macaroni, rice, or semolina that had once been considered somewhat exotic were served as well.

Dinner downstairs also involved a sweet. These were often starch-based dishes, such as rice pudding, tapioca pudding, macaroni pudding, and cornstarch blancmange, which were simple to make, forgiving in terms of timing, and easy to vary with a spoonful of jam or some puréed fruit. The rather indefinable and quintessentially British term *pudding* was almost universally applied to these working-class sweets, and while it often meant something boiled in a pudding dish, for the purposes of the servants' hall, it could also be a baked dish. The servants' hall ran on puddings, and though many of them are now forgotten or derided, they were often very good.

The usual drink in servants' halls was water or tea, though in some houses beer was still considered a necessary part of the daily allowance. Wine was very rarely consumed, or at least not officially. One of the well-known perils for butlers was alcoholism, generally brought on by easy and constant access to his lordship's port and wine. On special occasions, such as Christmas and New Year's, we see the Downton servants indulge in punch, though it would have been of a somewhat lower grade than the version upstairs.

TOAD-IN-THE-HOLE

The servants' hall table at Downton is usually laden with batter puddings, potatoes, stews, and vegetables that are cheap and filling. Rather than being carefully molded and garnished, the dishes are typically served in the vessel they were cooked in, and while some of them take a long time to simmer or bake, the effort and time involved in making them is minimal. Toad-in-the-hole was typical of servants' fare in the early twentieth century, as it was cheap, easy, and versatile. The name dates back to the eighteenth century, though it's unclear why the meat was called a toad—possibly because it peeps from the batter like a toad from its burrow.

SERVES 4

INGREDIENTS

I cup (240 ml) milk

I cup (115 g) flour

¼ teaspoon salt

2 eggs

Butter, lard, or pan drippings, for preparing the pie dish

I lb (450 g) bulk sausage meat or chopped raw sausages

Onion or meat gravy, for serving

To make the batter, whisk together the milk, flour, salt, and eggs in a bowl until thoroughly mixed. Set aside for 15–30 minutes.

Preheat the oven to 350°F (180°C). Butter a 9-inch (23-cm) pie dish.

Scatter the sausage over the bottom of the prepared dish. Put the dish into the oven for 10 minutes to render some of the fat and brown the sausage lightly. Remove from the oven, pour the batter over the sausage, and return to the oven. Bake until the sausage is cooked through and the batter has puffed up and browned, about 45 minutes.

Serve hot with gravy.

RECIPE NOTE

Batter puddings like these can be used with any filling, including fruit for a sweet version. Toads were frequently recommended for eking out small amounts of leftover meat and vegetables. During the food shortages of the First World War, one author suggested adding chopped tomatoes and onions to bulk out the "minced meat of any kind." If you are using leftover cooked sausage or small meatballs for this recipe, there is no need to brown them before adding the batter.

LAMB STEW WITH SEMOLINA

Stews are a staple of the servants' hall at Downton, as indeed they were in country houses more generally. They tend to be long cooked, use cheap cuts of meat, and are easy to make on the stove top or in the oven. In houses with several kitchen maids, the lowest maid would normally be in charge of making the servants' food, which was one step up from doing all the peeling, chopping, gutting, and plucking that was the lot of the scullery maid. It was a way of learning to cook without too much pressure, though servants could sometimes be as exacting as the family. This recipe comes from Mary Fairclough's *The Ideal Cookery Book* and is based on a rural French recipe that by the Edwardian period had climbed the social scale, been anglicized, and had descended yet again.

SERVES 6

INGREDIENTS

2 tablespoons butter

2 lb (1 kg) boneless lamb shoulder or leg, cut into 1-inch (2.5-cm) cubes

3 tablespoons flour

I small yellow onion, diced

6 cloves garlic, chopped

I teaspoon ground cloves

Salt and black pepper

4 cups (950 ml) meat stock, plus more if needed, heated

Bouquet garni of 3–4 fresh flat-leaf parsley sprigs, 2–3 fresh thyme sprigs, and I bay leaf, tied into a bundle with kitchen string

FOR THE SEMOLINA

I cup (170 g) semolina

3¾ cups (900 ml) lukewarm water

2 tablespoons olive oil

Ground nutmeg

Salt and black pepper

2 egg yolks

⅔ cup (160 ml) heavy cream

Juice of ½ lemon

Chopped fresh flat-leaf parsley and chopped or whole gherkins, for garnish

Melt the butter in a large, heavy-bottomed saucepan over medium-high heat. Add the lamb and fry briefly, turning the pieces as needed to brown. Sprinkle the flour over the lamb and continue to fry for another couple of minutes. Add the onion and garlic and fry briefly to soften. Sprinkle with the cloves, season well with salt and pepper, and pour in the stock. Add the bouquet garni and bring to a boil. Reduce the heat to a gentle simmer and cook, stirring occasionally and adding a little more stock if the pan begins to boil dry, until the meat is tender, 1½–2 hours.

About 30 minutes before the stew is ready, make the semolina. In a saucepan, whisk together the semolina, water, and I tablespoon of the oil until the semolina is dissolved and the mixture is free of lumps. Season with the nutmeg, salt, and pepper and bring to a gentle boil over medium-high heat, stirring occasionally. Reduce the heat to low and cook, stirring from time to time, until the mixture thickens, 4–6 minutes. It is ready if it leaves the sides of the pan dry as you drag a spoon through it and it clumps together in a soft, silky mass. Remove from the heat and stir in the remaining I tablespoon oil. Keep warm.

When the lamb is ready, using a slotted spoon, transfer it to a warmed plate. Strain the cooking liquid through a fine-mesh sieve into a pitcher and then measure ⅔ cup (160 ml) for the sauce (reserve the remainder for another use). Whisk the egg yolks briefly in a small, heavy-bottomed saucepan, then gradually add the cream and the ⅔ cup (160 ml) cooking liquid, whisking constantly. Place the pan over low heat and heat the mixture, stirring often, until thickened to a good sauce consistency (essentially you are making a savory custard), about 10 minutes. Remove from the heat and stir in the lemon juice. Pour into a warmed sauceboat.

You can serve the semolina separately or as a bed for the lamb. Garnish the lamb with the parsley and gherkins and serve the sauce alongside.

RECIPE NOTE

You can also use mutton (or goat) for this recipe. If you are not used to making custard, make the sauce in a bowl over a pan of simmering water, as there is less risk of it curdling this way. Alternatively, whisk 1 tablespoon cornstarch into the cold cream until dissolved before gradually adding the cream and the cooking liquid to the eggs, then heat, stirring, as directed. The sauce won't be as velvety but it will be slightly easier to make.

ETHEL: *What are we having?*

MRS. PATMORE: *Lamb stew and semolina.*

ETHEL: *Do you eat a lot of stews?*

MRS. PATMORE: *Don't you fancy that, dear?*

ETHEL: *Not all the time.*

~ SEASON 2, EPISODE 1

BEEF STEW WITH DUMPLINGS

Beef stew is a true servants' dish: cooked low and slow, hard to spoil, and filling for hungry bellies. This version comes with rib-sticking dumplings, so it's a real meal in a pot. It features several times on *Downton Abbey*, both as a dish in the servants' hall and at the soup kitchen, where it is set up for starving and injured soldiers in the episodes set during the Great War. The secret is to have a cut, such as brisket, that has some fat with it and that will benefit from long cooking. Beef was considered a symbol of Britishness, and a great deal of it was consumed both below and above stairs in country houses. In season 1, Daisy fails to sabotage the beef stew during her short-lived campaign to ruin the dishes so Mrs. Bird won't be seen as a better cook than Mrs. Patmore.

SERVES 8

MRS. BIRD: *There, there. There are worse crimes on earth than loyalty. Dry your eyes, and fetch the beef stew I was making for tomorrow. You've not had a chance to spoil that, I suppose.*

DAISY: *I was going to mix in some syrup of figs. But I've not done it yet.*

~ SEASON 1, EPISODE 7

INGREDIENTS

1 tablespoon lard or vegetable oil

½ lb (225 g) lardons

2 lb (1 kg) stewing beef, cut into 1–1½-inch (2.5–4-cm) cubes

1 small yellow onion, diced

1 tablespoon flour

2 tablespoons malt vinegar

1 tablespoon Worcestershire sauce or mushroom ketchup

1½ teaspoons black treacle (blackstrap molasses)

8 whole cloves

2 bay leaves

2 cups (480 ml) beer

Salt and black pepper

FOR THE DUMPLINGS

1 cup (115 g) flour

3 oz (90 g) shredded suet (about ¾ cup) or shredded cold butter

½ teaspoon baking powder

⅛ teaspoon salt

1 tablespoon minced fresh rosemary

Black pepper

Heat the lard in a heavy-bottomed pot over high heat and fry the lardons (bacon cut into strips about 1 inch/2.5 cm long and ¼ inch/6 mm wide and thick) and beef until browned. Reduce the heat to low, add the onion, and cook, stirring occasionally, until translucent, 3–5 minutes. Sprinkle everything with the flour and fry, turning all the ingredients regularly, for a few more minutes. Add the vinegar, Worcestershire sauce, treacle, cloves, bay leaves, beer, and water as needed just to cover the beef. Season with salt and pepper, bring to a boil, turn down the heat to low, and cook gently, stirring occasionally and adding a little more water if the pan begins to boil dry, until the beef is tender, about 3 hours.

Once the beef is cooking, make the dumplings: Stir together the flour, suet, baking powder, salt, rosemary, and a little pepper in a bowl, then mix in enough cold water (7–8 tablespoons/105–120 ml) to form a stiff paste. Divide the paste into eighths, shape each portion into a ball, and pop the balls into the pot to cook with the beef for about 2 hours.

At the end of cooking, using a slotted spoon, transfer the dumplings and beef to warmed individual plates. Turn up the heat and reduce the cooking liquid to a good sauce consistency, then spoon an equal amount over each serving.

STEAK AND KIDNEY PUDDING

Meat puddings of this type were a large part of middle- and working-class cookery. They were easy to make and could be left quite happily gently bubbling at the back of a range for several hours. The meat part-steams, part-boils inside, and as a form of slow cooking, the method is hard to beat. Early steak puddings were often flavored with oysters, rather than kidneys, but as the availability of oysters changed, and because these kinds of puddings are almost infinitely forgiving in terms of ingredients, the secondary flavor became mushrooms, and then kidneys. You can use the same technique for a wide variety of other fillings—pork and apple, sausage and leek—the choice is entirely yours.

SERVES 4

RECIPE NOTE

The slightly uric tang of the kidneys can be off-putting for the uninitiated, so if you are not a huge fan of kidneys, use sheep or veal kidneys instead of beef or pork and cut them up fairly finely. For slightly more texture, after removing the pudding from the water, bake it in a preheated 350°F (180°C) oven for 20 minutes to crisp the crust. You can bake the pudding instead of boiling it, too, but then it's really a pie and no longer a pudding.

INGREDIENTS

FOR THE PASTRY

1¼ cups (155 g) flour, plus more for the cheesecloth

2 oz (60 g) shredded suet (about ½ cup) or shredded cold butter

½ teaspoon salt

FOR THE FILLING

1½–2 lb (680 g–1 kg) mixed steak (chuck is ideal) and kidney, in the proportion of two-thirds steak to one-third kidney

2 tablespoons Worcestershire sauce or oyster sauce

A few mushrooms (optional)

Butter, for greasing

To make the pastry, stir together the flour, suet, and salt, then stir in enough cold water (about 1 tablespoon, or as needed) to make a malleable but not sticky dough. The dough does not need to rest before it is rolled out, but if it's a hot day, putting it in the fridge for 15 minutes will help to firm it up.

Butter a 2½-cup (600-ml) pudding mold. On a lightly floured work surface, roll out about two-thirds of the pastry into a round about ¼ inch (6 mm) thick. Line the prepared mold with the pastry, pushing it onto the bottom and up the sides and ensuring an overhang of at least ½ inch (12 mm).

To make the filling, cut the steak into 1½-inch (4-cm) cubes and the kidney into pieces slightly smaller. Put both meats into the lined dish. Add the Worcestershire sauce and mushrooms (if using) and toss to coat. Roll out the remaining pastry the same way and lay it over the top of the pudding dish, sealing it very well all the way around and dampening the edge, if needed, to ensure a tight seal. Trim off any overhang. Brush your fingers up the sides of the mold to make sure the pastry is neatly tucked into the basin and none is escaping over the sides.

Dampen a double thickness of cheesecloth or a clean kitchen towel and sprinkle it with flour, dusting off the excess. Make a fold across the center, lay it over the top of the pudding mold, and tie it firmly in place with kitchen string.

Fill a saucepan large enough to accommodate the mold with water to reach about two-thirds of the way up the sides of the mold once the mold is added. Bring the water to a boil and carefully lower the mold into the pan. Allow the water to come back to a full boil, cover the pan, and then turn down the heat so the water is still at a rolling boil but not bubbling so vigorously that it splashes over the rim. Boil the pudding for about 3½ hours, keeping an eye on the water level and adding more boiling water as needed to maintain the original level.

Turn off the heat and carefully remove the mold from the water. Take off the cloth and immediately cut a small triangle of pastry out of the middle of the top to allow the steam to escape. Serve hot. You can turn the pudding out of the mold if you like, but it can also be served from the mold, in which case the mold should be set on a plate before being dished out.

FOOD FOR THOUGHT

There's one reference to a pudding cloth in the medieval period, but the cloths don't creep into cookery books until the seventeenth century, after which they boom. Puddings boiled in cloths, and later in basins and molds, became one of the most representative dishes of British cuisine, and although plum pudding (now known as Christmas pudding) is the most well-known example today, there was a bewildering variety of both savory and sweet puddings for the discerning diner until the middle of the twentieth century, by which time they had gained a reputation for being stodgy and old-fashioned and had declined in popularity. Despite their position as a staple in the British diet, they are very hard to define, and puddings can include everything from sausages and haggis, to cheesecakes and molded ice cream.

CAULIFLOWER CHEESE

The recipe comes from *Everyday Cookery* by Isabella Beeton, who was long dead by 1913 when it was published. She was the author of the best-known historic cookery book in Britain, *Beeton's Book of Household Management*, first published in 1861 but in print continuously ever since. The original book, a mixture of strong, empowering language and utterly garbled recipes (Isabella plagiarized freely to compile her volume), dealt not only with cookery but also the running of a household. Aimed at the rapidly increasing urban middle classes, it set out to help women who had not necessarily been brought up with servants but who now found themselves married to businessmen and expected to hire and fire staff, care for their families, and put on impressive dinners in hope of climbing the social ladder. It was immensely popular, with some sixty thousand copies in its first year of publication. Beeton herself died only four years after it came out, but the book, which would not have been used for upstairs dishes but is perfect for the servants' hall, was regularly updated by its publishers. This version of cauliflower cheese is quite different from the original recipe.

SERVES 4 AS A SIDE DISH

INGREDIENTS

2 tablespoons unsalted butter, plus more for the baking dish

I large head or 2 small heads cauliflower, cut or broken into bite-size florets

2 tablespoons flour

¼ cup (60 ml) water

FOR THE SAUCE

2 tablespoons butter

¼ cup (30 g) flour

I cup (240 ml) milk, heated

Pinch of cayenne pepper

Ground nutmeg

Black pepper

½ cup (60 g) grated sharp Cheddar cheese

¼ cup (30 g) grated sharp Cheddar cheese, for topping

Preheat the oven to 400°F (200°C). Butter a deep 1½-quart (1.4-l) baking dish.

Melt the butter in a large, heavy-bottomed saucepan over medium heat. Add the florets, sprinkling them with the flour. Keep them moving until they start to brown, about 5 minutes. Add the water, stir well, turn down the heat to low, cover, and cook until tender but still fairly firm, about 5 minutes.

Meanwhile, make the sauce. Melt the butter in a saucepan over medium heat, then whisk in the flour until a smooth, thick roux forms. Reduce the heat to low and continue to stir until the roux is a very light brown, about 5 minutes. Add the hot milk, a little at a time, whisking vigorously after each addition so no lumps develop. When all the milk has been added and the sauce is smooth and creamy, season with the cayenne, nutmeg and black pepper. Add the cheese, stir until melted, and remove from the heat.

Drain the cauliflower and transfer it to the prepared baking dish. Pour the sauce evenly over the top and sprinkle with the cheese. Bake until the top is nicely browned and bubbling, 10–15 minutes. Let cool slightly before serving so the cheese crisps up and you don't burn your mouth on the molten sauce.

THE KITCHEN GARDEN

All country houses had a kitchen garden designed to supply most of the fruits, vegetables, and herbs required by the kitchen. When the Crawley family was away, for example at their London house, produce would be sent from the country garden by train. In the season 4 Christmas special, we see the upheavals the constant moves between country and town occasioned when the Crawleys decamp to Grantham House for Rose's first "season," including her debut ball.

In the Edwardian era, it was a mark of pride to serve out-of-season produce at the family table, as this showed both the skills of the gardeners and the wealth of the family. Producing nectarines in December required prolific amounts of coal to heat the hothouses and growing walls, while retarding the growth of grapes until March needed specialist equipment and plenty of patience. Fortunately, given the precarious state of the Crawleys' finances, fashions were changing by the 1920s, and there was a new emphasis on exquisite-looking seasonal fruits and vegetables, full of flavor and not quite as overcooked as their Victorian forbears.

The range of produce was extraordinary. The Victorians had been obsessed with plant breeding, leaving a legacy of thousands of varieties of apples and pears and hundreds of rhubarbs. Vegetables such as sea kale, skirret, and cardoons, which were common on the upper-class table, are barely eaten today, as they are difficult to grow and fiddly to prepare. Asparagus, once known as sparrowgrass, was common on the upstairs Christmas table, as were celery, truffles, and spinach. Vegetables were also plentiful downstairs, including potatoes, cabbage, and sometimes tomatoes, which had once been regarded as poisonous and grown only ornamentally but were now ubiquitous and often made into sauces.

DAISY: *Have you seen the kitchen gardens here?*
There's enough vegetables to feed an army.

~ SEASON 6, EPISODE 6

STEAMED TREACLE PUDDING

Steamed sponge puddings were a staple of servants' halls. Cheap and easy to prepare, they could be put on to steam at the back of the range and largely forgotten about. Ranges such as that at Downton were essentially huge blocks of cast iron, and although there were designated hobs (burners), including one directly over the central fire that had removable iron rings to increase or decrease the heat on the pan, the whole range operated as a giant piece of cooking apparatus. A gently bubbling pan could sit almost anywhere on it and still simmer merrily away.

SERVES 6 – 8

RECIPE NOTE

Treacle, a by-product of sugar refining, comes in a number of forms, from black molasses to light syrups. Golden syrup, the type used in dishes like this one, was invented in the 1880s specifically to make use of waste from sugar factories. By the Edwardian era, it was one of the cheapest forms of sugar available and was popular for cooking, for spreading on bread, and for adding to porridge.

INGREDIENTS

1 cup (40 g) fresh bread crumbs

1 cup (115 g) flour, plus more for the cheesecloth

⅔ cup (115 g) dried currants

¼ lb (115 g) shredded suet (about 1 cup), or ½ cup (115 g) solid vegetable shortening

1 tablespoon sugar

1 teaspoon ground ginger

1 teaspoon baking powder

½ teaspoon salt

1 egg, lightly whisked

⅔ cup (210 g) treacle (golden syrup)

½–1 cup (120–240 ml) water

Butter, for the mold

Combine the bread crumbs, flour, currants, suet, sugar, ginger, baking powder, and salt in a bowl and stir until well mixed. Add the egg, treacle, and ½ cup (120 ml) of the water and mix well, adding the remaining ½ cup (120 ml) water only if needed to form a batter that is moist but not too liquid.

Butter a 2½-cup (600-ml) pudding mold. Cut a piece of parchment paper for covering the top of the mold and butter one side of the paper. Pour the batter into the prepared mold and place the parchment, buttered side down, on top of the mold. Dampen a double thickness of cheesecloth or a clean kitchen towel and sprinkle it with flour, dusting off the excess. Make a fold across the center (to allow the pudding to rise as it cooks), lay it over the top of the pudding mold, and tie it firmly in place with kitchen string.

Fill a saucepan large enough to accommodate the mold with water to reach about halfway up the sides of the mold once the mold is added. Bring the water to a boil and carefully lower the mold into the pan. Allow the water to come back to a full boil, cover the pan, and then turn down the heat so the water is still at a rolling boil but not bubbling so vigorously that it splashes over the rim.

Boil the pudding for 2½ hours, keeping an eye on the water level and adding more boiling water as needed to maintain the original level. When the pudding is done, a skewer inserted into the center should show nothing more than a few moist crumbs.

Turn off the heat and carefully remove the mold from the water. Take off the string, cloth, and parchment and allow the pudding to cool on a rack for 10–15 minutes. Use a blunt knife to loosen the edges of the pudding from the mold before turning it onto a platter and serving. It is also good cold.

TREACLE TART

A mainstay of the servants' hall, treacle tart featured in English cookery books from the end of the Victorian period. It could be made with almost anything as long as treacle was included, and it came in deep and shallow crusts, with and without a lid. In this simple version, which comes from *Warne's New Model Cookery*, published in 1925, a thin layer of sweet filling is sandwiched between two sheets of flaky pastry. Because of its slender profile, this teatime treat required no fancy kitchen equipment and so was often baked on an ovenproof enamelware plate. Today, a shallow pie dish works just as well. It is good served with a drizzle of heavy cream or dollop of ice cream.

SERVES 6 – 8

RECIPE NOTE

Treacle tart is usually outrageously sweet, but in this recipe the lemon cuts through the sweetness. You can use orange instead, or you can mix lemon and orange. If you make the Asparagus Cups on page 173, the leftover brioche crumbs are ideal for making the filling called for here. You could also use rolled oats, a Yorkshire variant.

INGREDIENTS

FOR THE PASTRY

1⅓ cups (170 g) flour, plus more for the work surface

6 tablespoons (90 g) cold butter, cut into small cubes, plus more for the dish

2–3 tablespoons ice-cold water

FOR THE FILLING

¼ cup (10 g) fresh bread crumbs or cake crumbs

¼ cup (85 g) treacle (golden syrup)

Grated zest and juice of 1 lemon

To make the pastry, put the flour in a bowl, scatter the butter cubes over the top, and work the butter into the flour with a pastry blender or your finger just until the mixture is the consistency of coarse bread crumbs. Add just enough of the water, stirring and tossing it with the flour mixture, until the dough comes together in a rough mass. Shape into a ball, wrap in plastic wrap, and refrigerate for 20–30 minutes.

Preheat the oven to 400°F (200°C). Lightly butter a very shallow 9-inch (23-cm) round baking dish, pie pan, or pie dish. On a lightly floured work surface, roll out about two-thirds of the pastry into a 10-inch (25-cm) round about ⅛ inch (3 mm) thick. Line the prepared dish with the pastry round, allowing any overhang to drape over or extend up the sides of the dish. Trim away any ragged edges.

To make the filling, stir together the bread crumbs, treacle, and lemon zest and juice in a bowl, mixing well. Pour the filling into the lined dish and spread it out evenly, allowing at least a ½-inch border around the edges. Roll out the remaining pastry slightly larger than the top of the dish. Dampen the edge of the bottom crust. Lay the top pastry over the filling, folding the bottom overhang up and over the edges. Seal it very well all the way around by crimping with a fork. Slash 3 vents in the top pastry.

Bake the tart until the pastry is golden brown and cooked through, about 30 minutes. Let cool completely on a wire rack before serving.

RICE PUDDING

Starch-based puddings were extremely popular in the early twentieth century. They were staple nursery food, and the majority of children of most classes were raised on a steady diet of cornstarch blancmange, tapioca pudding, baked semolina, arrowroot pudding, and rice pudding. Of all of them, rice pudding has the most heritage, as boiled rice was eaten as a pricy and exotic dish in the medieval period, using rice imported from the Far East and flavored with sugar and spice. There are hundreds of recipes for rice pudding, and it was (and still is) possible to buy it fully prepared in cans. Best cooked low and slow, this recipe is ridiculously easy and virtually foolproof.

SERVES 4

RECIPE NOTE

The pudding can be served on its own, with a spoonful of jam, or with some fruit compote.

INGREDIENTS

½ teaspoon butter, for the dish

2½ cups (600 ml) milk

3 tablespoons short-grain white rice, such as risotto rice or pudding rice

2 teaspoons sugar

1 teaspoon pure vanilla extract, 1 strip lemon peel, or 1 cinnamon stick

Preheat the oven to 300°F (150°C). Butter a shallow 4-cup (950-ml) ovenproof dish.

Combine the milk, rice, and sugar in a bowl and whisk together well, then mix in the vanilla. Pour the mixture into the prepared dish.

Bake the pudding for 3 hours. Halfway through baking, slide a spoon under the skin that will have formed on top and give the pudding a brief stir (this is optional). You'll know the pudding is done when the skin is browned and hard and the pudding itself is thick and unctuous. Serve warm or at room temperature.

FOOD FOR THOUGHT

English puddings and American puddings are different. In America, pudding is a specific term for a custardy confection, which to the British would be called custard when served in glasses or blancmange if molded. A British pudding, on the other hand, can be sweet or savory and is usually steamed or boiled in a pudding basin or mold but can also be baked in a dish, set in a mold in the fridge, or, in the case of iced puddings, set in a mold in the freezer. Sometimes puddings aren't molded at all, though they do nearly always have some form of container at some stage in their preparation. Technically, sausages might be puddings, given the early ones were boiled in stomachs (haggis, boiled in a sheep's stomach, is definitely a pudding). They can also be boiled in cloths, though the basin largely replaced the cloth in the eighteenth century. Mainly, they are turned out of the mold (or cloth) to serve, but there are exceptions. Oh, and just to add to the confusion, pudding in England in the twenty-first century is often used as a generic term for the sweet course (as is dessert), though this is really a bit of a betrayal of the brilliance (and distinctiveness) of British puddings.

SPOTTED DICK

Essentially just a plain suet dumpling with added fruit, spotted dick had been the cause of sniggers around the downstairs dinner table since it was first put into print in the middle of the nineteenth century. The term *dick* came from a dialect word for dough, and the spots refer to the dried fruit. It was a popular nursery dish, too, and a staple of school dinners in the twentieth century. It was sometimes called a bolster, after a type of long pillow, but you can also make it in a pudding basin. Spotted dick is vaguely related to another servants' hall classic, the roly-poly, in which suet dough was rolled out into a rectangle, spread with a savory or sweet filling—often jam—rolled up like a jelly (Swiss) roll, and then wrapped in a cloth and boiled. Custard to accompany it is obligatory.

SERVES 6 – 8

INGREDIENTS

FOR THE DICK

1⅓ cups (170 g) flour, plus more for the work surface and cheesecloth

3 oz (90 g) shredded suet (about ¾ cup)

⅔ cup (115 g) dried currants

2 tablespoons sugar

1 teaspoon baking powder

½ teaspoon ground cinnamon

Generous pinch of ground nutmeg

½ cup (120 ml) milk

FOR THE CUSTARD

3 egg yolks

1½ teaspoons cornstarch

1¼ cups (300 ml) milk

1½ tablespoons sugar

Orange flower water, pure vanilla extract, or brandy, for flavoring (optional)

To make the dick, combine the flour, suet, currants, sugar, baking powder, cinnamon, and nutmeg in a bowl and stir to mix well. Add the milk and stir until a stiff, slightly sticky dough forms. On a lightly floured work surface, flatten the dough into a rectangle about 7 inches (18 cm) long, 5 inches (13 cm) wide, and 1 inch (2.5 cm) thick. You can use your hands to flatten the dough, as it should be soft and malleable. Starting from a long side, roll up the rectangle into a log, leaving it seam side down. Dampen a double thickness of cheesecloth, butter muslin (similar to cheesecloth but with a finer weave), or a kitchen towel and sprinkle it with flour. Roll up the dough log in the cloth and tie the ends with kitchen string so it looks like a big boiled sweet. You can loop an extra piece of string between the ends to use as a handle, but make sure there is lots of slack, as the log will expand.

Bring a saucepan filled with water to a rolling boil and carefully lower the pudding into the pan. Allow the water to come back to a full boil, cover the pan, and then turn down the heat so the water is still at a rolling boil but not bubbling too vigorously. Boil the pudding for 2 hours, keeping an eye on the water level and adding more boiling water as needed to keep the pudding submerged.

Meanwhile, make the custard, which for this recipe should be thick and gloopy. Lightly whisk together the egg yolks and cornstarch in a heatproof bowl until the cornstarch dissolves. Combine the milk and sugar in a saucepan over medium heat and bring just to a boil, stirring to dissolve the sugar. Remove from the heat and slowly pour the hot milk into the egg yolks while whisking constantly. Pour the mixture back into the pan, add a little flavoring if you like (2 or 3 teaspoons will do), and return the pan to very low heat. Stir the mixture continuously until it starts to thicken. If you have a thermometer, the custard should start to thicken at about 160°F (74°C) and will start to curdle at 175°F (80°C). Remove the custard from the heat and keep stirring for another few minutes until it stops cooking. If you don't need the custard immediately, cover it with plastic wrap, pressing the plastic directly against the surface to prevent a skin from forming.

When the dick is done, carefully remove it from the pan, let it rest for about 10 minutes, and then gently turn it out of the cloth onto a serving plate and cut into slices to serve. Pour the warm custard into a pitcher and serve on the side.

RECIPE NOTE

Many versions of spotted dick don't include sugar, partly because the dish was invented when sugar was still relatively expensive and partly because it's intended to be served with a sweet sauce. If you don't like custard, melted butter with sugar works. For a more decadent version of the pudding, soak the currants in warm brandy before adding them to the dough, or add crystallized ginger or candied citrus peel to the dough.

MRS. HUGHES: *I hear you're getting on well with your mathematics, Daisy.*

BAXTER: *An extra feather in your cap.*

DAISY: *Yes, it is. But now I wonder . . .*

CARSON: *You wonder what?*

DAISY: *Well, should I stop there?*

MRS. PATMORE: *That's enough, Daisy. Come and carry the spotted dick!*

~ SEASON 5, EPISODE 3

SUMMER PUDDING

Summer pudding has become a British classic. As stated in one 1920s book, "everyone knows this dish, all like it." It started life in the mid-nineteenth century as "hydropathic pudding," though there were a number of recipes in circulation that were similar. In theory, as the healthy-sounding name suggested, it was good for those trying to watch their weight, since it uses bread and not pastry as the base. Given that most recipes then suggested serving it with heavy or whipped cream, ice cream, or custard, its usefulness as a diet food is debatable. It is a great way to use up slightly stale bread, however, large loaves of which we regularly see on the table in the Downton servants' hall.

SERVES 6–8

ROSAMUND: *There's nothing like an English summer, is there?*

MARY: *Except an English winter.*

~ SEASON 1, EPISODE 7

INGREDIENTS

1 lb (450 g) raspberries, plus more for garnish

10 oz (285 g) other fresh fruit, at least half made up of ripe red, black, and/or white currants and other soft fruits such as gooseberries, pitted cherries, or blueberries (see Recipe Note)

2 tablespoons sugar

1 tablespoon water

6–7 slices good-quality white bread, no more than ¼ inch (6 mm) thick, crusts removed

Heavy cream, for serving

Pick any stems off the fruit, then put all the fruit into a saucepan with the sugar and water. Heat gently over low heat until the currants and gooseberries start to burst and yield their juice and the whole thing looks like a luscious red soup. Let cool.

Meanwhile, line a 2½-cup (600-ml) pudding mold with plastic wrap (you could also use a charlotte mold or other vessel of similar size). Using the base of the mold as a template, cut out a piece of bread to fit and place it on the bottom. Cut enough of the bread slices into strips the height of the mold and about 3 inches (7.5 cm) across the top to line the sides. If using a conventional pudding basin, you should taper them slightly at the bottom. If using a charlotte mold or straight-sided dish, cut them to fit that instead. Line the sides of the mold with the bread strips, with no overlap and no significant gaps. Stand the mold in a large bowl.

Using a slotted spoon, transfer the fruit from the pan to the bread-lined mold. Most of the juice will go in too, and that's fine. When all the fruit is in, pour any remaining juice on top, stopping when it just starts to overflow. Cut out a lid from the remaining bread slices (this usually requires a couple of slices) and lay it on top of the mold. Put a plate, the bottom of which just fits inside the rim of the mold, on top of the bread lid. Weight this down with old-fashioned metal weights or a heavy jar or can. Juice will flow out (hence, the surrounding bowl). Refrigerate overnight to set.

The next day, take off the weights and plate, using a table knife to free the plate if necessary. Trim off any excess bits of bread. To serve, upend the mold onto a deep serving plate, lift it off, and peel off the plastic wrap. If there are white gaps in the bread, use some of the juice that collected in the bowl to cover them (strain or scoop out any bits of errant bread first). Otherwise, simply pour the juice on top. Garnish with berries and serve with cream.

RECIPE NOTE

The secret to this pudding is the quality of the bread, and sadly, a long-life ready-sliced loaf simply won't work. You can use the Cottage Loaf on page 242 or a loaf from a good bakery. The leftover bits from the slices will make excellent bread crumbs. You can use a variety of red fruits, but the base should really be raspberries and currants. Do not use strawberries, as they will turn mushy and make the pudding too soggy. Do taste the fruit filling before you put it into the bread mold. It should be fairly tart and palate cleansing, so be careful not to use fruits that will make it too sweet.

JAM AND CUSTARD TARTS

A fixture at fairs, fetes, and festivities of all kinds, jam tarts and custard tarts appear at the Carson-Hughes wedding, as well as at the countless village events of *Downton Abbey*. Jam tarts are possibly the easiest thing anyone can make, and in a house like Downton, they were very useful for using up nub ends of pastry from other dishes. Custard tarts remain one of the traditional offerings at old-fashioned bakeries. Here, the two fillings are combined, a trick of the day. Slightly more decadent than just jam or custard, it's the kind of thing that upper servants would have eaten, while those below them made do with the simple versions.

MAKES 12 TARTLETS

RECIPE NOTE

You can easily flavor the custard with anything else you fancy, too. Also, swapping out the jam topping for a layer of fruit under the custard will elevate the tarts to a point where you could just about serve them as an upstairs dish. If you prefer the jam to be more obvious, you can spread a layer on top of the tarts after they come out of the oven—useful for disguising any splits or burnt bits as well.

INGREDIENTS

FOR THE PASTRY

1½ cups (185 g) flour, plus more for the work surface

½ teaspoon salt

6 tablespoons (90 g) cold unsalted butter, cut into cubes

3–5 tablespoons ice-cold water

FOR THE CUSTARD

1⅓ cups (325 ml) milk

4 egg yolks

¼ cup (50 g) superfine sugar

¼ teaspoon pure vanilla extract

½ cup (140 g) good-quality jam

To make the pastry, put the flour and salt into a bowl and mix well. Scatter the butter cubes over the flour mixture and, using a pastry blender or your fingers, work in the butter until the mixture is the consistency of bread crumbs. Add 3 tablespoons of the water and stir and toss just until the dough comes together in a rough mass, adding more water if needed. Shape into a ball, wrap in plastic wrap, and refrigerate for 30 minutes.

Have ready 12 tartlet pans, each about 3 inches (7.5 cm) in diameter and ¾ inch (2 cm) deep. On a lightly floured work surface, roll out the pastry as thinly as possible. Using a small, sharp knife or cookie cutter, cut out 12 rounds ¾–1 inch (2–2.5 cm) larger in diameter than your pans. If needed, gather the pastry scraps and re-roll to make enough rounds. Transfer the pastry rounds to the pans, pressing them onto the bottom and up the sides and trimming away any excess. Refrigerate the pastry-lined pans for 30 minutes.

To make the custard, warm the milk in a saucepan over medium heat just until bubbles appear around the edges of the pan. Meanwhile, whisk together the egg yolks and sugar until well blended. Gradually whisk the warm milk into the egg mixture until well-mixed. Whisk in the vanilla.

Preheat the oven to 400°F (200°C). Place the chilled tartlet shells on a large sheet pan. Divide the custard mixture evenly among the pans, pouring about 2 tablespoons in each. Do not overfill. Bake until the pastry is golden and the custard is puffed and lightly browned at the edges, about 20 minutes. Let cool completely in the pans on a wire rack, then use the tip of a small, sharp knife to ease the tartlets from the pans.

SUPPER & TEA

SUPPER AND TEA IN THE SERVANTS' HALL WERE much more informal meals than dinner. At Downton, we frequently see just a few servants at a time having tea, with the others busy about their duties. The core of the meal was, of course, the tea itself, brewed in large quantities and drunk hot, strong, sweetened with sugar, and with a generous splash of milk. Whereas the tea for the family may well have been Chinese, or perhaps the finest Indian tea, downstairs the brew would have been stronger and punchier. Leaves were used until there was no more flavor or color left in them. By the Edwardian period, tea had come down in price sufficiently that there was very little profit to be derived, as had been the case in previous centuries, from cooks selling off the used tea leaves (they were "upcycled" into tea for the very poor, with the addition of dried hedgerow leaves, colorants, and anything else that came to hand). The spent leaves were, however, used by the housemaids for cleaning carpets.

Both tea and supper were cold meals, and both centered around the staples of working-class life: bread, butter, and cheese, with ham and other cold meats if they were available. Leftovers from the servants' dinner could also be expected to appear, and at supper, the upper servants would often get to clean up any remains from the upstairs dinner, provided the cook could find no better use for them. This is graphically illustrated in season 1, when Mrs. Patmore feeds the nub ends of the crêpes Suzette to the dog, rather than let Ethel try them. Status, as ever, was paramount.

Tea could also involve pickles, chutneys, and jams from the still room, all concoctions that not only helped preserve fruits and vegetables, ensuring nothing from the kitchen gardens went to waste, but were also invaluable on the table for enlivening plain foods. Cheese and pickles, ham and piccalilli (relish), cold beef and horseradish were all solid parts of the British repertoire, easily stuffed into a sandwich and eaten speedily before the family had their more delicate tea, around five o'clock.

Also on the table for supper were savory biscuits or crackers, for it was intended to be a light meal before bed. It was generally served around nine, as the family upstairs reached dessert and then turned to port and cigars or to tea for the ladies. At this point, the footmen would be dismissed and be free to come downstairs for supper before returning upstairs to clear the dining table.

ANNA
William! What a treat to see you and how smart you look. Welcome.

WILLIAM
Thanks.

ANNA
Supper won't be long. I'm just going up to clear the dining room.

~ SEASON 2, EPISODE 2

DIGESTIVE BISCUITS

A thinly veiled attempt by bakers to market their wares to the gastrically challenged, digestive biscuits are based on whole-wheat flour and, generally, oats. They were designed as bland, wholesome biscuits for the nursery or for those who believed that a lack of flavor meant they must be good for you. At Downton, they regularly appear at the servants' hall supper, for, although they are quite plain alone, they are a good foil for cheese.

MAKES 26 BISCUITS

2⅓ cups (285 g) whole-wheat flour, plus more for the work surface

4 tablespoons (60 g) cold butter, cut into small cubes

¾ cup (75 g) rolled oats

2 tablespoons firmly packed light brown sugar

1 tablespoon plus 2 teaspoons arrowroot or cornstarch

½ teaspoon baking soda

Pinch of salt

1 egg, lightly whisked

About ½ cup (120 ml) milk

Preheat the oven to 350°F (180°C). Line two sheet pans with parchment paper.

Put the flour into a bowl, scatter the butter cubes over the top, and, using a pastry blender or your fingers, work in the butter until the mixture is the consistency of coarse bread crumbs. Add the oats, brown sugar, arrowroot, baking soda, and salt and stir to mix. Stir in the egg and enough milk to make a firm but malleable dough.

On a lightly floured work surface, turn out the dough and knead several times to form a disk. Cut the dough in half and roll out ⅛ inch (3 mm) thick. Using a 2½-inch (6-cm) round cookie cutter, cut out 13 rounds, gathering up the scraps and rerolling as needed. Transfer them to the prepared pans, spacing them about 1 inch (2.5 cm) apart, and prick each round with a fork. Repeat with the remaining half of the dough.

ROBERT: *Now this takes me back. Did I ever tell you about our cook when I was a boy? Mrs. Yardley.*

CORA: *Many times.*

ROBERT: *She was quite a cross patch but she was always kind to me. She used to let me hide down here when I was in trouble, and she kept a box of biscuits and sweets, just for me. Rosamund was furious.*

~ SEASON 6, EPISODE 1

RECIPE NOTE

These biscuits go well with both sweet and savory accompaniments. Modern digestives, which are much sweeter, are often sold with a chocolate topping, and these are also good dipped in milk or dark chocolate.

COTTAGE LOAF

The bread that is consumed on a daily basis in the Downton servants' hall is significantly less refined than that provided for the family upstairs. The working classes consumed an enormous amount of bread in the early twentieth century, and it was, quite literally, the stuff of life. The local bakery would deliver to country houses like Downton on a daily basis: delicate rolls and enriched breads for upstairs and huge, comforting loaves for downstairs. This recipe is from Swift's Bakery of Clee Hill, which has been in the same family, and has used largely the same recipes for traditional loaves like this one, since 1863.

MAKES 1 LARGE LOAF, ABOUT 2 LB (1 KG); SERVES 14–16

RECIPE NOTE

The dough can also be baked in two 1-lb (450-g) loaf pans (8½ x 4½ inches/ 21.5 x 11.5 cm). This bread is suitable for all the recipes in this book that require bread or bread crumbs. Bread is not very forgiving when it proofs, and it is hard to re-cover it if it proofs too long, so this is one recipe for which you definitely need to remember to preheat your oven well in advance.

INGREDIENTS

FOR THE SPONGE

1¾ cups plus 2 tablespoons (225 g) flour

1½ teaspoons salt

¼ teaspoon active dry yeast

½ cup plus 1 tablespoon (135 ml) cold water

FOR THE LOAF

5¾ cups (710 g) bread flour, plus more for kneading and dusting

1 tablespoon plus ½ teaspoon salt

1 tablespoon plus ½ teaspoon active dry yeast

About 1¾ cups (425 ml) cold water

Butter, for the bowl and pan

To make the sponge, combine all the ingredients in a bowl and mix well. The mixture will appear dry and somewhat crumbly. Cover the bowl with plastic wrap or a damp kitchen towel and leave at room temperature overnight.

The next day, make the loaf. In a large bowl, combine the bread flour, salt, and yeast. Gradually mix in enough of the water to incorporate all the flour so that the mixture comes together. Add the sponge, cutting it up with scissors or using your fingers to break it into small pieces to make it easier to mix in, and mix well until the dough begins to form a ball. Now knead the dough until it is smooth and elastic. You can do this by hand on a lightly floured work surface for 10–15 minutes or in a stand mixer fitted with a dough hook on low speed for 7–10 minutes. Shape the dough into a ball.

Dust a large bowl with flour and put the dough into it. Cover the bowl with plastic wrap or a damp kitchen towel, set aside in a warm spot, and let the dough rise until it doubles in size, about 1½ hours.

Punch down the dough, re-cover it, and leave to rise again until puffed and doubled in size, about 45 minutes.

Position a rack in the lower third of the oven and preheat the oven to 425°F (220°C).

Butter a sheet pan or line with parchment paper. Punch down the dough and knead a few times on a lightly floured surface. Form the dough into a thick rectangle, then cut off about one-third of it and set aside. Shape the remaining two-thirds into a sphere, tucking the edges under until the top is smooth. Place on the prepared pan. Press the sphere into a 7–8-inch (18–20-cm) disk about 1–1½ inches (2.5–4 cm) thick. Shape the smaller portion of dough into another smooth sphere, using the same technique. Now flatten the smaller sphere into a disk about 5 inches (13 cm) in diameter and position securely on top of the larger disk. Hold together your middle finger and forefinger and dust them lightly with flour. Press those fingers down firmly through the center top of the loaf, right down to the bottom, sealing the 2 dough disks together and creating the characteristic hole in the middle of the loaf. (If you have large hands, use just your thumb.)

Using a very sharp knife, make slashes all the way around the loaf, on both the top and the bottom portion, spacing the slashes about 1 inch (2.5 cm) apart and cutting about ½ inch (12 mm) deep.

Cover with plastic wrap and leave to rest for 10 minutes. Then, just before the loaf goes into the oven, lightly dust it all over with flour and press your fingers into the top, as before, to make sure the hole in the top is well formed and the 2 dough disks have no chance of coming apart in the oven.

Bake the loaf until golden brown and it sounds hollow when thumped on the bottom, about 45 minutes. If you have a thermometer at hand, the center of the loaf should register 200°–205°F (93°–95°C) when the bread is done. Let cool completely on a wire rack before slicing.

FOOD FOR THOUGHT

The cottage loaf was a standard shape for loaves designed for working people, and it is ubiquitous in photographs of bakeries from the mid-Victorian era onward. It largely died out in the latter half of the twentieth century, as bakeries became more mechanized and more and more bread was bought from highly industrialized factories via supermarkets.

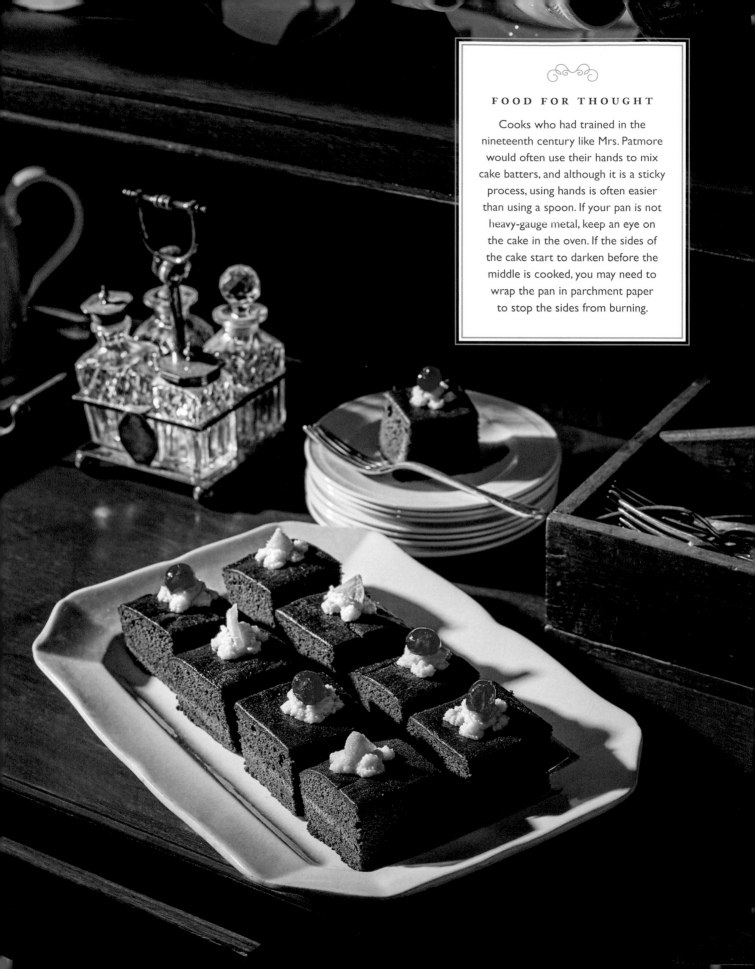

GINGERBREAD CAKE

Ginger was one of the cheapest spices in the past, so gingerbreads were very popular among the working classes. Nearly every European country had its own version, and in England there were many regional types. In Yorkshire, where *Downton Abbey* is set, a type called Parkin, which was made with rolled oats, was popular. However, the staff at such houses would have expected slightly better food than the locals were eating, so this version uses only flour. This recipe is adapted from a handwritten book kept by Avis Crocombe, a Victorian cook who, like Mrs. Patmore, worked in a large country house. The cake is very practical for busy cooks, as it keeps for months, which means it can be made well in advance and stored until needed.

SERVES 8–10

RECIPE NOTE

This cake can also be baked in a rectangular pan. The round cake would be carried to the table whole and sliced into wedges for serving. The rectangular cake can be cut into small squares and the top of each square decorated with a little icing and a glacéed cherry or a piece of crystallized ginger, as shown left. The batter can also be baked in a muffin pan and decorated with piped cream or frosting.

INGREDIENTS

1 cup (225 g) butter, at room temperature, plus more for the pan

3¾ cups (450 g) flour, plus more for the pan

Superfine sugar, for the pan

2 tablespoons plus 2 teaspoons ground ginger

1 teaspoon baking soda

Pinch of salt

1 cup (225 g) firmly packed dark brown sugar

2 eggs, lightly whisked

1 can (1 lb/450 g) black treacle or 1⅓ cups blackstrap molasses

½ cup (120 ml) milk

Preheat the oven to 325°F (165°C). Butter the bottom and sides of a 9-inch (23-cm) round springform pan. Line the bottom with parchment paper and generously butter the paper. Dust the bottom and sides of the pan with equal parts of flour and superfine sugar, tapping out the excess.

In a medium bowl, combine the flour, ginger, baking soda, and salt. Whisk gently to blend.

Put the butter into a large bowl and beat until pale and creamy. Add the brown sugar and beat until light and fluffy. Add the eggs and continue to mix vigorously until incorporated. Add the treacle gradually and carefully (as it is rather messy) and beat until incorporated. Add the flour mixture in three batches alternately with the milk in two batches, beginning and ending with the flour mixture and mixing well after each addition. Spoon the batter into the prepared pan.

Bake until a skewer inserted into the center comes out clean, 1¼–1½ hours. (If the edges of the cake begin to darken before the center of the cake is cooked, cover the pan loosely with parchment paper.) Remove from the oven and let cool completely in the pan on a wire rack. Loosen the edges of the cake from the pan sides with a blunt knife and unclasp the pan sides. Carefully slide the cake onto a serving plate, peeling away the paper, and serve.

SEED CAKE

Seed cake has a long history in Britain, and it probably started life in the Tudor period as a cake distributed to workers when they were seed sowing. It originally contained caraway comfits, sugar-coated seeds that were used as breath fresheners by the upper classes. Ironically, one of the reasons for poor dental health among the rich was their consumption of the very sugar that coated the seeds they used to disguise bad breath. Skeletal analysis has shown that, until sugar started to come down in price in the seventeenth century, you had to be quite well-off to afford to have cavities. The poor, in contrast, had worn-down teeth from their more fibrous diet. By the eighteenth century, the seeds were added without their sugary coating, and the cake became an absolute staple of both the tea table and the late-afternoon tippling spot, as it goes very well with fortified wines. Charles Dickens mentions it, as do the Brontës in their novels. Plain, popular, and easy to make, it features in many *Downton* scenes, especially in the servants' hall and at village fetes.

SERVES 6

INGREDIENTS

¾ cup (170 g) butter, at room temperature, plus more for the pan

3¾ cups (450 g) flour, plus more for the pan

Superfine sugar, for the pan

¾ cup plus 1 tablespoon (170 g) firmly packed dark brown sugar

1 teaspoon baking powder

½ teaspoon mixed spice

1¼ cups (300 ml) milk

2 tablespoons caraway seeds

2 eggs

Preheat the oven to 350°F (180°C). Butter an 8-inch (20-cm) square cake pan, then dust with a mixture of equal parts of flour and superfine sugar, tapping out the excess.

Put the butter into a large bowl and beat until pale and creamy. Add the brown sugar, baking powder, and mixed spice and beat until light and fluffy. Add the flour in three or four batches, beating well after each addition. (The batter will appear very dry and crumbly at this point.) Pour in the milk, add the caraway seeds, and beat until thoroughly mixed. Whisk the eggs in a small bowl until pale and frothy, then, while mixing constantly, gradually add them to the batter. Continue to beat the batter vigorously until well blended, thick, and smooth, about 15 minutes. Alternatively, beat the batter in a stand mixer fitted with the paddle attachment for 6–8 minutes. Scrape the batter into the prepared pan.

Bake until a skewer inserted into the center comes out clean, about 1 hour. Let cool in the pan on a wire rack for 15 minutes, then turn out of the pan onto the rack, turn upright, and let cool completely before serving. This cake tastes best if allowed to sit 1 day before serving. Cut into squares or into slices ½ inch (12 mm) thick.

MRS. PATMORE: *I know the popular fantasy is that you can feed six strong men from a single seed cake, but you and I know better.*

~ SEASON 2, EPISODE 3

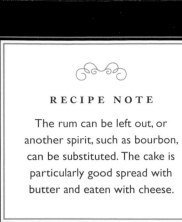

RECIPE NOTE

The rum can be left out, or
another spirit, such as bourbon,
can be substituted. The cake is
particularly good spread with
butter and eaten with cheese.

PORTER CAKE

Ideal for any servants' hall, this cake was not only cheap to make but kept for weeks. Servants at houses like Downton Abbey who did not accompany the family on trips received an allowance called "beer money," which was to cover their food when it wasn't being provided by the kitchen (cooks nearly always traveled with their employers). The term dates from a time when the staple drink in Britain was beer, with a low-alcohol type known as small beer the drink of servants and manual laborers everywhere. Although water was the cheapest and easiest drink to obtain, it was boring and associated with poverty, so drinking beer showed you were in the employ of a decent person. By the Victorian period, the staple drink of servants was tea, but the name of the allowance didn't change. Porter was an eighteenth-century commercial beer, strong, dark aged, and slightly sweet. Its popularity had waned by the twentieth century, and it nearly died out after the Great War—except in cakes.

SERVES 10-12

INGREDIENTS

1⅓ cups (225 g) dark raisins

1⅓ cups (225 g) golden raisins

¾ cup (180 ml) porter

¼ cup (60 ml) rum

½ cup (115 g) butter, at room temperature, plus more for the pan

3¾ cups (450 g) flour

1 teaspoon baking soda

1 teaspoon ground allspice

1 teaspoon ground nutmeg

Pinch of salt

½ cup (100 g) firmly packed dark brown sugar

Grated zest of 1 lemon

3 eggs, lightly whisked

Combine the dark raisins, golden raisins, porter, and rum in a saucepan, bring to a simmer over medium heat, and simmer for 5 minutes. Remove from the heat and let steep for at least 30 minutes but preferably for 2–3 hours. (They can easily be left overnight.)

Preheat the oven to 275°F (135°C). Butter the bottom and sides of a 7-inch (18-cm) or 8-inch (20-cm) round cake pan. Line the bottom with parchment paper and generously butter the paper.

In a bowl, combine the flour, baking soda, allspice, nutmeg, and salt. Whisk gently to blend.

In a large bowl, using a handheld mixer on medium speed or a wooden spoon, beat together the butter, brown sugar, and lemon zest until light and creamy. Add the eggs together with a spoonful of the flour mixture to stop the mix from curdling and beat until light and fluffy. Add the remaining flour mixture in three batches, beating after each addition until incorporated. Add the raisins and their steeping liquid and beat just until well mixed. The batter should be firm. Spoon the batter into the prepared pan.

Bake until the cake is nicely browned on top, the edges are beginning to pull away from the pan sides, and a skewer inserted into the center comes out clean, about 2 hours. Remove from the oven, turn out onto a wire rack, peel off the parchment, turn upright, and let cool completely. Store in an airtight container at room temperature for 1–3 days before serving. Cut into slices with a serrated knife.

THE STILL ROOM

UNLIKE KITCHENS, STILL ROOMS WERE CLEAN, quiet spaces, away from the heat and bustle of the main cooking space. They were presided over by the housekeeper, who in very large houses had a still room maid to assist her. As the name suggests, the rooms were originally intended for the distillation of spirits and housed stills. At that time, in the Tudor era, distilled liquors were seen primarily as medicines, and often the mistress of the house would play an active role in preparing medicinal cordials and spirits for the household. However, in the seventeenth and eighteenth centuries, distilled spirits became far more about drinking for pleasure, and the role of the still room changed to encompass anything that was outside the area of daily cookery, thus jams and other preserves, as well as drying flowers and candying fruits, flowers, and peels. Sometimes it also doubled as a confectionery room, for the preparation of sugar craft and fine cookies and wafers.

By the time *Downton Abbey* opens, only very large houses continued to have a still room, and the role of the still room maid was often in abeyance. The preparation of jellies, jams, and candied items had largely passed to the cook, and this was hastened by the Great War, which led to a servant shortage and the kind of financial retrenchment we see very graphically in the series. In the world of *Downton Abbey*, it is Mrs. Patmore who takes on the responsibility for all the traditional still room dishes, and so as viewers, we see them being prepared in the kitchen rather than elsewhere by a still room maid. However, they do form a distinct area of cookery, for they cannot be classified into dishes for breakfast, lunch, dinner, and tea. Instead, they are things to be made when the cook has a spare moment and are then kept for use at a future time.

In the twentieth century, jams and jellies, sauces, and pickles were widely available to buy, though many families still made their own. Any household with a vegetable garden or orchard suffered gluts, and waste was utterly frowned on. Early autumn, when the harvest was at its peak, was also the time when a number of aristocratic families chose, like the Crawleys, to decamp to Scotland for the shooting season. The cook was then able to make the most of the time she or he had without them to preserve, pot, and jam. The results could be stored in a dry larder for several years.

MRS. PATMORE

I know it's cheating but I think I might get a jar of horseradish. It really isn't bad now.

DAISY

That's not like you.

MRS. PATMORE

True. But we could use it in sandwiches and such without having to go through the whole palaver.

~ SEASON 6, EPISODE 2

APPLE CHEESE

In season 3, calamity occurs in the kitchen when the oven breaks down midway through the day of the showdown between the two matriarchs of Downton Abbey: Robert's mother, Violet, and Cora's mother, Martha. Coal-fired ovens were notorious for their unpredictability, especially when the wind was blowing in the wrong direction, so the problem would have been one that many cooks and their employers faced. Happily for the hungry guests, Martha turns the planned grand dinner into an impromptu picnic, sending the downstairs staff scrambling for things to serve. This dish, which has its roots in Tudor medicinal marmalades, is exactly the kind of thing they would have found lurking in the back of a larder, as it is easily prepared and lasts a long time—ideal for sudden culinary emergencies. The term *cheese* simply refers to the texture. Although the dish was popular served with custard, it's equally good as part of a cheese board or with yogurt.

SERVES 6–8

INGREDIENTS

2¼ cups (450 g) sugar

1¼ cups (300 ml) water

2 lb (1 kg) apples, peeled, cored, and roughly chopped

Grated zest and juice of 1 large or 2 small lemons

Butter, for the mold

2–3 tablespoons slivered blanched almonds

Custard, cream, or cheese, for serving

Combine the sugar and water in a large saucepan and bring to a boil over medium-high heat, stirring to dissolve the sugar. Reduce the heat to a simmer and continue to heat, stirring, until the sugar is dissolved. Add the apples and lemon juice and simmer until the apples are cooked through and start to fall apart (see Recipe Note). Raise the heat to high and boil the mixture, stirring continuously, until it thickens and dries out, 10–15 minutes. It will probably brown slightly as well, and that's fine. It is ready if, when you drag the spoon across the bottom of the pan, it leaves a dry trail behind it that only gradually closes up. Add the lemon zest, stir to mix, and remove from the heat.

Lightly butter a 5-cup (1.2-l) ceramic or glass mold and pour the apple mixture into it. If you prefer a block that you can cut slices from, use a square dish or a square pan lined with parchment paper. Cover and leave to set at room temperature overnight.

The next day, unmold the cheese onto a serving plate. (It should slip out easily, but if it doesn't, run a knife along the edges to help unmold it.) Decorate with the almonds and serve with custard. The cheese will keep for a year in the fridge if you cover the top with parchment paper or a thin layer of jam paraffin.

RECIPE NOTE

How long your cheese takes to cook will depend on your apples. If you use Bramleys, it will take forever, for they contain a lot of water. The Edwardians would have been able to choose from around three thousand apple varieties; older ones bred before the distinction between cooking and eating apples came in during the middle of the nineteenth century work best. If you can't get such wonderfully named apples as James Grieve, Ashmead's Kernel, or Nonesuch, then Cox's Orange Pippin will work just as well. Newer types, such as Pink Lady and Royal Gala, tend to be sweeter.

MARROW AND GINGER JAM

Huge marrows (outsize summer squashes) are often in the background in the kitchen at Downton, just as preserving jars and neatly labeled jams appear both on the table and in the kitchen cupboards. Gardeners were constantly at loggerheads with cooks in the Edwardian house: cooks wanted young, delicate vegetables suitable for the family table, whereas gardeners wanted to grow big, prizewinning specimens. Gardening and produce shows were part of country life, and the top prizes, unsurprisingly, often went to the gardeners from the local country house who had the expertise, staff, and equipment to really go to town. Sadly, marrows are virtually inedible, as they tend to be watery and flavorless, and recipes like this, which uses marrow to eke out the more expensive ginger, show the ingenuity of cooks at the time.

MAKES 6–7 PINT (480-ML) JARS

RECIPE NOTE

Don't be put off by the fact that this recipe is based on marrow: the end result is more like a melon and ginger jam, with the main flavor being ginger. If you haven't let your zucchini grow into marrows, or can't locate a big marrow, zucchini will also work. However, it's actually worth letting one zucchini grow enormous just to do this recipe.

INGREDIENTS

1 marrow, about 4 lb (1.8 kg), peeled, seeded, and cut into 1–2-inch (2.5–5-cm) chunks

3½ lb (1.6 kg) sugar (8 cups)

¼ lb (115 g) fresh ginger, peeled and finely chopped

2 oz (60 g) stem ginger in syrup, finely chopped

Grated zest and juice of 2 lemons

2 pouches (3 fl oz/90 ml each) Certo brand liquid pectin (or equivalent)

Pile the marrow chunks on a steamer tray and steam over boiling water for 10 minutes, Alternatively, boil the chunks in water for 10 minutes, then drain well. Transfer the marrow to a large bowl, add the sugar, both gingers, and the lemon zest and juice and mix well. Cover the bowl and leave it in a cool place overnight.

The next day, puree about three-fourths of the marrow mixture with an immersion blender or a stand blender. (You want to leave some out so you have jam with chunks in it.) Transfer the marrow mixture to a preserving pan and add the pectin.

Have ready sterilized canning jars and flat lids and screw bands (see Recipe Note on page 255). Bring the marrow mixture to a boil over high heat and boil until it registers 217°F (103°C) on a candy thermometer. (The temperature is 2–3 degrees lower than normal due to the addition of the liquid pectin.) As a rough guide, when the foam on top disappears and the bottom starts to caramelize, it's ready.

Ladle the jam into the hot, sterilized jars, filling them to within ½ inch (12 mm) of the rim. Wipe the rim of each jar clean, then top with a flat lid and twist on the screw band. Let cool, then test for a good seal: press on the center of each lid; if it remains concave, the seal is good. Label the jars with the contents and date and store in a cool, dark place for up to 1 year. Refrigerate any jars that failed to seal properly and use within 3 weeks.

PICCALILLI

An eighteenth-century English riff on Indian pickles, piccalilli is frequently seen on the servants' hall table among the condiments. It goes brilliantly with ham and other cold meats, can be used as a sandwich filling (if chopped finely), or can simply sit on the side of a supper plate. You can use any hard vegetables, and it's another good way to put away small amounts of fresh vegetables for use in the winter. This recipe makes quite a lot, but some people like to eat half a jar at a sitting, so it's worth it.

MAKES 4–5 PINT (480-ML) JARS

INGREDIENTS

8–10 cups chopped pickling vegetables, in 1–1½-inch (2.5–4-cm) chunks, such as green beans, cauliflower, broccoli, zucchini, beets, cabbage, carrots, cucumbers, and onions

6 tablespoons (50 g) kosher salt

5 cups (1.2 l) distilled white vinegar

2 tablespoons plus 2 teaspoons mustard powder

1 tablespoon ground turmeric

¼ head garlic, cloves separated and peeled

1½ tablespoons chopped shallot

½ fresh horseradish root, peeled and chopped, or 1 tablespoon prepared horseradish

1 oz (30 g) fresh ginger, peeled and chopped

1½ tablespoons black peppercorns

1 tablespoon plus ¾ teaspoon ground allspice

4 whole cloves

Put all the chopped vegetables in a large bowl and sprinkle them with the salt. Cover and leave in a cool place for 2 days, turning them twice a day. Rinse the vegetables thoroughly, then drain and dry them.

Have ready sterilized canning jars and flat lids and screw bands (see Recipe Note on the opposite page). Mix together 2 tablespoons of the vinegar, the mustard powder, and the turmeric in a small bowl and set aside. Pour the remaining vinegar into a saucepan, add the garlic, shallot, horseradish, ginger, peppercorns, allspice, and cloves, and bring to a boil over high heat. Reduce the heat to a simmer and simmer for 2–3 minutes. Remove from the heat and mix in the mustard mixture.

Using a slotted spoon, fish out the majority of spices from the vinegar mixture and mix them roughly in with the vegetables. Spoon the vegetables into hot, sterilized jars and ladle in the hot vinegar mixture, filling to within ½ inch (12 mm) of the rim. Wipe the rim of each jar clean, then top with a flat lid and twist on the screw band. Let cool, then label and refrigerate for 1 month before eating. It will keep up to 6 months.

PICKLED GREEN TOMATOES

The monotony of servants' meals could sometimes lead to grumbling. Indeed, some cooks found the servants as picky as their employers. Preserves and pickles were easy ways to pep up plain meals and were also vital for using up gluts of produce from the gardens. This recipe is particularly useful, as it uses up the inevitable load of unripe tomatoes left on the plants when the sun's warmth fades at the end of autumn.

MAKES 2–3 HALF-PINT (240-ML) JARS

RECIPE NOTE

To sterilize the jars, first wash them with hot, soapy water, then boil them for 15 minutes in water to cover, run them through a dishwasher on a hot cycle, or put them in a preheated 275°F (135°C) oven for 20 minutes. If you are using two-part canning lids—flat, rubber-lined lid and screw band—sterilize them in simmering water for 10 minutes. Never put them in boiling water or in the oven. It's fine to reuse canning jars free of chips and the like and unmarred screw bands, but always use new flat canning lids. If you will be storing any of the preserving recipes in this chapter in the refrigerator, any good jar and undamaged lid can be used.

INGREDIENTS

1 lb (450 g) green tomatoes, thickly sliced

2 tablespoons kosher salt

3 tablespoons plus 1 teaspoon sugar

¾ teaspoon yellow mustard seeds

¾ teaspoon whole cloves

¾ teaspoon black peppercorns

¾ teaspoon peeled and finely minced fresh ginger

1–2 fresh red Thai chiles, chopped

1 cup (240 ml) distilled white vinegar

Layer the tomato slices in a bowl, sprinkling each layer with the salt. Cover and leave in a cool place overnight.

The next day, have ready sterilized canning jars and flat lids and screw bands. Drain the tomatoes and transfer them to a saucepan. Add the sugar, mustard seeds, cloves, peppercorns, ginger, chiles, and vinegar and bring to a boil over high heat. Reduce the heat to medium-low and simmer gently until the tomatoes are soft and tender but not pulpy, 8–10 minutes.

Ladle the tomatoes into the hot, sterilized jars, filling them to within ½ inch (12 mm) of the rim. Wipe the rim of each jar clean, then top with a flat lid and twist on the screw band. Let cool, then label and refrigerate for 2 weeks before eating. The tomatoes will keep for up to 6 months.

FLAVORED BUTTERS

A handy pantry fallback, ideal for sudden oven emergencies or spontaneous picnics, flavored butters were one of the key elements of a cook's arsenal in busy environments such as country houses. They first appeared in cookery books in the 18th century, when chopped herb butters were particularly in vogue, together with sweet butters perfumed with citrus and ground nuts. They were valued both for their flavor and their look, and served both on bread, in sandwiches, and as an accompaniment to meat, fish, and vegetables.

INGREDIENTS

SAVORY BUTTERS

ANCHOVY BUTTER

½ cup (115 g) unsalted butter, at room temperature

2 anchovy fillets in olive oil, finely minced

I teaspoon minced fresh flat-leaf parsley

LOBSTER BUTTER

½ cup (115 g) unsalted butter, at room temperature

Coral from I lobster

Pinch of salt

Pinch of cayenne pepper

MONTPELLIER BUTTER

½ cup (115 g) unsalted butter, at room temperature

Leaves from I small bunch watercress, finely minced

Salt and black pepper

HERB BUTTER

½ cup (115 g) unsalted butter, at room temperature

4 teaspoons finely minced fresh herbs, such as sage, rosemary, and/or oregano

Pinch of salt

I teaspoon crushed garlic (optional)

SWEET BUTTERS

FAIRY BUTTER

½ cup (115 g) unsalted butter, at room temperature

¼ cup (50 g) superfine sugar

2 hard-boiled egg yolks

I teaspoon orange flower water

ORANGE BUTTER

6 tablespoons (90 g) unsalted butter, at room temperature

⅓ cup (70 g) superfine sugar

½ cup (60 g) ground almonds

I teaspoon orange flower water

I teaspoon grated orange zest

All of these butters are made using the same method: Combine all the ingredients in a bowl and work them together with a fork or wooden spoon until the ingredients are evenly distributed. Press the flavored butter in a small dish, making sure it fills it completely. Cover tightly and chill until needed. You can also form the butter into a log, wrap it tightly in plastic wrap, chill it, and then slice it as needed.

An alternative means of displaying the flavored butter—and a very period-specific one—is to mix and chill it as directed and then push it through a colander or squeeze it through loosely woven cloth onto a small plate so it resembles very thick spaghetti.

The savory butters can be used exactly as you would plain butter: spread on bread, stirred into mashed vegetables, slipped into baked potatoes, or tossed with hot pasta. They are also good slid under the skin of birds before they are roasted, to ensure crisp skin and succulent flesh. Sweet butters go well on toast or as an accompaniment to rice pudding, pancakes, and simple cakes.

RECIPE NOTE

You can make pretty much anything into a flavored butter as long as it's not too runny. Always use unsalted butter, and make sure it's good quality, for it's the primary ingredient. Margarine or anything low fat will not yield the same result.

BIBLIOGRAPHY & FURTHER READING

ORIGINAL SOURCES USED IN THIS BOOK

Eliza Acton, *Modern Cookery for Private Families* (1845)

Dorothy Allhusen, *A Book of Scents and Dishes* (1927)

'A Cordon Bleu', *Economical French Cookery for Ladies* (1902)

Anon., Unpublished manuscript cookbook (c. 1860-1890) [in author's collection]

Anon., *Recipes for High Class Cookery, as Used in the Edinburgh School of Cookery* (1912)

Anon. [Maria Rundell], *Domestic Cookery and Household Management* (nd., c. 1911)

Anon., *Be-Ro Home Recipes* (nd., 1930)

Mrs. S. Beaty-Pownall, *The 'Queen' Cookery Books, no. 11: Bread, Cake and Biscuits* (1902)

Isabella Beeton, *The Book of Household Management* (1888)

Margaret Black, *Household Cookery and Laundry Work* (nd, c. 1899)

Margaret Black, *Superior Cookery* (1887)

X. Marcel Boulestin, *Simple French Cooking for English Homes* (1923)

Phyllis Browne [Sarah Sharp Hamer], *The Dictionary of Dainty Breakfasts* (1899)

May Byron, *How to Save Cookery Book* (1915) [republished as *The Great War Cookbook*, 2014]

Cassell's Dictionary of Cookery (1878) [introduction by Arthur Payne, almost certainly another pseudonym of Sarah Sharp Hamer]

George Cox, *The Art of Confectionery* (1903)

Henry Craddock, *The Savoy Cocktail Book* (1930)

Avis Crocombe, unpublished manuscript cookbook (c. 1870-1910) [at Audley End, English Heritage]

Aubrey Dowson (ed.), *The Women's Suffrage Cookery Book* (c. 1908)

Auguste Escoffier, *Le Guide Culinaire* (1921)

Mary Fairclough, *The Ideal Cookery Book* (c. 1911)

Charles Elmé Francatelli, *The Modern Cook* (1896)

Catherine Frances Frere (ed.), *The Cookery Book of Lady Clark of Tillypronie* (1909)

Theodore Garrett (ed.), *The Encyclopedia of Practical Cookery* (c. 1885)

Florence George, *The King Edwards's Cookery Book* (1901)

T. Herbert, *Salads and Sandwiches* (1890)

J. W. Hoffman, *Cyclopedia of Foods* (ca.1890)

Catherine Ives, *When the Cook Is Away* (1928)

Florence Jack, *The Good Housekeeping Cookery Book* (1925)

Agnes Jekyll, *Kitchen Essays* (1922)

Mary Jewry, *Warne's Model Cookery and Housekeeping Book* (c. 1870)

Colonel Arthur Robert Kenney-Herbert ('Wyvern'), *Picnics and Suppers* (1901)

Mrs. E. W. Kirk, *Tried Favourites* (1929)

John Kirkland, *The Modern Baker, Confectioner and Caterer* (1907)

Hilda Leyel and Olga Hartley, *The Gentle Art of Cookery* (1925)

Ruth Lowinsky, *Lovely Food* (1931)

Agnes Marshall, *The Book of Ices* (1885)

Agnes Marshall, *Cookery Book* (c. 1888)

Alice Martineau, *Cantaloup to Cabbage* (1929)

Alice Martineau, *Caviare to Candy* (1927)

Katharine Mellish, *Cookery and Domestic Management* (1901)

Edith Milburn (ed.), *Cookery Book* (1913)

M. M. Mitchell, *The Treasure Cookery Book* (1913)

Marion Harris Neil, *How to Cook in Casserole Dishes* (1914)

Arthur Gay Payne, *The Housekeeper's Guide to the use of Preserved Meats, Fruits, Condiments, Vegetables &c* (ca.1886)

Lillie Richmond, *Richmond Cookery Book* 1897)

Frank Schloesser, *The Cult of the Chafing Dish* (1905)

Charles Herman Senn, *The New Century Cookbook* (1904)

Alfred Suzanne, *La Cuisine et Pâtisserie Anglaise et Americaine* (1904)

Frederick Vine, *Saleable Shop Goods* (1907)

Frederick Vine, *Savoury Pastry* (1900)

Georgina Ward, Countess of Dudley, *The Dudley Recipe Book* [*The Dudley Book of Cookery and Household Recipes*] (1913)

Mabel Wijey (ed.), *Warne's New Model Cookery* (1925)

Lucy H Yates, *The Country Housewife's Book* (1934)

Mollie Stanley Wrench, *Complete Home Cookery Book* (1930)

ETIQUETTE BOOKS

Anon., *Party-Giving on Every Scale* (1881)

G.R.M. Devereux, *Etiquette for Men* (1904 and subsequent editions)

OTHER USEFUL READING

Mary Anne Boermans, *Déjà Food* (2017)

Elizabeth Driver, *A Bibliography of Cookbooks Published in Britain 1875-1914* (1989)

Louise Foxcroft, *Calories and Corsets: A History of Dieting over 2000 Years* (2012)

Jane Grigson, *English Food* (1974)

Pamela Horn, *Country House Society* (2013)

Nicola Humble, *Culinary Pleasures* (2005)

Kaori O'Connor, *The English Breakfast* (2013)

Helen Saberi & Alan Davidson, *Trifle* (2001)

Fortune Stanley, *English Country House Cooking* (1972)

Adrian Tinniswood, *The Long Weekend: Life in the English Country House between the Wars* (2016)

Regula Ysewijn, *Pride and Pudding* (2016)

ANNIE GRAY is one of Britain's leading food historians. She holds degrees from the University of Oxford, as well as York and Liverpool, and is an honorary research associate at the University of York. She is the author of a culinary biography of Queen Victoria, *The Greedy Queen: Eating with Victoria* (2017), and of the forthcoming *Victory in the Kitchen: The Story of Churchill's Cook* (2020), a biography of Georgina Landemare, Winston Churchill's longest-serving cook. She is the resident food historian on the popular BBC Radio 4 food panel show, *The Kitchen Cabinet*, and has both presented and consulted for various British television productions, including the recent *Victoria & Albert: The Wedding* (shown on PBS) and *The Sweet Makers*. She is also a consultant for the *The Victorian Way* series, featuring Mrs. Crocombe, for the English Heritage channel on YouTube. She works more generally as a consultant to the heritage industry on historic food and dining, and worked for many years as a costumed interpreter, leading the service wing team at the award-winning Audley End House (English Heritage). She is a huge fan of a proper suet pudding.

ACKNOWLEDGMENTS

Thanks firstly to my agent, Tim Bates, who, along with Annabel Merullo, got me involved with this book. Thanks also to Amy Marr and Roger Shaw at Weldon Owen, copyeditor Sharon Silva, and designer Debbie Berne. The many people at Carnival Films and NBCUniversal who have been involved at the commissioning and editing stage have been crucial to the final structure of the book, as well.

My personal advisory and tasting panel of Emily O'Brien, Laura Gale, Kathy Hipperson, Richard Gray, Katharine Boardman-Hims, Rebecca Lane, and Matt Howling all need thanking effusively, as does Jess Smith for sterling work with highlighter pens. I apologise to the unsuspecting enthusiasts at the Greedy Queen launch for an entire table of Downton party food and no crisps. Thanks to Lisa Heathcote, the food stylist on the show, for responding to my queries. A special mention to Bex and Charlie Harris-Quigg, who went well beyond the call of cake and cocktail duty. And, lastly, thanks to Ben Hipperson for letting me drive his combine harvester, thereby fulfilling my childhood dream.

INDEX

weldon**owen**

President & Publisher Roger Shaw
Associate Publisher Amy Marr
Creative Director Kelly Booth
Designer Debbie Berne
Art Director Lisa Berman
Photo Shoot Art Director Marisa Kwek
Managing Editor Tarji Rodriguez
Production Manager Binh Au
Production Designer Carlos Esparza
Food Photographer John Kernick
Food Stylist Cyd Raftus McDowell
Prop Stylist Suzie Myers

Produced by Weldon Owen
1045 Sansome Street
San Francisco, CA 94111
www.weldonowen.com

Downton Abbey is available on Blu-ray and
DVD. To purchase, visit shop.pbs.org

Library of Congress Cataloging-in-Publication
data is available.

ISBN: 978-1-68188-369-4

Printed and bound in China
First printed in 2019
10 9 8 7 6 5 4 3 2 1

Weldon Owen wishes to thank the following
people for their generous support in producing
this book: Rizwan Alvi, Lisa Atwood, Lesley
Bruynesteyn, Peggy Fallon, Rishon Hanners,
Rae Hellard, Rachel Markowitz, Joan Olson,
Elizabeth Parson, Nico Sherman, Sharon Silva,
and Angela Williams.

Weldon Owen also wishes to thank:
Gareth Neame, Aliboo Bradbury, Charlotte Fay,
and Nion Hazell at Carnival Films; Dominic
Burns at NBCUniversal; Annabel Merullo and
Laura McNeill at Peters Fraser and Dunlop;
Adrian Botterell and Steven Rowley at Royal
Crown Derby; and Jay Hering, Jeffrey Millar,
Whitney Sinkule, and Vince Quarta at Imagine
Exhibitions.

Cover image: Darley Abbey plate designed by
Jane James and manufactured by Royal Crown
Derby, an English Bone China Manufacturer.
www.royalcrownderby.co.uk
Photo by Laura Flippen